Praise for

Meanings of Bandung is an outstand.
points, engage anticolonial sensing of that world-shaping event in 1955, as well as its decoloniz-ing legacies. The collection provides a brilliantly illuminating window into a diversity of interna-tional relations and world orders. It is a must read for all who seek to think international relations otherwise than as an American social science – and even more importantly for those who do not.

—**Raymond D. Duvall**, Professor, University of Minnesota

Meanings of Bandung takes up one of the most significant and undervalued moments in the history of international relations when anticolonial politics intersected with decolonial visions to produce some of the most inspired possibilities for a truly global politics. A formidable col-lection of critical and postcolonial International Relations scholars examines the multivalent politics, aesthetics and ethics that emerged from the 1955 Bandung Conference when leaders of newly independent African and Asian states dared to imagine an alternative global order in which global peace, social justice and human dignity were more than just rhetorical masks for the exercise of realpolitik. Readers will come away both inspired and humbled by the sharp analyses and profound lessons that Bandung continues to provide us for crafting more just and plural worlds in our contemporary times. This volume should be a must-read for all students of International Relations.

—**Shampa Biswas**, Paul Garrett Professor, Whitman College

Sixty years ago, the Bandung Conference seemed to open up the possibility of a new world of racial equality and global justice. But as this valuable collection makes clear, the event also had even more far-reaching aspirations. Bandung offered a revolutionary decolonial revisioning of the affective sensibilities, dominant temporalities and official corporealities of the planetary body politic. It is a vision we urgently need to recover.

—**Charles W. Mills**, Professor, CUNY Graduate Center

This pioneering volume retrieves Bandung's entangled histories. By combining work on the intimate solidarities that sustained the conference along with chapters on the importance of Bandung for narrating conspicuously global histories, *Meanings of Bandung* represents a major advance. The book will be of significant interest to those working on colonial and postcolonial histories, the politics of development and the terrain of "lived" international relations.

—**George Lawson**, Associate Professor, London School of Economics

It is not frequent to read, in the social sciences, expressions such as "Meanings of Bandung" and "Sensing Bandung," as this excellent volume unapologetically does. The Bandung Con-ference is the equivalent to the French Revolution for the history of Europe. Bandung was a signpost and will remain so for the growing presence in the planetary scene of people, states and regions, shattered by the consolidation of Eurocentrism to which the French Revolution contributed so much.

—**Walter D. Mignolo**, William H. Wannamaker Professor and Director, Center for Global Studies and the Humanities, Duke University

Robbie Shilliam and Quỳnh N. Phạm place the lens on an iconic moment for the postcolonial world in global politics. Invaluable for both research and teaching, this collection of essays reveals the layers of meaning contained in this moment, as well as the paradoxes and tensions faced by those who sought to recreate the international beyond the legacies of the colonial era.

—**Vivienne Jabri**, Professor, King's College London

Kilombo: International Relations and Colonial Questions

This is the first series to mark out a dedicated space for advanced critical inquiry into colonial questions across International Relations. The ethos of this book series is reflected by the bricolage constituency of Kilombos – settlements of African slaves, rebels and indigenous peoples in South America who became self-determining political communities that retrieved and renovated the social practices of its diverse constituencies while being confronted by colonial forces. The series embraces a multitude of methods and approaches, theoretical and empirical scholarship, alongside historical and contemporary concerns. Publishing innovative and top-quality peer-reviewed scholarship, Kilombo enquires into the shifting principles of colonial rule that inform global governance and investigates the contestation of these principles by diverse peoples across the globe. It critically re-interprets popular concepts, narratives and approaches in the field of IR by reference to the "colonial question" and, in doing so, the book series opens up new vistas from which to address the key political questions of our time.

Series Editors

Mustapha K. Pasha, Aberystwyth University
Meera Sabaratnam, SOAS University of London
Robbie Shilliam, Queen Mary University of London

Titles in the Series

Meanings of Bandung: Postcolonial Orders and Decolonial Visions, Quỳnh N. Phạm and Robbie Shilliam
Decolonizing Intervention: International Statebuilding in Mozambique, Meera Sabaratnam (forthcoming)
Politics of the African Anticolonial Archive, Shiera S. el-Malik and Isaac A. Kamola

Meanings of Bandung

Postcolonial Orders and Decolonial Visions

Edited by Quỳnh N. Phạm
and Robbie Shilliam

ROWMAN &
LITTLEFIELD
——————— INTERNATIONAL

London • New York

Published by Rowman & Littlefield International Ltd
Unit A, Whitacre Mews, 26-34 Stannary Street, London SE11 4AB
www.rowmaninternational.com

Rowman & Littlefield International Ltd. is an affiliate of Rowman & Littlefield
4501 Forbes Boulevard, Suite 200, Lanham, Maryland 20706, USA
With additional offices in Boulder, New York, Toronto (Canada), and Plymouth (UK)
www.rowman.com

British Library Cataloguing in Publication Data
A catalogue record for this book is available from the British Library

ISBN: HB 978-1-7834-8564-2
       PB 978-1-7834-8565-9

Library of Congress Cataloging-in-Publication Data
Names: Phạm, Quỳnh N., 1985- editor. | Shilliam, Robbie, 1969- editor.
Title: Meanings of Bandung : postcolonial orders and decolonial visions / edited by
    Quỳnh N. Phạm and Robbie Shilliam.
Description: London : New York : Rowman & Littlefield International, [2016?] |
    Series: Kilombo : international relations and colonial questions | Includes
    bibliographical references and index.
Identifiers: LCCN 2016037016 (print) | LCCN 2016037836 (ebook) |
    ISBN 9781783485642 (cloth : alk. paper) | ISBN 9781783485659 (pbk. : alk. paper) |
    ISBN 9781783485666 (electronic)
Subjects: LCSH: Asian-African Conference (1st : 1955 : Bandung, Indonesia) |
    Decolonization–Africa. | Decolonization–Asia. | Asia–Foreign relations. |
    Africa–Foreign relations. | Afro-Asian politics.
Classification: LCC DS35.2 .M43 2016 (print) | LCC DS35.2 (ebook) | DDC 325.6–dc23
LC record available at https://lccn.loc.gov/2016037016

∞™ The paper used in this publication meets the minimum requirements of American
National Standard for Information Sciences—Permanence of Paper for Printed Library
Materials, ANSI/NISO Z39.48-1992.

Printed in the United States of America

Contents

About the Contributors

Anna M. Agathangelou teaches Political Science at York University, Toronto. She is the author of *The Global Political Economy of Sex: Desire, Violence, and Insecurity in Mediterranean Nation-States* (2004) and co-editor with Kyle D. Killian of *Time, Temporality and Violence in International Relations: (De)fatalizing the Present, Forging Radical Alternatives* (2016).

Khadija El Alaoui is an Assistant Professor at Prince Mohammad bin Fahd University, Saudi Arabia. Previously, she was a visiting scholar at the Department of Islamic Studies at McGill University in Montreal, a Mellon postdoctoral fellow in Peace and Justice Studies in the American Culture Program at Vassar College, NY, and a visiting assistant professor at the Center for American Studies and Research at the American University of Beirut, Lebanon. She received her MA and PhD in American Studies from the Technical University of Dresden, Germany. Her published articles deal with representational practices in American and Arab visual economies, the mutations of colonialism, and poetry and politics in the recent Arab uprisings.

Siba N. Grovogui is a professor of international relations theory and law at Africana Studies and Research Center at Cornell University, New York.

Budi Hernawan is a social scientist, a lecturer at Paramadina Graduate School of Diplomacy in Jakarta, and a research fellow at Abdurrahman Wahid Centre of Universitas Indonesia. He was awarded PhD from the Australian National University in Canberra in 2013. His research areas cover anthropology of violence, historical justice and memory, peacebuilding, and human rights with regional foci of Indonesia, Papua and the Pacific. His recent publications include "Torture as a Mode of Governance: Reflections on the

Phenomenon of Torture in Papua, Indonesia" in M. Slama and J. Munro, eds., *From "Stone-Age" to "Real-Time": Exploring Papuan Temporalities, Mobilities and Teligiosities* (2015); Budi Hernawan and Pat Walsh, "Inconvenient Truths" (2015); and "Torture in West Papua (Indonesia): A Spectacle of Dialectics of the Sovereign and the Abject" in P. King, J. Elmslie and C. Webb-Gannon, eds., *Comprehending West Papua* (2011).

Aida A. Hozić is an Associate Professor of International Relations and Colonel Allan R. and Margaret G. Crow Professor, College of Liberal Arts and Science, University of Florida (2015–2016). Her research is situated at the intersection of international political economy, cultural studies and international security. Much of her research thus far has been focused on the political economy of media industries and their relation to power, violence, and warfare. She is currently working on several projects linking arts, narratives, and international politics – from illicit trade in the Balkans to American modernism in Europe – aiming to broaden our notion of "the political" and affirm the importance of "peripheral visions" in International Relations.

Rosalba Icaza is a Mexican feminist academic–activist who conducts research and teaches on social movements, epistemic justice and indigenous people resistance and autonomy. Her pedagogical practice has been focused on making the classroom as space to share ideas-as-incarnated-experiences about the academy as a colonizing institution and/or emancipatory possibility. Her latest publication in English is "The Permanent People's Tribunals and indigenous people's struggles in Mexico: Between coloniality and epistemic justice?," *Palgrave Communications Journal*, available at: http://www. palgrave-journals.com/articles/palcomms201520. She is senior lecturer in Governance and International Political Economy at the Institute of Social Studies, Erasmus University of Rotterdam. Her email address is icaza@iss.nl.

Narendran Kumarakulasingam is honorary research fellow at the School of Built Environment and Development Studies, University of KwaZulu-Natal, Durban and a visiting scholar with the Centre for Refugee Studies, York University, Toronto. He is the editor of the special issue on "Decolonial Temporalities" (forthcoming) and his recent publications have appeared in *Journal of Narrative Politics* and *Journal of Agrarian Change*. He is currently working on a book on the poetics of savage and civilizational violence in international politics.

Rachmi Diyah Larasati is a scholar from Indonesia and an Associate Professor who teaches cultural theory and historiography in the Department of Theatre Arts & Dance, University of Minnesota, Minneapolis, US.

Currently the Dance Director at College of Liberal Arts, she is also an affiliated graduate faculty in the Department of Gender, Women, and Sexuality Studies (GWSS), the Interdisciplinary Center for the Study of Global Change (ICGC), and the Department of Asian Languages and Literatures (ALL). She is the author of *The Dance that Makes You Vanish: Cultural Reconstruction in Post-genocide Indonesia* (2013) and more than fifteen articles. She is currently writing her second book, *Dancing in the Forest: Modern Machine and Audio Politics of Land Narrative.* Her latest writings (2016) include "The Rethinking of Remembering, Who Lays Claim to Speech in the Wake of Catastrophe, and Is It Important?" in *Surviving Genocide: Politics of Representation*, and "The Dancing Goddess: Ecological Memory, Technique and the Inquiry of Value in Globalized Space" (Smithsonian, DC. Collection in *Indonesian Series*). As an Indonesian dancer who dedicates her inquiry to the study of female citizenship, politics of the body, and critical ethnography, her research focuses on the aesthetic and politics of globalism.

Himadeep Muppidi is Betty G. C. Cartwright Professor of Political Science & International Studies at Vassar College, New York. He is the author of *Politics in Emotion: The Song of Telangana* (2015), *The Colonial Signs of International Relations* (2012), and *The Politics of the Global* (2004). He is also the co-editor, with Andrew Davison, of *Europe and Its Boundaries: Words and Worlds, Within and Beyond* (2009) and *The World is My Home: A Hamid Dabashi Reader* (2011).

Craig N. Murphy is Research Professor in the Department of Conflict Resolution, Human Security, and Global Governance at the University of Massachusetts, Boston.

Amy Niang is a lecturer in International Relations at the University of the Witwatersrand in Johannesburg and a visiting research fellow at the Princeton Institute for International and Regional Studies (PIIRS). Her research is a theoretical investigation into notions of statehood, sovereignty, order and community, and an empirical and historical investigation in state and social processes in the West African region, particularly the Sahel. Some of her works have been published in *Alternatives: Global, Local, Political, African Economic History, Politics*, and *Afrique Contemporaine.*

Sam Okoth Opondo is an Assistant Professor of Politics and Africana Studies at Vassar College, New York. His research focuses on the dynamics of "mediating estrangement" and co-habitation in colonial, settler colonial and postcolonial societies. He has written journal articles and book chapters on the often-overlooked amateur diplomacies of everyday life, postcolonial cities, aesthetics, ethics, and cultural translation in Africa and its diasporas.

Mustapha Kamal Pasha is Chair and Professor in International Politics at Aberystwyth University, UK. He was Sixth Century Chair and Head of International Relations at the University of Aberdeen from 2006 to 2013. He specializes in International Relations theory, Human Security, Globalization, and Contemporary Islam.

Randolph B. Persaud is an Associate Professor at the School of International Service, American University, Washington, D.C. He has written extensively on race and international relations. Recent publications include "Neo-Gramscian Theory and Third World Violence: A Time for Broadening," *Globalizations*, Vol. 13, No. 5, 2016; and Randolph B. Persaud and Christine B. N. Chin, "From Sexation to Sexualization: Dispersed Submission in the Racialized Global Sex Industry," *Cambridge Review of International Affairs*, Vol. 29, No. 1, March 2016.

Quỳnh N. Phạm is a doctoral candidate in Political Science at the University of Minnesota. Her dissertation examines the mutually constitutive relationship between subaltern power and world order, and situates "local" struggles of peasant subalterns within a global politics of worlding. Her publications include "Enduring Bonds: Politics and Life Outside Freedom as Autonomy," *Alternatives*, Vol. 38, No. 1 (2013); "Decolonial Designs: José Martí, Hồ Chí Minh, and Global Entanglements," *Alternatives*, Vol. 40, No. 2 (2015, co-authored with María José Méndez); and chapters (co-authored with Himadeep Muppidi) in Tarak Barkawi and Keith Stanski, *Orientalism and War* (2012); Arlene Tickner and David Blaney, *Claiming the International* (2013); and Naeem Inayatullah, *Autobiographical International Relations: I, IR* (2011).

Rahul Rao is a Senior Lecturer in Politics at SOAS, University of London. He is the author of *Third World Protest: Between Home and the World* (2010), and of numerous articles in the fields of gender and sexuality, critical theory and international relations. He is currently working on a book on queer postcolonial temporality. He has a law degree from the National Law School of India University, and a doctorate in international relations from the University of Oxford.

Giorgio Shani, PhD, is Professor of Politics and International Relations at International Christian University, Tokyo and visiting senior fellow at the Centre of International Studies at the London School of Economics and

Political Science (LSE). He is author of *Sikh Nationalism and Identity in a Global Age* (2008) and *Religion, Identity and Human Security* (2014). He is a series editor of *Critical Perspectives on Religion in International Politics* and currently serves as president of the Asia-Pacific region of the International Studies Association.

Robbie Shilliam is Professor of International Relations at Queen Mary University of London. He is author of *The Black Pacific: Anti-Colonial Struggles and Oceanic Connections* (2015) and co-convener of the *British International Studies Association*'s Colonial/Postcolonial/Decolonial working group.

Tamara Soukotta is currently a PhD researcher at the International Institute of Social Studies in The Hague. At the moment, Tamara is mainly interested in coloniality, border epistemology and decolonial option/thinking/doing, as well as actively pushing the boundaries of academic research to make space for other ways of knowing.

Heloise Weber is Senior Lecturer in International Relations and Development Studies at the School of Political Science and International Studies, The University of Queensland, Australia. She has published articles and book chapters on the theory and politics of development, inequalities, poverty reduction strategies, as well as methodological problems. She is the co-editor (with M. T. Berger) of *Recognition and Redistribution: Beyond International Development* and editor of *Politics of Development*. She is co-author (with M. T. Berger) of *Rethinking the Third World – International Development and World Politics*.

Acknowledgements

As editors, we find Bandung an important moment of global politics from which diverse, albeit subalternized, ways of imagining and living international relations may be discerned. Over the past few years, we have organized a set of round-table panels at the annual conventions of the International Studies Association (ISA) to invite reflections on the memories and meanings of Bandung. We owe special thanks to all the panelists and audiences for stirring lively energies and generating thought-provoking discussions, which carried on far beyond the clock time of the panels. In particular, we are thankful to Noer Fauzi Rachman (who came all the way from Indonesia), Charles W. Mills, and Timothy M. Shaw, whose presentations did not become chapters in this book but contributed significantly to the broader conversations and debates on Bandung and decolonization. We also want to acknowledge the Global Development Section of the ISA as the nurturing space within which these conversations and relationships were developed over a number of years.

The image on the front cover belongs to the painting *El Tercer Mundo* ("The Third World") by Wifredo Lam (1902–1982). For a book on meanings of Bandung, we could not find a more wonderful match for the cover than a painting created on the occasion of the nonaligned meeting of the peoples of Africa, Asia and Latin America – commonly known as the Tricontinental Conference – in Havana, Cuba in 1966. Furthermore, Bandung can be said to be embodied in the diverse crossings and confluences that constituted Wifredo Lam's inheritances, life paths, political awareness, and decolonial approach to arts. We are grateful to the National Museum of Fine Arts in Havana, Cuba (Museo Nacional de Bellas Artes de La Habana) for generously granting us the permission to use the image of Lam's painting without charge. We thank Mr. Heriberto Rodriguez Pérez, the Vice Director of the

Department of International Relations, Business Management and Communication at the Museum, for his invaluable assistance and María José Méndez for her helpful translation in the process of obtaining this permission. It is regrettable that the full image of the painting cannot be printed on the front cover. However, it is reproduced for viewing after the index.

Thanks are due to two anonymous reviewers for their suggestions at the initial stage of the project. We would also like to thank Dhara Patel, Tanuja Krishna Kumar, Anita Singh, Michael Watson, Anna Reeve, Sinéad Murphy, and other staff at Rowman & Littlefield International for their hard work in helping to make the production a relatively fast and smooth process.

And of course, we owe tremendous thanks to the contributors for turning their reflections into such rich essays and for making this collective project a meaningful and convivial endeavour to be part of.

INTRODUCTION

Chapter 1

Reviving Bandung

Quỳnh N. Phạm and Robbie Shilliam

INTRODUCTION

"[T]his hall is filled not only by the leaders of the nations of Asia and Africa; it also contains within its walls the undying, the indomitable, the invincible spirit of those who went before us," declared Indonesian president Sukarno, as he hosted twenty-nine nations of Asia and Africa from April 18 to 24 in 1955 (*Asia-Africa Speaks* 1955). These newly independent nations met in Bandung, Indonesia, to discuss the present condition and future prospects of international relations. Upon reading the news of this historic gathering a few months before, African American writer Richard Wright, even from remote Paris, instantly realized its empire-shaking significance: "[T]his is the human race speaking" (Wright 1956: 11–13). Wright felt compelled to go and witness "the agenda and subject matter" that "had been written for centuries in the blood and bones of the participants." Both Sukarno's solemn tribute to "those who went before" and Wright's thrilled "stream of realizations" that "[t]his smacked of something new, something beyond Left and Right" suggest that the meanings of the event, what is known nowadays as the "Bandung Conference" or simply "Bandung," far exceed the standard narratives of geopolitics, diplomacy and ethics.

It is not that certain conventions of international relations cannot be read into the conference. It has been argued that among the major concerns for its five original sponsors – Burma, Indonesia, India, Ceylon and Pakistan – were diffusing growing tensions between China and the United States, decreasing polarization between the two ideological poles of the Cold War, and addressing the destructive power of nuclear and thermo-nuclear explosions (e.g. Kahin 1956). However, it is telling that the few engagements with Bandung in the field of International Relations have tended to place it entirely within

3

already-existing theoretical problematiques. Apart from the predominant focus on strategic self-interest and statesmanship, Bandung was, in the estimation of English Schooler Martin Wight (1987: 224–225), an example of "Kantian moral solidarity" in action, that is, an attempt to "sweep away evil" from international society (see also Jackson 2005: 66). More recently, Roland Burke (2010: 13–34) has placed Bandung as a landmark in the evolution of the United Nations and its mission to promote universal human rights. Alternatively, others past and present have seen in Bandung something less of a global Kantian revolution or human rights evolution and more of an emergent Asian "regionalism" (Brecher 1963; Tan & Acharya 2008).

Nevertheless, it is possible to glean in some scholarly interventions a resonance with Richard Wright's reading of Bandung and its reverberation in both the Global North and South. For example, in a special issue of *Daedalus* published in the aftermath of the infamous Watts Riots in Los Angeles in 1965, Robert Gardiner (1967: 302) suggested that Bandung signalled a "renewed self-respect" of colonized peoples in their vehement rejection of the "white man's standards." Likewise, in the aftermath of the so-called race riots in London, Birmingham, Leeds and Liverpool in 1981, Robert Vincent (1982: 668) contextualized Bandung within a global politics of race that sought to dismantle "white superiority" in the service of "the principle of racial equality." Although primarily filtered through a lens of "race" and "colour," these direct allusions to global systems of colonial rule mark a crucial hermeneutic excess that Bandung holds for IR.

This book examines the excess of meanings invoked by Bandung in order to understand and reflect on the affinities, visions and projects of decolonization that shaped international relations in the twentieth century, and that continue to do so. Moving away from conventional frames, we, as editors, are convinced that Bandung, while important in and of itself as a diplomatic event, is also a political and affective touchstone that can help to illuminate *the life of other international relations*, besides those of the hegemonic West and its theoretical narrations of global order. These other international relations are not "other-worldly"; they operate in this world, but through non-conventional points of departures, thought systems, archives, sensibilities, aspirations and practices that variously contest, provincialize or re-entangle themselves with the global-colonial projection of power and order. They are populated by peoples who connect, who resonate – sometimes disharmoniously – across diverse but relatable perspectives, stories and projects. These international relations may not always be visible or audible, but they are lived, and thus make a difference to the way the world is imagined, inhabited and adjusted to multiple life practices, convivialities and globalities.[1]

In pursuit of this retrieval of meanings, the book is divided into two sections. Addressing the affective-corporeal relations with regard to the

Asian-African Conference of 1955 as well as what comes before and after it, the first section explores Bandung as a way of sensing international-as-intimate relations. Here the chapters trace what Walter Mignolo (2011) calls the "body-politics of knowing/sensing/understanding" in his discussion on decoloniality, the Bandung Conference and the Third World more broadly. Contributors to the first section walk us into an international relations experienced through the memories, speeches, songs, names, symbols, poetry, fragrances and smells that texture, often contentiously, Bandung's political and cultural intimacies. Notably, these intimacies have been in the making long before the 1955 conference.

The second section seeks to resituate Bandung in both historical and contemporary contexts, and to reintroduce pivotal, albeit forgotten or maligned, contexts to the study of international relations. This section locates Bandung beyond the narrow Cold War security framework commonplace in IR scholarship in order to approach the conference as a conspicuous episode in a long history of rallies against old and new forms of colonial domination. Contributors examine the diverse ethico-political imaginaries of the global that both made Bandung possible and emerged out of it. As they do so, they critically investigate the affinities and alliances as well as the tensions and contradictions that permeated Bandung.

We propose that working through the multiple senses and lineages of Bandung helps to cultivate understandings of international relations that are better attuned to the postcolonial predicaments and decolonizing impulses that frame contemporary struggles over global order. As editors, we are attentive to the intricate dynamics of these predicaments and impulses within colonial orders. Indeed, recent investigations disclose the many strictures, tensions and ambiguities between local, national and global projects that intersected at the conference (see Lee 2010; McDougall & Finnane 2010; Vitalis 2013; Roberts & Foulcher 2016). At the same time, we are committed to the premise that the colonial order never was – and never is – all encompassing. Hence, the contributions across both sections engage with Bandung beyond romantic or pessimistic gestures in order to capture the complexity of the promises and processes of decolonizing international relations.

In what follows, we provide a primer for both sections of the volume and introduce the individual contributions. First, we dwell on the affective and temporal dimensions of Bandung to consider the ways in which sensing it intimately generates meanings that exceed those garnered solely from a focus on self-interested or ideological engagements. Having traced this broader and deeper constellation of meanings, we then sketch out the lineages of struggle within which Bandung can be situated as a crucial intervention into global order, lineages yet to be grasped in IR.

SENSING BANDUNG

The Bandung Conference is remarkable insofar as it provided the first diplomatic space in twentieth century international relations that promised an intimacy among colonized and postcolonized peoples. This space, in significant ways, defied the geopolitical borders that most attendees inherited from colonial cartographies. In particular, the conference resonated far beyond the diplomatic circles that largely constituted its immediate audience. Intensely felt, the resonance spoke to existing intimacies that bore many names, ranging from friendship to companionship, from solidarity to brotherhood/sisterhood, from neighbourliness to kinship. Invoked by statesmen and commoners alike, sung in prose-poetry and diverse vernacular tongues, these intimacies, we propose, are vital to both the making and the making sense of Bandung. Emerging out of profound bonded and bonding histories, these intimacies embody political sensibilities. They entwine with wide-ranging emotions and experiences, including euphoria as well as anguish, and fidelity as well as estrangement.

To borrow the image from Egyptian poet Fuad Haddad, "the white dove from Bandung sp[oke] in rhyme" across the world. In her chapter, Khadija El Alaoui draws from Algerian thinker Malek Bennabi to argue that Bandung represented the opportunity for both the moral renewal of colonized societies and a global politics of grounding with neighbours. In her critical analysis, poets and dissidents kept the promises of Bandung alive despite, paradoxically, authoritarian punishment by anti-colonial leaders such as Egypt's Abdel Nasser. Where statesmen and intellectuals of North Africa fail to pursue decolonial aspirations to full effect, El Alaoui turns to "Street Bandung," especially in the vernacular rhyme of people's poets who "embody Bandung in their conversations" with neighbours across traditions and across struggles for justice. If artistic media such as poetry has been crucial to the transmission of the Bandung spirit, Rachmi Diyah Larasati's chapter alerts us to the duality of the artistic form, especially in the contemporary dominant order. She provocatively asks, "Is it possible to hold the political value of the artistic form as an embodiment of memory and a decolonizing process while functioning in a neoliberal spatial configuration?" Recollecting the suppressed memories of Bandung in the context of Indonesia's silenced past and her own family's experiences, Larasati ponders the layered and displaced meanings of images of Che Guevera and the song "Guantanamera" in Indonesia.

Bandung reverberated even in the West. Despite mainly hostile and condescending reactions from its dominant representatives, "the despised, the insulted, the hurt, the dispossessed" who resided there felt the extraordinary nature of Bandung (Wright 1956). This subaltern excitement was exemplified, for instance, in Richard Wright's report *The Color Curtain* (1956: 12): "It was the kind of meeting that no anthropologist, no sociologist, no political scientist would ever have dreamed of staging; it was too simple, too elementary. ... There was something extra-political, extra-social, almost extra-human about it; it smacked of tidal waves, of natural forces. ..." Less well known than Wright's now popular account was the enthusiasm that Bandung aroused among African American editors and journalists, some of whom applied for passports to attend only to be rejected by the US State Department (Plummer 1996: 248). Likewise, rejections were visited upon W. E. B. Du Bois and Paul Robeson who sent messages of support instead (Fraser 2003: 135).[2] "How I should have loved to be at Bandung," began Robeson's "heartfelt greetings" and deep regrets at missing this momentous (re)union. "In your midst are old friends I knew in London years ago, where I first became part of the movement for colonial freedom" (Foner 1978: 398–400). Inspired by Bandung, Malcolm X (1963) considered it a model to create unity among black people in the United States. The African American press hailed the conference as a "product of 500 years" of European colonial atrocities (Rogers 1966) and a "clear challenge to white supremacy" that "might well prove to be a turning point in world history" ("Afro-Asian Conference" 1955). The press also asserted that Bandung enabled the subsequent "whippings" of colonial states at the United Nations over issues of self-determination such as the freedom of Algeria from France (Hicks 1955a, 1955b).

The profound and visceral attachments to Bandung around the world are steeped in long and violent histories. They become intelligible only if we understand the 1955 conference as a formally diplomatic expression of anti-colonial sentiments and connections that long preceded the Cold War context of decolonization. Some brief examples will be instructive.

The Haitian Revolution (1791–1804) is now well known for resonating with anti-colonial movements near and far. Independent Haiti gave material aid to Bolivar's struggles for independence in Latin America; meanwhile, the revolution proved instructive for the Māori King Movement's wars against settlers in 1860s' Aotearoa (New Zealand). Likewise, the victory of Ethiopian forces over the Italian army at Adwa in 1896 demonstrated to the Māori the vulnerability of European colonial forces, and a commentary on Emperor Menelik II's victory even appeared in the newspaper of the Māori Parliament movement (Shilliam 2015a: 117). After Adwa, the sovereign independence of Ethiopia took on especial importance for those in the African diaspora who had long prophesied through Psalms 68:31 their redemption from enslaved pasts and impoverished presents: "Princes shall come out of Egypt, Ethiopia shall soon stretch her hands towards God" (see Shilliam 2013; Jonas 2011). And when Italy returned to invade Ethiopia in 1935 with a fascist army, pro-Ethiopian sentiments were evident across the world. T. B. Allotey, an itinerant merchant from Accra, even managed to establish an Ethiopian Society in Tokyo ("An African British Subject Tells of Ethiopia" 1936).

These anti-colonial affections variously carried on into the Cold War era and were thus contemporaneous with Bandung. They were echoed in Frantz Fanon's affirmation of the global significance of Điện Biên Phủ – the battle that decisively won the Vietnamese liberation from colonial France:

> The great victory of the Vietnamese people at Điện Biên Phủ is no longer strictly speaking a Vietnamese victory. From July 1954 onward the colonial peoples have been asking themselves: "What must we do to achieve a Điện Biên Phủ? How should we go about it?" A Điện Biên Phủ was now within reach of every colonized subject. (Fanon 2004: 30–31)

It was revealing when African American activist and singer Paul Robeson declared in 1954: "Ho Chi Minh is the Toussaint L'Overture of Indo-China" (Foner 1978: 377–379). Che Guevera (1967) would go further and claim that solidarity with the Vietnamese struggle was "not a matter of wishing success to the victim of aggression, but of sharing his[/her] fate." When the hands and feet of colonized peoples were still shackled, battles like Điện Biên Phủ and revolts elsewhere actualized for them the dance for and of freedom. Witnessed Guyanese poet Martin Carter (1951):

> And no matter where I turn
> the fierce revolt goes with me
> like a kiss
> The revolt of Malaya
> And Viet Nam
> The revolt of India
> And Africa
> Like guardian.
> Like guardian at my side
> Is the fight for freedom –
> And like the whole world dancing
> For liberation from the slave maker

For the colonized around the world, the Haitian Revolution, Ethiopia's independence and the Vietnamese liberation were never only national victories; they were apprehended and remembered as global struggles too.[3] Aside from strategic utility, their binding power evinces affective and even spiritual identifications and commitments across colonial and other borders. Naming these identifications and commitments "poetic solidarities," Anna M. Agathangelou's chapter emphasizes the transformative possibilities of past and present anti-colonial internationalisms, from Bandung to contemporary indigenous, feminist, queer and anti-racist movements. Taking Bandung to be a vital site of revolutionary visions and intimate solidarities, her analysis focuses on not only the conceptual logics of Bandung speeches but also their literary dimensions, visceral charges and desires for a world otherwise. In his chapter, Narendran Kumarakulasingam also attends to the intimate and poetic journeys that the colonized take towards each other, an undertaking he calls "de-islanding." If a key effect of colonization is "islanding," that is, the compartmentalization of "natives" into particularity and non-relation, Kumarakulasingam argues that Bandung materialized in and as a worlding process of de-islanding. He dares to connect Sri Lanka with Martinique in an affective solidarity guided by the need for islanded peoples to incline to listen to each other, beyond colonial History and beyond programmes of salvation. Sam Okoth Opondo's chapter also highlights "ways of sensing and making sense of the (third) world" that exceed colonial scripts as well as postcolonial state practices and national narratives. Opondo collects "intimate and colossal" fragments of Bandung speeches and other philosophical, literary and extra-literary texts in order to draw our attention to "multiple communities of sense, some of them dissensual."

The hermeneutic challenge regarding such ways of sensing and de-islanding emanates, at least partly, from the way in which they defied the colonial cartographies that outlawed the colonized from relating to one another on their own terms. In these cartographies, all developmental paths had to follow the "reason" of Europe: bodies, knowledges, trade routes and God travelled one way back to imperial centres. But numerous anti-colonial movements rudely interrupted this logic with inspirations that pointed elsewhere and conversed with each other. Carefully parsing the hermeneutic challenge that Bandung presents, Himadeep Muppidi's chapter cautions against quarantining its meaning within colonial/modern language. Engaging with the ways in which European radical philosopher Jean-Paul Sartre and African American writer Richard Wright "strain against the borders of Europe" in their encounters with (post)colonized peoples, Muppidi discerns both their perceptiveness and limitations in making sense of the intimate coming together of diverse postcolonial bodies *and* "political imaginaries." The global meanings and transformative nature of Bandung remain elusive, Muppidi suggests, if we do not begin to fathom its "kinship producing, world constituting" elements. His sympathetic critique of Wright resonates with those made by Indonesian writers and artists contemporaneous with Wright's visit and recently published in English.[4]

Approaching anti-colonial alliances from a differently intimate angle, Rahul Rao reminds us that they "could serve *both* progressive and reactionary ends, often at the same time." Delving into his own family history to glean the pan-Asianisms before Bandung, Rao finds that when non-European modernizing elites were impelled by European colonialism to look across regions for strategies of empowerment, they would channel their pan-Asian inspirations and resources not only against an imperial West but also against the "restive lower orders at home." From yet another perspective, Aida A. Hozić, too, cautions us about the prospects for solidarities and alternative political imaginaries when/if built upon histories of exclusion. Her reflection on the entwined political histories of Non-Aligned Yugoslavia and "Comrade Jovanka" warns us of entrenched, often gendered, practices of exclusion and silencing. Yet, what can we learn about gendered agency and the power of Bandung on the global imagination and the self-understanding of political actors when Jovanka Broz vividly recollected her participation at Bandung although neither Yugoslavia nor she had been (invited) there?

We maintain that it is difficult to grasp the meanings of Bandung without understanding the constitutive depth of its collective affective politics. Its contentious and multiple meanings arise in good part from the "bonding through bondage" (Phạm & Méndez 2015) that composes an often invisible substrata of international relations. Indeed, Bandung spoke from and to the gut of colonized bodies, one could say. Wasn't it the gut speaking when even a most loyal ally of the United States at the conference – General Carlos P. Romulo, the head of the Philippine delegation – rebuked the West in no equivocal terms:

> We have known, and some of us still know, the searing experience of being demeaned in our own lands, of being systematically relegated to subject status not only politically and economically, and militarily – but racially as well. ... Few of the Western countries were willing to go far enough in condemning the racial practices of the Government of the Union of South Africa. They have yet to learn, it seems, how deeply this issue cuts and how profoundly it unites non-Western peoples who may disagree on all sorts of questions. (Romulo 1956: 68–69; see also Espiritu 2006)

Bandung's range of emotions, from searing hurts to felt solidarities, must be appreciated as political sensibilities that disrupt the self-referential calculus of European "reason" so fundamental to imperial expansion and colonial administration. As former Sri Lankan prime minister Sirimavo R. D. Bandaranaike (1976: 28) affirmed, albeit in the later context of the Non-Aligned Movement (NAM), "[t]he fight against injustice cannot but be emotional and it will help mutual understanding if this simple truth is remembered." If Bandung was felt in the gut, it was because it spoke to deep colonial wounds and expressed a struggle that stretched back over hundreds of years for those whose humanity had been mutilated (see Grovogui 2006). We submit, then, that the meanings of Bandung cannot stay within the bounds of its attendees and formal proceedings, and its communiqué cannot be translated solely into the conventional language of IR. State representatives at the conference, perhaps more than anyone else, understood this excess, which was thus articulated:

> Why did we meet? Some persons called the Prime Ministers of five countries invited you. Do you think that is the reason why [we] met? They were the conscious or unconscious agents of other forces. We met because there is an irrepressible urge amongst the people of Asia and Africa for us to meet. We met because mighty forces are at work in these great continents moving millions of people, creating a ferment in their minds, and urges and passions and a desire for a change from their present conditions. So, however big or small we might be, we represented these great forces. (*Asia-Africa Speaks* 1955: 183; see also ibid.: 138)

LINEAGES OF BANDUNG

The sensibilities that we have sketched out above allow students of international relations to understand how the temporalities and politics of Bandung well exceed the self-interested pursuit of political and/or economic power. With such an expanded understanding, we now wish to consider how the lineages of Bandung can be extended back, forward and elsewhere.

The Asian-African Conference took place at a time when superpower conflict violently interfaced with independence projects whose transformative natures were grounded in entrenched decolonization struggles and would outlast the Cold War era (see Saull 2005). Crucially, attendees at Bandung introduced anti-colonialism and anti-racism as constitutive principles of a new world order rather than as background aspirations in a bipolar rivalry of great powers. Likening the Bandung moment to an "estuary" that forever altered the ecology of world politics, Siba N. Grovogui's chapter traces the diverse political streams crested at the conference to deep-rooted anti-colonial historical formations and comraderies. Moreover, his analysis demonstrates that the multitude of political movements and traditions from Asia and Africa have within themselves, pre- and post-Bandung, the normative and institutional resources to cohere with "universal aspirations while allowing for their respective singularities." In the face of persistent hierarchies and injustices on both international and national terrains, the politics of Bandung reverberates, Grovogui insists, in today's ongoing battles against reinventions of the colonial order in new guises, and in future efforts to enact "new modes of governance and related institutions of subjectivity as foundation for justice, global solidarity, and coexistence."

The story of Eugene Bernard Achan referenced in Grovogui's chapter is suggestive for us: a Trinidadian of mixed ancestry heeded Sun Yat-Sen's appeal to go to revolutionary China and advised him on anti-imperialist foreign policies while also editing the bilingual *Peking Gazette* and founding the *Shanghai Gazette* in the 1910s. Among other things, the story reminds us that antecedents of Bandung lay not only in salient movements and armed struggles in which colonized peoples joined forces, but also in all sorts of incredible and consequential intercolonial crossings and collaborations that are lesser known and often less traceable (e.g. West, Martin and Wilkins 2009; Raza, Roy and Zachariah 2015; Goswami 2012; Shilliam 2015a). For instance, more than half a century before Bandung, Haitian intellectual and statesperson Anténor Firmin spoke of "an undeniable affinity" that he and Cuban independentista José Martí felt for one another. With the help of Puerto Rican revolutionary Dr Ramón Emeterio Betances, they met in Cap Haitien in 1893 to discuss "the great question of Cuban independence and the possibility of a Caribbean Federation" (cited in Phạm & Méndez 2015: 158; see also Plummer 1998). Firmin also fondly recalled "an affinity of views and aspirations that produced a powerful and consistent bond" with Dr Betances, whom he first encountered at the Society of Latin American Unity (Chaar-Pérez 2013: 13).[5] Another Haitian statesperson and poet Benito Sylvain travelled to Ethiopia after the Battle of Adwa in 1896 to meet with Emperor Menelik II. At the first Pan-African Conference, held in London in 1900, Sylvain's enthusiasm perhaps got the best of him when he also decided to unofficially represent himself as aide de-camp of the Ethiopian emperor ("Pan-African Conference" 1900).

By the early twentieth century, these "powerful and consistent" bonds were increasingly organized and institutionalized by various pan-African, pan-Asian and other movements and networks (see, e.g. Assie-Lumumba 2015; Armstrong 2016; Ghazal 2010; Blain 2015).[6] In fact, the meeting in 1927 in Brussels of the League against Imperialism and Colonial Oppression was acknowledged at Bandung by the host of the conference as a formative influence wherein "many distinguished Delegates who are present here today met each other and found new strength in their fight for independence" (*Asia-Africa Speaks* 1955: 20). In his chapter, Randolph B. Persaud seeks to explain the way in which these movements and networks were connected through a "racial dynamic" mutually constituted through histories of oppression and projects of emancipation. Although the actual Bandung Conference involved the Asian far more than the African world, Persaud argues that the anti-colonial and anti-racist norms that structured Bandung were cultivated and transmitted by various pan-Africanist movements that preceded the conference by at least fifty years. Also noteworthy, albeit sorely understudied, were global fora that constituted women's internationalism before and after Bandung, such as the 1928 Pan-Pacific Women's Association's first conference in Honolulu, the 1931 All-Asian Women's Conference in Lahore, the

1944 Pan-Arab Feminist Conference in Cairo, the 1949 Conference of the Women of Asia in Beijing (with guests from North and West Africa), the 1958 Asian-African Conference of Women in Colombo, and the 1961 Afro-Asian Women's Conference in Cairo (see Armstrong 2016; Bier 2011: 154–176; Prashad 2007: 51–61; Paisley 2009).

Since the coming together of political subjectivities and aspirations at Bandung had long been fermented by decolonization movements, all state representatives at the 1955 conference, despite quite different ideological and geostrategic positions in the global order (Kahin 1956), were acutely aware of the intervention that they were making into international relations. "We do not intend to be the playthings of others," proclaimed Indian prime minister Jawaharlal Nehru at the Asian Relations Conference in New Delhi in 1947 (cited in Ampiah 2007: 29). Eight years later at Bandung, Indonesian president Sukarno echoed Nehru's declaration in the conference's opening speech: "[Previously colonized peoples] are no longer the victims of colonialism. They are no longer the tools of others and the playthings of forces they cannot influence. Today, you are representatives of free peoples, peoples of a different stature and standing in the world" (*Asia-Africa Speaks* 1955: 21).

With this new stature and standing, Bandung established the position of "non-alignment" vis-à-vis a Cold War framework of two blocs. Formally instituted in Belgrade in 1961, non-alignment did not mean "neutrality" as often translated into the conventional dichotomy of dis/interest and im/partiality. A simple question from President Sukarno would render this translation untenable: "How is it possible to be disinterested about colonialism?" (ibid.: 23) Rather, non-alignment referenced an independent stand that refused, as Nehru made clear in his Bandung speech, to be "dragged in, and tie ourselves to Europe's troubles and Europe's hatreds and Europe's conflicts" (ibid.: 185) Although newly independent states were entangled with the contending poles of capitalism versus communism, non-alignment enunciated an anti-colonial politics that was more fundamental: an international relations in which Asians and Africans could no longer be treated as the anonymous, obedient, or chaotic "rest" in the shadow of the West. Representatives at Bandung announced that they were now global actors in their own right, with their own purposes, trajectories, ideals and visions of how the world ought to be. Hence, Bandung's intervention lies not only in the resolve to not be "camp-followers," but simultaneously, in the (co)authoring of a new "we" of the global order:

Are we copies of Europeans or Americans or Russians? What are we? We are Asians or Africans. We are none else, and for anybody to tell us that we have to be camp-followers of Russia or America or any country of Europe, is, if I may say so, not very creditable to our new dignity, our new independence, our new freedom and our new spirit and our new self-reliance. (ibid.: 186)

Crucially, this new "we" had no illusion about the many forms that colonialism could take even in an international system constituted by formally independent states. President Sukarno famously warned in his opening address:

> I beg of you do not think of colonialism only in the classic form which we of Indonesia, and our brothers in different parts of Asia and Africa, knew. Colonialism has also its modern dress, in the form of economic control, intellectual control, actual physical control by a small but alien community within a nation. It is a skillful and determined enemy, and it appears in many guises. It does not give up its loot easily. (ibid.: 23)

While the delegates at Bandung covered a spectrum of economic systems between capitalist, communist and otherwise, the conference as a whole addressed the fact that a global-colonial division of labour persisted even in a postcolonial state system. This challenge of political-economic transformation was subsequently taken up in the United Nations by the campaign for a New International Economic Order (NIEO) (see Anghie 2004; Murphy 1984; Benjamin 2015; Nesadurai 2008). In her chapter, Heloise Weber argues that Bandung serves as an alternative archive of development that allows us to foreground past and present struggles for restorative justice while evaluating the continuing strictures of the colonial order. Weber's analysis of the conference and especially the NIEO identifies how critical challenges to the colonial division of labour were undermined by Western capitalist states and are epistemically erased by hegemonic narratives of liberal internationalism in IR. Yet, Weber maintains, the spirit of Bandung can be found in the ongoing struggles for development otherwise in fresh sites such as the Bolivarian Alliance for the Peoples of Our America and various social movements.

Attentive to more than economic structures of inequality, Bandung delegates understood that colonization proceeded not only through conquest and exploitation but also through cultural estrangement. Accordingly, one of the pillars in Bandung's final communiqué was cultural cooperation among the rich cultures of Asia and Africa in order to renew old contacts and develop new ones, against colonial suppression and segregation (*Asia-Africa Speaks*: 161–169). Aimé Césaire, famous poet of Negritude, commented that "the historic conference in Bandung can be said to have been not only a great political event; it was also a cultural event of the first order, because it was the peaceful uprising of peoples hungry not only for justice and dignity but also for what colonization had taken away of the greatest importance: culture" (Césaire 2010: 131). Amy Niang's chapter demonstrates how the challenge presented by Bandung of meaningful self-determination was at once cultural and political. Niang investigates how members of the Francophone

Rassemblement Démocratique Africain (RDA) drew constructively on the Bandung convention at their third and largest congress in 1957 in Bamako, Mali. Bandung informed the RDA debates about two interrelated challenges that French West Africa faced in relation to the empire: First, how might decolonizing peoples negotiate association with or autonomy from the colonizer?; and, second, how might Africans stop obsessing about the need to prove their political competency to the colonizer and speak, instead, to themselves about themselves?

In all these respects, Bandung contrasted with and provided an alternative to the Cold War calculus of superpower conflict manifested, for instance, in the contemporaneous South East Asia Treaty Organization (SEATO), which sought merely to promote US geopolitical, economic and military dominance in the region (Jones 2005). It can be argued that an international conference of statespeople and interested parties convened exclusively by Asians and Africans, unlike SEATO, sent a message that, as African American writer James Baldwin (1998) put it, "[t]his world is white no longer, and it will never be white again." In other words, if Western colonial powers had hitherto monopolized the "international community," they were now kept out of a global convention "of almost all of the human race living in the main geopolitical center of gravity of the earth" (Wright 1956: 12). Furthermore, as the host of the conference noted, this union did not take place in European metropoles, as by necessity before, but on Asian land (*Asia-Africa Speaks* 1955: 19), land upon which the majority of humanity lived. Such a fresh political locale and composition undoubtedly divulged a shift in the geo/body-political as well as imaginative terrain of international relations.

Claiming to represent the majority of humanity, the Bandung communiqué spoke of a different international relations ordered along the lines of equality and mutual respect over hierarchy, world peace and justice over war and domination, non-interference over aggression and self-determination over political subjugation and economic dependency.[7] Vijay Prashad hears the echo of this "Bandung Spirit" in the subsequent NAM as well:

> From Belgrade to Tokyo, from Cairo to Dar es Salaam, politicians and intellectuals began to speak of the "Bandung Spirit." What they meant was simple: that the colonized world had now emerged to claim its space in world affairs, not just as an adjunct of the First or Second World, but as a player in world affairs. Furthermore, the Bandung spirit was a refusal of both economic subordination and cultural suppression – two of the major policies of imperialism. (Prashad 2007: 45–46)

So conceived, the Bandung spirit can be linked to a broad array of political, economic, and cultural initiatives such as the Afro-Asian People's Solidarity

Organization that resulted from the 1957 conference in Cairo; the Tricontinental Conference in Havana in 1966, which launched the Organization of Solidarity with the People of Asia, Africa and Latin America (OSPAAAL); the Congresses of Black Writers and Artists in 1956 and in 1959; the series of Afro-Asian Writers Conferences which started with the first in Tashkent in 1958; and the Third World Approaches to International Law, to name just a few (Farid 2016; Eslava, Fakhri & Nesiah 2016). Furthermore, as many have suggested, the Bandung spirit is revived today in non-state-centric articulations of global order and solidarity.

Ultimately, Bandung's intervention into international relations was to reclaim the dignity *and* affinity of those whom colonial powers had attempted for generations to subjugate, humiliate, disregard and partition from one another. Bandung redefines the very idea of international relations in terms of *who constitutes the global and what constitutes the political.* The unconcealable nervousness and exasperation that it provoked in the uninvited albeit "super-powerful" Western states confirmed the felt challenge posed by Bandung.[8] (The CIA even proposed to assassinate President Sukarno to sabotage the conference, but did not carry out the plan [Wardaya 2005]. There were also assassination plots against Chinese Premier Chou En-lai, one of which was executed without success [Bidwai 2005; Datta-Ray 2015].)

It is critical, though, to remember that all the colonial strictures and divisions that Bandung opposed were inflected through the conference itself. Indeed, while arguing for a radical transformation of the political, economic and cultural structuring of international relations, most of the attending statespeople had inherited precisely such structures of governance. For one, the unanimous desire for development led newly independent states to carry out projects of modernization that reproduced the hierarchy of civilization over backwardness (see Herrera 2005; Chakrabarty 2010). Moreover, the call for collective self-determination at Bandung was inescapably entangled with lineages of the modern nation-state and all its colonially inherited pitfalls. These include, in particular, the violence exercised upon minoritized nationalities and the inability to recognize it as internal colonialism (see Chatterjee 2005; Nandy 2005; Dirlik 2015; Persaud 2003b). In his chapter, Giorgio Shani points out these pitfalls in relation to the global capitalist economy, nation-state homogenization as well as Enlightenment-inspired developmental progress. Significantly for Shani, the promise of Bandung, yet to be realized, lies in the possibility of redefining international relations along post-Western, post-secular lines. Such an international relations would be "based on different conceptions of sovereignty and development embedded in *their own* religio-cultural traditions" instead of relying on the Judeo-Christian conception of secular time and transcendence.

Most notably, in its final communiqué, the conference recognized Indonesia's claim over West Irian, then still under Dutch administration. In 1961, indigenous activists started to call this land West Papua as part of their movement for self-determination. In 1969, Indonesia annexed West Papua and has since undertaken a violent suppression of the self-determination movement. In his chapter, Budi Hernawan investigates in detail the "colonisation by other means" of the peoples of West Papua through and after the transfer of the territory to Indonesia. He carefully documents the many forms of state violence against Papuans as well as their persistent contestations against Indonesia's sovereignty over Papua. Hernawan suggests that the decolonial impulse at Bandung resides now in the liberation movements of Papuans and those who support them, such as the Melanesian Spearhead Group. In their chapter, Rosalba Icaza and Tamara Soukotta also discuss this violent disjuncture between the decolonizing imperative of Bandung and the postcolonial predicament of Indonesia. They highlight plural, even conflicting, ways of relating to Bandung by taking into account its various dimensions as an event/place and its presence/absence in relation to their own positionalities. In their dialogue, it becomes clear that the plotting of Bandung in global lineages of decolonization must always reckon with its concomitant implication in lineages of postcolonial state consolidation.

CONCLUSION

We take these paradoxes, contradictions and – some would say – betrayals extremely seriously; in fact, we would argue that they reveal the central importance of Bandung as a nexus where commitments to decolonization meet the challenges and practices of postcolonial politics. In this respect, the diverse and often contentious meanings of Bandung help us better understand the cardinal points of international relations in the twentieth and, we would suggest, the twenty-first century. Bandung inaugurated impassioned collective endeavours by newly independent countries to democratize world order across political, economic and cultural spheres. As Mustapha Pasha argues, the "Bandung impulse" (Pasha 2013) of these endeavours exceeded their postcolonial limitations in terms of enlivening both historical memories and contemporary imaginations.

And yet, notwithstanding some of the literature referenced in this introduction, the Bandung Conference remains woefully understudied in IR, and in the Euro-American academia at large.[9] Why? Building on the points we have made above, we would argue that in theory and practice alike, peoples in the so-called Third World or Global South have been continually treated as objects, usually of interventions, and are rarely conceived as co-authors of and in international relations, who collectively practice their own visions of political order and just relations. Within this framework of objectification, Bandung cannot but be a "non-event" (Trouillot 1997). In the few cases in which Bandung is broached, it is often located within a context of Cold War rivalry and ideologies, and shorn of its deeper-determining colonial coordinates. What is more, Bandung, if mentioned, is mostly subalternized as it is made to fit ready-made categories of Hobbesian strategic self-interest, Kantian or liberal idealism, interstate diplomacy and/or regional norms and policies.

Over the past few years, we have organized a set of roundtable panels at the annual conventions of the International Studies Association to invite reflections on the meanings of Bandung and, most importantly, to refuse its subalternization. The result is this book wherein all the contributors variously consider Bandung as a nexus through which different globalisms are enunciated, and in the poetic words of Jahlani A. H. Niaah (2016), as "part ghost of the past forefathers [and foremothers] and part echo of a future gestation." Bandung emerges from these investigations as an archive of sensibilities, desires as well as fears, wherein decolonizing impulses and postcolonial predicaments constantly entangle, join and break to form the matter of international relations. In the conclusion to this book, Mustapha Kamal Pasha dwells on the tensions imbibed within and the openings promised by this archive – what he calls "the Bandung within" – for continuing decolonial struggles in the world, including in the academy and especially in the discipline of IR. And in an afterword, drawing from the book chapters, Craig N. Murphy proposes that rich paths of research remain to be explored by scholars of both past and future Bandungs by digging – often right where you are standing – for stories, people, memories and aspirations that have been overlooked in global politics, and for the profound and most unexpected connections among them.

NOTES

1. We have in mind the sense of adjusting and conviviality in Bush, Davison and Muppidi (2009).

2. See Robeson's "Greetings to Bandung" in Foner (1978): 398–400; Du Bois' greetings "The Bandung Conference" in Aptheker (1982): 236–37.

3. Pankaj Mishra (2012: 1–11) tells us about similar reverberations of Japan's victory over Russia in 1905.

4. Among other things, their accounts note that Wright's visit was funded in large part by a CIA front. As a result, he met with writers and artists to whom US cultural diplomacy would be amenable while avoiding others, especially Islamic-oriented ones. See Roberts and Foulcher (2016).

5. We thank Jason Vargas for this reference.

6. It is important to note that Caribbean and pan-American anticolonial and anti-slavery transnational networks were formed much earlier. See for example Arroyo (2013); Kamugisha (2013); Reyes-Santos (2013).

7. In addition to the final communiqué, see "Address by Ali Sastroamidjojo, President of the Conference" in *Asia-Africa Speaks* (1955: 31–39); Chatterjee (2005); Lee (2009); Amin (2015); Berger (2004: 47–55).

8. Aside from the literature referenced above see also Parker (2006); Tarling (1992).

9. With the exception of a few publications since its fiftieth anniversary in 2005. In addition to the above-referenced literature, see also Mackie (2005); Rey (2014); Young (2005); Abraham (2009, 2014).

Part I

SENSING BANDUNG

Chapter 2

The Elements of Bandung

Himadeep Muppidi

EARTH

When I think of Bandung, it is not Indonesia's Sukarno, India's Jawaharlal
Nehru or Egypt's Gamal Abdel Nasser I think of first, though they, along with
the delegates of two-thirds of the world, were all there, from April 18 to April
24, 1955, and multiple photographs speak, in black and white, to that huddle
of colour at the first Asian-African Conference. When I think of Bandung,
it is not the writer Richard Wright I think of first, though Wright rushed to
Bandung on reading about it in a small section of a newspaper in Paris and,
even decades later, his black-, yellow- and turquoise-covered report on the
conference, *The Color Curtain*, is the source text for many. Nor do I think
first, when I think of Bandung, of the mighty Paul Robeson, brother Paul, who
desperately wanted to come to Bandung – "How I should have loved to be at
Bandung! ... How I would love to see my brothers from Africa, India, China,
Indonesia and from all the people represented at Bandung" (Foner 1978,
398–400) – but was stopped by a fearful and nervous US State Department
that impounded his passport because its impoverished worldview could only
see a short-run embarrassment but not the deeper one awaiting it in history.[1]

When I think of Bandung, I think first, perhaps a bit strangely, of an orientalist scene, a scene of nativity, of natives gathered in the night, a scene
evoked by a European philosopher, Jean-Paul Sartre. Why does Sartre's word-
image of a native huddle come to mind rather than the photographs from the
week-long conference in Bandung or the report of Wright or the greetings and
global longings of a Robeson for Bandung? Is it the sheer/queer pleasure of
revisiting postcolonial beginnings through the anxiety of European eyes? Or,
is it that Europe, stirred properly, that is, against the flow of its provincial currents, spills its colonial secrets readily? Either way, when I think of Bandung,

what comes to mind, first, are Sartre's words prefacing Frantz Fanon's *The Wretched of the Earth* (2004) and the centrality of one scene, one image, in the introduction, that those words sketch very beautifully.

Introducing Fanon, Sartre warns his "fellow Europeans" of the postcolonial futures headed their way; futures that will situate them as the objects, not the subjects, of new histories. Depicting himself as "a European" "stealing [his] enemy's book and turning it into a way of healing Europe," Sartre wants Europeans to make "the most of it," of this theft, in order to heal themselves. Heralding Fanon, Sartre addresses Europeans primarily: warns them, advises them, instructs them to read (Fanon) for their own good, for their own, postcolonial, recovery. He confesses to stealing for them, from "the enemy," so that they, his fellow Europeans, can cure themselves. Why does Sartre, the radical philosopher, steal from the postcolonial writer/fighter to heal colonial Europe first? How does he justify this renewed looting of the colonized? A postcolonial may, perhaps, be excused for wondering if Europe hasn't "made the most" of it one too many times, already.

What compels Sartre's thievery here? Is Sartre's gift motivated by a concern that the once colonized might not be that interested in healing Europe? Is he worried that Europe, left to itself, would not know, until it was too late, how to tread the postcolonial currents rushing its way? Or, is the "stealing" a rhetorical feint, driven by a sense that advice stolen from "the enemy," advice taken by stealth, advice served as booty, tastes sweeter to a colonial tongue? Whatever the tastes flavouring the theft, Europe needed help – the sort of help that the US State Department could also have benefited from when dealing with Paul Robeson – and Sartre is ready, reading the words, meanings and forces of the decolonizing world as well as the difficulties in sloughing off his illusions of himself: "You see," he tells us, "I, too, cannot lose my subjective illusion. I, too, say to you [Europeans], 'All is lost unless …'."

Curating Fanon's prophetic text – the "Bible of decolonization" in Stuart Hall's words (Bhabha in Fanon 2004, xvi) – Jean-Paul Sartre traces carefully the changes in the "subjective illusions" of the natives who, once upon a colonial time, were "fabricate[d]" and "fully doctored" in the metropolitan capitals of Europe. Once home, this "native elite" was expected to diligently echo, "somewhere in Africa and Asia," Sartre tells us, whatever was voiced in Paris, Amsterdam and London. That is, the subjective illusions of the natives were engineered in colonial capitals, and they were then sent off to serve as industrious echoers of colonial wisdom around the empire. Ostensibly.

The enunciatory centrality of European metropolises ("Paris, Amsterdam, London") as against the shapelessness of the colonies ("somewhere in Africa and Asia"), the monopolistic dissemination, from colonial centres, of magical mantras/philosophical concepts ("Parthenon," "Fraternity") as against their inchoate echoes on the peripheries ("… thenon," "… nity") portray well the passivity and pathetically "dependent" nature of the colonized: their amorphousness, one could say, within this framing of the colonial international. In this colonial international, the native elite depended on the energies and desires from the colonial centres to acquire a form – What am I? Am I a human? – and secure a recognizable subjectivity. Indeed, colonial power could not but, through regular surges, help shore up the native in this fabrication. Sartre calls this, sarcastically no doubt, a "golden age," for the colonial centres.

But golden ages age and expire also. And so through the 1940s and 1950s, decolonization battles rearranged this golden age and de-formed these relations between Europe and its colonies. It was Europe that, in confrontations with the colonized, faced relative dispossession and was discharged of its self-imposed burdens: dislocated steadily but forcefully from places such as Điện Biên Phủ. Bandung comes, when it comes, after Điện Biên Phủ.

Reading this temporality of progressive dispossession, Sartre exhorts Europeans to pay heed to the voices of *The Wretched of the Earth*: "Europeans, open this book, look inside." Sartre is encouraging his fellow Europeans to head away from their own borders of illusion and seek the unfamiliar outside through the words of the wretched. If they take heed, what will they see in this new space? "After taking a short walk in the night you will see strangers gathered around a fire, get closer and listen." Though Sartre begins the preface with native talk, what Europe sees as it walks away (from its historical self) are strangers, not natives. Sartre is teaching Europe how to lose, on this walk, the fabricated subjectivity of the non-European that Europe has long clung to: the non-European as a passive, pathetic and dependent being, that is, a native.

The stranger that Europe will see, if it heeds Sartre, is not a native. This new being is an unfamiliar figure; its unfamiliarity is a positive sign of the limits of European knowledge when it comes to the diversity of the world. Europe has, of course, seen strangers before but recognized them only on its own terms. Stories of colonization are also, often enough, stories that tame the unfamiliar as the familiar; scripts that frame the unknown stranger as the known native. Europe had long cultured a sensibility that allowed it the illusion that it knew the natives well, probably better than the natives knew themselves. And crucial to that colonial myth were the natives' seeming awe of and desire for Europe itself, that is, its indispensability.

But the new strangers that Europe sees, in Sartre's reading of *The Wretched of the Earth*, are indifferent to Europe. They do not, as Europe walks towards them, defer to it: "They might see you, but they will go on talking among themselves without lowering their voices." They do not invite it into their circle. Sartre acknowledges here the changes in the "subjective illusions" of the decolonizing generations: natives are no longer natives but have reverted to being strangers. They do not defer. Colonial intimacy has morphed into postcolonial unfamiliarity. And, in that reconfiguration of a subjective illusion, there is the promise of a new beginning, potentially as between equals, between Europe and these strangers.

Mapping these dramatic changes in the "psycho-affective" (Bhabha in Fanon 2004) relationship between European subjectivities and the natives-turned-strangers, Sartre observes: "Their indifference strikes home. ... You, standing at a respectful distance, you now feel eclipsed, nocturnal and numb." He presses the point: "The sons [and daughters] ignore you." This is a world that has turned strange and become indifferent to Europe. This is a world in which Europe has moved from the centre to an ignorable locale. It has become dispensable.

The daughters and sons, while indifferent to the presence of Europe, are, however, engrossed in talking to each other. They talk in order to reduce their unfamiliarity with each other. They talk in order to move from being strangers to being neighbours. They talk in order to establish friendships and acknowledge kinships. Cousins through colonization, they become cousins in conversation. Cairo, Djakarta, Beijing, Rangoon, Colombo, Hà Nội and New Delhi talk to each other without Paris or London or Amsterdam coming in between or having a say or having anything to say. But what world is this in which Europe is ignored and London and Paris and Amsterdam have no say? What world is this in which Europe stands at a "respectable distance," "feeling eclipsed, nocturnal and numb"?

BLOOD AND BONES

Even from faraway Europe, Richard Wright hears the chatter and smells the sizzle of the "extra," "extra," "extra" ordinary elements going into the making of Bandung. *The Color Curtain* (1956) begins with Wright, post-Christmas, idly "thumbing" a newspaper and his bafflement as he snags on an item about an Asian-African Conference, a bafflement that induces him to do some "rapid calculation of the populations" involved. I wonder why Wright so quickly translates twenty-nine nations into their population equivalents. Why does he not take the nations as the face of the international? That is, what about his way of inhabiting the world allows him to read it not just as an association of nation-states but also as an agglomeration of peoples? Whatever those reasons may be, Wright's calculation turns quickly into a "stream of realizations" of the "ex-colonial" character of the peoples and political leaders implicated in this conference, which morphs in turn, into a snap judgement of how this "meeting of the rejected" was a "kind of judgment upon [the] Western world."

Barely pausing in the transition from bafflement to judgement, Wright notes the "extra-," "extra-," "extra-," nature of the meeting itself. "There was," he says, "something extra-political, extra-social, almost extra-human about it." And then, as if to give form and weight to this triple extra dimension, this excess that he cannot quite name precisely, he adds: "It smacked of tidal waves, of natural forces. ..." In intensely feeling and conceptually presenting the excess that Bandung emanated – an excess in terms of the political, social and human aspects of our world – Wright reaches for the elements: "tidal waves" and "natural forces." And, just in case "tidal waves" and "natural forces" were still inadequate, Wright stretches the making of Bandung across centuries while infusing it, simultaneously, into the bodies of "ex-colonial peoples": "The agenda and subject matter had been written for centuries in the blood and bones of the participants."

Though not a participant himself, Wright speaks of the emotional forces, within his own body, that were surging towards Bandung: his expressly "felt" need to go to Bandung; his sense that he, somehow, brought a special understanding to it; his desire "to go anyhow," even though he "represented no government." He plans to go as a reporter, even though he had no idea whom he would report for. But that ignorance of his likely audience wouldn't matter since, notwithstanding a general weariness in Europe about these places, he would still be reporting on the speech of "the human race" ("I don't know. For somebody. ... I know that people are tired of hearing of these hot, muddy faraway places filled with people yelling for freedom. But this is the human race speaking. ..."). Wright is also unclear how he would report the meeting but he is certain that his "life has given [him] keys to what they [the human race] would say or do."

In the course of a few pages, Wright conveys to us Bandung's power to "smack" a seasoned writer with the force of multiple elements. Richard Wright, of course, is not just any seasoned reporter but also an African American writer who sees his race, class, religious and rebellious political experiences and emotions as allowing him a special access to what "these people," "think and feel and why." His own life, as an African American, has given him "keys" to the voices and actions of those gathering in Bandung. What we feel in *The Color Curtain* then is Wright's own "blood and bones" response to the elemental forces, the blood and bones, of the wretched of the earth, pooling at Bandung.

Ensconced in Europe, shuttling between Paris and Madrid, Wright senses the wretched of the earth and wants to get closer to them by getting to Bandung. Is reporting on Bandung – even when unsure about his audience and unclear about his mode of reporting – just the cover Wright needs to escape the colonial metropolis for more colourful climes? If Sartre feels European and steals the words of the wretched to enlighten Europe, is Wright, all native blood and bones, stealing himself into darker-cooler spaces? What does he think he will find in these shades? What does he hope to?

RACE AND RELIGION

Even as the elemental forces constitutive of Bandung tug at him, Wright sees
the limitations of his own "subjective illusions." In preparing for Bandung,
as he does his homework on Asian realities, Wright delineates what he sees
as the differences between a white Western, an African American and an
Asian subjectivity when it comes to talking with each other. As an African
American, he is conscious of the advantages of colour/race he possesses when
interacting with Asians on the meanings of Bandung (Wright 1956, 25): "In
my questioning of Asians I had had one tangible factor in my favor, a factor
that no white Westerner could claim. I was 'colored' and every Asian I had
spoken to had known what being 'colored' meant. Hence, I had been able to
hear Asians express themselves without reserve; they had felt no need to save
face before me. ..." The shared understanding of being coloured made for
less inhibited conversations between African Americans and Asians.

This advantage of colour is compounded by the profound limitations that
Western subjectivities might already face in making sense of the meanings
of Bandung (Wright 1956, 82): "I soon realized that American newsmen
had at least two grave disabilities when trying to grasp what was happening:
one, they had no philosophy of history with which to understand Bandung;
two, they were trying to understand actions initiated by someone else and
they could not quite grasp the nature of the terms in which those actions
were being projected." This reading of the West's limitations foreshadows,
in a way, Sartre's warning to Europe that it was clueless about the postcolonial currents coming its way, currents that would situate it as the object
rather than the subject of history. Wright's reading is also echoed by Nehru
(2001, 84–85), who says that the newspapermen from "other countries" took
a "superficial view" of Bandung, focusing on "personalities" and framing
Bandung in terms of Cold War politics rather than by grasping the "ferment
in Asia" and "the forces at work there." Nehru and Wright merge in saying
that the "real meanings of Bandung," were only gradually being understood
and only by particular subjectivities.[2]

But Wright also notes some limits to the African American perspective
when compared with the Asian perspective in relation to the West. Though
the African American subjectivity has a distinct edge over the white Western
one in grasping the meanings of Bandung, as well as the "ferment" and
"forces" at work in Asia and Africa, it lacks something that the Asian subjectivity has, namely the "absoluteness" with which "many Asians hated
the West." This was "an absoluteness that no American Negro could ever
muster," and it was one that reduced the differences between white Western
and African American subjectivities to the "status of a family quarrel."[3] In
other words, notwithstanding the affinity and "advantage" of colour, Wright

puts the African American and white Western subjectivities in the same "family," while drawing an absolute line of difference – a border marked by hate – between that family and the world of coloured and ex-colonial people outside.

This is a distinction that I find appealing as well as disturbing. That an Asian subjectivity musters an "absoluteness" in its opposition to the West speaks to the power of decolonizing struggles and postcolonial imaginations to wrest themselves away, to "de-link," as it were, from the pre-fabrications and modular diffusions of Europe (Amin 1990; Chatterjee 1991). But that this negation of colonial imaginaries, of the seemingly "normal" "conditions of life" as scripted by the West, is interpreted as "hate" (or in racial and religious terms) is troubling. It is troubling because it seems to deny that the absoluteness of the opposition could stem from any basis other than hatred; that it could, for instance, be based on other imaginations of the necessary "conditions of life."

It is precisely a history of these other imaginations that postcolonial leaders such as Nehru were specifically evoking at the conference: "Has it come to this, that the leaders of thought who have given religions and all kinds of things to the world have to tag on to this kind of group or that and be hangers on of this party or the other carrying out their wishes and occasionally giving an idea?"[4] Bandung makes its meaning from a shared understanding that Asia and Africa had a long history of original contributions to the world of thought and that there was no need to meekly follow either the United States or the USSR in thinking the global. Moreover, the postcolonial leaders gathered at Bandung deliberately avoided conjuring up either "racialism" or "hate" as the central factors of relevance and kept the focus on political issues of anti-colonial struggles and peaceful coexistence.[5]

Why then does Wright deploy this distinction?

In reading Wright's interpretations closely, it is clear that there is a disjuncture between what he feels corporeally about Bandung and what he is able to say about it. It is as if he can think the postcolonial imaginary at play in Bandung only as an extension of certain significantly limiting concepts: race, religion and emotion. However powerful these might be, and however positively he may read them, Wright cannot but see them as the obverse of reason, that is, as forms of irrationality. Here is Wright, for instance, commenting on the world on display at Bandung: "It was no accident that most of the delegates were deeply religious men representing governments and vast populations steeped in mystical visions of life." Wright also claims, subsequently, that race and religion were the "only realities" that postcolonial leaders could "appeal to," though these were also "two of the most powerful and irrational forces in human nature": "Sukarno was appealing to race and religion; they were the only realities in the lives of the men before him that he could appeal to. And, as I sat listening, I began to sense a deep and organic relation here in Bandung between race and religion, *two of the most power-ful and irrational forces in human nature.* Sukarno was not evoking these twin demons; he was not trying to create them; he was trying to organize them. ... The reality of race and religion was there, swollen, sensitive, turbu-lent."[6] In thus seeing race and religion as having a "deep and organic relation" to each other, as "powerful but irrational forces" and as the "twin demons" that were being "organized" by postcolonial leaders such as Sukarno at Bandung, Wright's reading evacuates the Asian-African Conference of its political history. It effectively reduces the historical and social and economic aspects of nationalist and decolonization struggles to the management of tur-bulent nature and natural forces by a few leaders.

Even less surprisingly, Wright ends up seeing most of the political speeches at Bandung as structured around the themes of race and religion and perceives rationality in them only on rare occasions (1956, 148–149): "Only when Mr. Tatsunosuke Takasaki, principal Japanese delegate, rose to speak did the tone sink to the level of the rational. But even he had to speak in a confessional tone." Wright's inability (or unwillingness) to conceptual-ize the excess he senses in Bandung in a language other than that of "race," "religion," "emotion" or "irrationality" is, therefore, a serious constraint on his accessing the historical significance and meanings of Bandung.

How do we read Wright's failure in understanding the political imaginar-ies constitutive of Bandung? Do the familial connections he draws between African American and white Western subjectivities ensure that "[o]nce his particular grievances were redressed the [African American subject] reverted to a normal Western outlook"? And that it is this "normal Western outlook" that is framing Wright's readings of the speeches at Bandung? Do African American subjectivities necessarily take for granted the normalcy of the West in a way that the colonized outside of the West do not? Is the African American forced to inhabit the US nation, and hence the Western family, in a way that other colonized subjects do not have to? Or, is it, as I believe is more likely the case, that Wright is held back by the language of colonial modernity, even as he tries, in multiple ways, to make sense of Bandung? And that language cannot but see race, religion and emotion as negative forces, forces that can be organized but do not, on that account, necessarily lose their "irrationality"?

Whatever be the different sources of their overall limitations, we can see that both Sartre and Wright strain against the borders of Europe in ways that both facilitate and limit what they can imagine of the politics of other actors in the world. Hailed as a European, Sartre is pulled back into dressing its wounds and finding a way to heal it. Pulled intensely by the world that lies beyond Europe, Wright pushes against his inherited languages to draw attention to its excess, and yet falls back on the "normalcy of the Western outlook," with its binary of rationality/irrationality as the marker of an essential difference between the West and multiple other actors.

What is missing in both Sartre and Wright then is a richer and deeper sense of the politics that much of the world (i.e. the human race) is capable of, that is, the political imaginaries productive of Bandung. Both Sartre and Wright see and feel the "darker nations" gathering outside the West but are unable to read the range of colours constitutive of their politics. The language of an alternative global politics – a worldview that crystallizes later on as non-alignment but whose core elements were very much at play in Bandung – thus eludes both Sartre and Wright. Maybe this is because they are still beholden to an epistemology of light/dark, rationality/irrationality, reason/emotion and, necessarily, of course, West/Rest.

But rather than despair of the West, once more, rather than mark yet another distinction of absoluteness, I wonder if it might be possible to rework these relations drawing on the spirit of Bandung itself: a spirit oriented towards finding the global, moral commons. Perhaps Sartre and Wright, reread more hospitably, might give us some hope for not giving up on the West's ability to see beyond itself, beyond its own play of light and shade.

FIRE

Bandung pictures the world anew. But when presented with complex political colours, the West sees only shadows. The shadows – its ostensibly darker selves – seem to be meeting, moving, talking, agitating outside Europe. If the West looks outside and expects to see only puppetry, that is, the play of its shadows, then any autonomous movements of these darker selves, is likely to strike anxiety and terror into its heart. Its "philosophy of history," as recognized by both Wright and Sartre, cannot accommodate non-Western forms of political agency: How can these shadows be meeting and moving on their own? And, how are they able to do that without Europe, somehow, masterminding the show?

That this anxiety is no figment of Sartre or Wright's literary imagination is evident in the criticisms that Bandung encountered in many Western sites. Nehru refers to such criticisms in the course of a speech to his political party on the historical significance[7] of Bandung: "If you have read any of the criticisms in foreign newspapers, and which I have been reading since I came back, mostly they have been angry criticisms: 'What business have these people to meet without their elders and mentors! Oh! they are going to meet like children away from their teacher, they want to play about and misbehave,' – this kind of extraordinary mental approach." What is, of course, evident in these Western criticisms is a colonial imaginary that infantilizes non-Europeans or shades them into selves perennially dependent on European enlightenment.

Familiar with such a colonial imaginary, Sartre has an answer to an anxious and nervous Europe: "The fire that warms and enlightens them," Sartre reveals to Europe, "is not yours." This is an answer that explains the shadows but probably doesn't calm European anxieties. I, on the other hand, find in its explanation a clarity that hundreds of black and white photographs of chatty and smiling postcolonial leaders and the parade of their costumed delegations or the content of their agreements and disagreements cannot quite convey about Bandung: the wretched of the earth have circled around their own fire.

If the wretched of the earth have kindled and gathered around their own fire, then Bandung, from a colonial perspective, is the warning of a trauma to come: the trauma of witnessing one's dispensability, one's irrelevance, in a world supposedly centred on the colonial self. Therein lies its terror. If the wretched of the earth have gathered around their own fire, then Bandung, from a postcolonial perspective, is the very real possibility of "a world (or worlds) of our making." It is the initiation of a new multiplicity. Of new fires and new gatherings. Of "polycentricity." Therein lies its appeal.

Fascinated by the terror as well as the appeal, scribbling a Post-it to the tangible pulls and archival pleasures of the Asian-African Conference in Bandung, I wonder about the imaginaries that compel such primal gatherings. In *Things Fall Apart*, Chinua Achebe ([1959] 1994, 166–167), writing around the same period as Bandung, shows me one way to think that question: "A man who calls his kinsmen to feast does not do so to save them from starving. They all have food in their own homes. When we gather together in the moonlit village ground, it is not because of the moon. Everyman can see it in his own compound. We come together because it is good for kinsmen to do so."

Kinsmen and kinswomen come together; the human race gathers itself; we call or come together for a feast, because it is good for kinfolk to do so. We do not do so because we lack food in our nations or because we cannot see the moon from our capitals. Achebe reminds me that there are worlds of our making where coming together is not always a function of instrumental, self-interest driven, actions: we come together because it is good to do so. But if kinfolk come together because it is good to do so, that coming together also produces new bonds and nourishes old ties. That is, coming together is also constitutive and transformative of relationships. Wright, to his credit, grasps this. He too understands that Bandung is a transformative experience and not just the implementation of prior agendas (Wright 1956, 129): "It was my impression that, with the exception of Nehru, Chou En-lai, and U Nu, no other delegations or heads of delegations came to Bandung but with the narrowest of parochial hopes and schemes. But when they got to Bandung, with their speeches in their pockets, something happened that no Asian or African, no Easterner or Westerner, could have dreamed of." Something happens in collective gatherings that no one initially dreams of. We are otherwise than what we had prepared our speeches for.

Bandung, looking through the eyes of an Achebe, is a feast, a coming together of postcolonial kith and kin. It is a festive gathering where Asia and Africa meet and look forward to meeting other Americas and other Europes. If Europe is not on the guest list, it is only because it is not yet willing to see itself as kith and kin to the once colonized. Not because race or religion or irrationality or hate keep it out "absolutely" from an Asian-African Conference.

A Bandung feast stages the times and places to come when European supremacy disappears from global politics. Postcolonial and Western subalterns read hope in that disappearance. A Bandung feast is the social construction of another world, "a world of our making" (Onuf 2012). Accompanying this other construction, this coming together because it is good to do so, is a scripting of "the moral commons" of the international system.[8]

Reducing Bandung to instrumental policy implementation concerns or analysing it through a consequence-driven social science framework misses its deeper significance. Bemoaning that Bandung was a high point but all is lost now, or that nothing was gained at Bandung, or that what was gained at Bandung was somehow sadly frittered away over time misses the profoundly constitutive nature of this coming together as well as its kinship-producing, world-constituting, aspects. What was being shaped and given voice at Bandung was a worldview, a global political imaginary in the making.[9]

When I think of Bandung then, when I think of the Asian-African Conference of 1955, I think of once-upon-a-time natives, from across the world, who have now, in the first flush of freedom, gathered for a festivity, a political celebration of their newly achieved independence. I think of strangers who have come together in a prominent city in Indonesia, not just "somewhere in Africa or Asia," strangers talking and warming themselves around a conference fire, strangers talking to each other, and finding themselves becoming otherwise: changing from being strangers to each other to becoming neighbours and friends and brothers and sisters.[10] Bandung as a gathering is a feast of conversations – about what was and what might be in the world and not just in one's own national home or in the regional neighbourhood. This feast has its arguments, its animosities and its intrigues. That is in the nature of feasts.[11]

When I think of Bandung, I think of the place where representatives of the human race huddled together and sought to enlighten themselves about each other while imagining another world of their collective making. When I think of Bandung, I think, of how this city had become for a week, as Nehru observed, "the capital of Asia and Africa." I think, when I think of Bandung, of how an inchoate "somewhere" of Asia and Africa acquired its own fire, a fire that enlightened subsequent postcolonial confabulations about the world; a fire that warmed hands, the hands of diverse colours, the hands of those who were once slaves and coolies and miners and farmers and subalterns of multiple kinds.

Earth and fire, blood and bones, colours and costumes, feasts and festivities are the elements that go into the real meanings of Bandung in historical time. The elements this time, the fires this time, are profoundly postcolonial.

ACKNOWLEDGEMENT

I am very grateful to the editors of this volume for their close reading and perceptive comments on an earlier version of this essay. Naren Kumarakulasingam and Quỳnh Phạm have also, through multiple discussions, debates and Skype sessions, made working on this chapter a true labour of love.

NOTES

1. Robeson writes in his "Greetings to Bandung" (April 1955): "And I might have come as an observer had I been granted a passport by the State Department whose lawyers have argued that 'in view of the applicant's frank admission that he has been fighting for the freedom of the colonial people of Africa ... the diplomatic embarrassment that could arise from the presence abroad of such a political meddler [*sic*] travelling under the protection of an American passport, is easily imaginable!'" (Foner 1978, 400).

2. "Many of the newspapermen who came to Bandung from other countries had preconceived notions. Because of these ideas they tended to judge everything accordingly. They attached importance to personalities rather than to the ferment in Asia and to the forces at work there. They tried to look at Bandung as another arena for the cold war. No doubt some of the statements made there supported this viewpoint and much was made of them. But, as a matter of fact, all this was rather a superficial view and gradually the real meaning of Bandung is being understood" (Nehru 2001).

3. "As a frank and sometimes bitter critic of the Western world, I've been frequently dubbed 'extreme.' ... Well, what I heard from the lips of many Asians startled me, reduced my strictures to the status of a 'family quarrel.' ... I found that many Asians hated the West with an absoluteness that no American Negro could ever muster. The American Negro's reactions were limited, partial, centered, as they were upon specific complaints; he rarely ever criticized or condemned the conditions of life about him as a whole. ... Once his particular grievances were redressed the Negro reverted to a normal Western outlook. The Asian, however, had been taken from his own culture before he had embraced or pretended to embrace Western culture; he had, therefore, a feeling of distance, of perspective, of objectivity toward the West which tempered his most intimate experiences of the West" (Wright 1956).

4. Jawaharlal Nehru, "World Peace and Cooperation," Speech in the closed session of the Asian-African Conference, Bandung, April 22, 1955. File SI/162/9/64-MEA.

5. "You will have noted that the proceedings of the Conference and certainly our approach have not been characterised by any race hatred or anti-Western attitudes. This is true also of the Chinese delegation. ... The Conference has strengthened the feeling that the new Asia can and will make a contribution towards world cooperation and peace, and in doing so, is not animated by any continental compartmentalism or by racial and anti-Western feeling." Nehru's message to Anthony Eden. New Delhi. April 29, 1955. V. K. Krishna Menon papers (Nehru 2001).

6. "Thus, a racial consciousness, evoked by the attitudes and practices of the West, had slowly blended with a defensive religious feeling; here, in Bandung, the two had combined into one: *a racial and religious system of identification manifesting itself in an emotional nationalism which was now leaping state boundaries and melting and merging, one into the other.*" (Wright 1956, 139–140, original emphasis).

7. "And therefore the Bandung Conference really was very important in the context of history, because these various forces, urges, etc., were given a certain shape by the Conference, a certain focal point, a meeting point. The Bandung Conference by itself could have done nothing unless there were these urges; it was because these urges were there, we met, and Bandung gave it a shape and formulation. None of us who went to Bandung, none of the countries that went to Bandung, are quite the same now." Nehru, "Recollections of the Conference," Speech at a closed-door meeting of members of the Congress Parliamentary Party, May 3, 1955. From AICC tapes. Extracts.

8. "The mistakes of my country and perhaps the mistakes of other countries here do not make a difference; but the mistakes the great powers make do make a difference to the world and may well bring about a terrible catastrophe. ... [W]e countries of Asia have to consider whether we can, all of us put together certainly not singly, prevent the great powers or big countries going to war. We certainly cannot prevent the big countries going to war if they want to but we can make a difference. ... It is with military force we are dealing now but I submit that moral force counts and the moral force of Asia and Africa must, in spite of the atomic and hydrogen bombs of Russia, the USA or another country, count! ... Therefore, are we, the countries of Asia and Africa, devoid of any positive position, except being pro-communist or anti-communist? Has it come to this, that the leaders of thought who have given religions and all kinds of things to the world have to tag on to this kind of group or that and be hangers on of this party or the other carrying out their wishes and occasionally giving an idea?" Jawaharlal Nehru, "World Peace and Cooperation," Speech in the closed session of the Asian-African Conference, Bandung, April 22, 1955. File SI/162/9/64-MEA.

9. "We are a little tired of the conflicts and hatreds of Europe and see no reason why we should succumb to them. The Bandung Conference was the first clear enunciation by the countries of Asia especially that they have an individuality and viewpoint which they are not prepared to give up because of the views or pressure from other countries." Nehru, "The Spirit of Bandung," Answers to a questionnaire sent by Louis Gibarti, a Hungarian communist, May 23, 1955 (Nehru 2001).

10. "But, of course, what happened at Bandung was much more important than the mere preparation of a joint statement. Daily contacts and our being together day

after day for long hours toned us all down and we tended to become rather a friendly gathering, in spite of our differences. Strangers to each other almost became friends, or at any rate behaved as such." Nehru, "Letter to Lady Mountbatten," April 30, 1955 (Nehru 2001).

11. "Then the discussions there were, on the whole, fairly frank. These discussions, undoubtedly, made all of us understand the fears and apprehensions of various countries. So it was an enormously educative Conference and in spite of what you might read in the papers about conflicts in the Conference, really it was a very friendly conference. Conflicts there were in the sense that in argument somebody said something, somebody replied but it was a very friendly Conference and people were constantly meeting not only in the Conference but in large numbers of parties. Every delegation was giving party; every evening there were five or six parties and people going from one to the other. Some were of course very lavish parties, some were simpler. So it did create a sensation of some commonness of purpose in Asia and Africa which is a tremendous thing. On the whole, there was no, what might be called anti-European or anti-American feeling. There was no racial feeling, not much anyway, very little. But there was very definitely a pro-Asian feeling, a pro-African feeling, that is, a positive side was present there with a feeling of Asia standing on its own feet and not being pushed this way or that by Europe or America." Nehru, "Recollections of the Conference," Speech at a closed-door meeting of members of the Congress Parliamentary Party, May 3, 1955. From AICC tapes. Extracts.

Chapter 3

Entanglements and Fragments "By the Sea"

Sam Okoth Opondo

I [then] drew attention to what I called the "Life-line of Imperialism." This line runs from the Straits of Gibraltar, through the Mediterranean, the Suez Canal, the Red Sea, the Indian Ocean, the South China Sea and the Sea of Japan ... the territories on both sides of this lifeline were colonies, the peoples were unfree, their futures mortgaged to an alien system. Along that life-line, that main artery of imperialism, there was pumped the life-blood of colonialism.

—Sukarno, Bandung Conference (*Asia-Africa Speaks* 1955)

New maps were made, complete maps, so that every inch was accounted for, and everyone now knew who they were, or at least whom they belonged to. These maps, how they transformed everything.

—Abdulrazak Gurnah (2002, 15)

What the map cuts up, the story cuts across.

—Michel de Certeau (1984, 129)

FRAGMENT 1: ON INTIMATE AND COLOSSAL FRAGMENTS

"We will begin by making ours the art of the fragment because life is too complex to be seized in its entirety." With this provocative remark, Abdourahman Waberi (2005, 85–86) invites readers of his *Intimate and Colossal Fragments* to engage in a philosophico-literary practice that proceeds by "parasitizing, cannibalizing official discourses ... by reducing them to their percussive echoes in this world where indignation is calculated according to suffering."

Predicated on the desire to "learn the craft of being men," the "art of the fragment" creates and retrieves more life-affirming acts by echoing, crafting, negotiating and juxtaposing human and non-human beings in a manner that "accounts for the past and casts a critical eye on the present" (Garane's Introduction in Waberi 2005, xi–xxix, xxviii).

Heeding the insights from Waberi's *art of the fragment*, the narratives that follow cannibalize and parasitize the official programme of Asia-Africa relations as presented at the 1955 Bandung Conference while seeking out the echoes of its promise. Rather than mapping the Bandung instruction of sovereignty, solidarity and non-alignment based on romantic and tragic narratives, the following fragments map the tension between "consensual communities" and their codes of identification, and multiple communities of sense (or a *sensus communis*) – some of them dissensual – and their forms of dis-identification.[1] By juxtaposing quotes from some of the Bandung speeches with philosophical, literary and extra-literary texts, the fragments map the conflict between different "regimes of sense/sensory worlds." The hope is that by inter-articulating the promise and programme of Bandung with other world/historical events, objects and peoples, we will be better placed to retrieve ways of sensing and making sense of the (third) world that encourage experimentation with modes of relation and intelligibility that exceed the practices of states or the narratives of nations.

FRAGMENT 2: FRAGRANT ENTANGLEMENTS BY THE SEA

"I speak to maps. And sometimes they say something back to me. ... Before maps, the world was limitless ... maps made places on the edges of the imagination graspable." What a profound proclamation by Saleh Omar, the protagonist of Abdulrazak Gurnah's novel *By the Sea* (2002, 35). Through a meditation on maps and the ways in which "geography became biology" and then history, Omar offers a narrative cartography of beautiful things and human pains that enables us to capture the complex Afro-Asian encounters, colonial displacements and entanglement of beings in Indian Ocean worlds. Among the numerous stories he recounts is an object biography of a mahogany casket containing incense (*ud-al-qamari*) of the best quality, which ties his life story to the history and geography of East Africa and the Indian Ocean at large:

> *Ud-al-qamari*: its fragrance comes back to me at odd times, unexpectedly, like a fragment of a voice or the memory of my beloved's arm on my neck. Every Idd I used to prepare an incense burner and walk around my house with it, waving clouds of perfume into its deepest corners, pacing the labors

it had taken me to possess such beautiful things, rejoicing in the pleasure they brought – incense burner in one hand and a brass dish filled with ud in the other Aloe wood, *ud-al-qa-mari*, the wood of the moon. That was what I thought the words meant, but the man I obtained my consignment from explained that qamari was really a corruption of Qimari, Khmer, Cambodia, because that was one of the few places in the world where the right kind of aloe wood was to be found. … I had obtained the *ud-al-qamari* from a trader who had come to our part of the world with the *musim*, the winds of the monsoons, he and thousands of other traders from Arabia, the Gulf, India and Sind, and the Horn of Africa. They had been doing this every year for at least a thousand years. In the last months of the year, the winds blow steadily across the Indian Ocean toward the coast of Africa, where the currents obligingly provide a channel to harbor. (ibid., 14)

The above fragment from Gurnah's novel remaps a cosmological/spiritual connection to a cosmopolitical/oceanic relation. Omar's initial understanding of the *ud-al-qamari* as the "wood of the moon" is based on an Islamic interpretation of *qamar* primarily derived from the *Surah-al-qamar* from the Quran that is concerned with the cleaving of the moon (*shaqq al-qamar*). However, his encounter with a trader brought to Zanzibar by the *musim* of 1960 exposes him to a story that opens the meaning of *qamar* to a world of translation and travel that reveals new meanings, other knowledges, and other worlds connected to his own thus giving it a historical depth and geographical breadth that had hitherto remained imperceptible. Through the fragrance and intimate family relations, Omar maps a long history of Indian Ocean trade that ties the East African coast to Persia, Qimari (Khmer Cambodia), Arabia, the Gulf, India and Sind, and the Horn of Africa. Losing his most prized possession to the immigration officer at Gatwick forces him to recall the history of plunder of the same islands by the Omanis, Portuguese, Germans, French and British, thus revealing that "postcolonial migration, of people and things" is best read in this "historical context, rather than as a product of the more recent and publicized trend of globalization as something new" (Cooper 2008, 90).

The smells (fragrances) that Omar summons invoke a sensory world that complicates religious narratives and disturbs the nation-state's attempt to manage bodies or fix "historical narratives as well as territorial space" (Shapiro 2000, 82). By mapping and unmapping family narratives, the violence of nativist politics, and demotic cosmopolitan entanglements between lives in the Indian Ocean island of Zanzibar and the world at large, the novel calls up co-presences, practices and relations that a presentist, statist geophilosophy disavows, and explores ways of being-in-common that existed elsewhere in another time (before colonialism) and can still be explored in the here and now "after empire."

FRAGMENT 3: SUKARNO'S OPENING SCRIPT

To get a sense of how invoking common pasts and lines of connection/dis-connection can interrupt an imperial consensus, let us return to the epigraph above from President Sukarno's opening speech to the delegates of the 1955 Asian-African Conference in Bandung. With attentiveness to lines that connect different seas and polities, Sukarno maps "the life-line of imperialism" and the space within which numerous peoples were subjected to Europe's colonial rule and brutality (*Asia-Africa Speaks* 1955, 23). His speech also draws a line that offers a diagnostic that resonates with, yet exceeds, the oft-cited characterization of the colour line provided by W. E. B. Du Bois (1917) during his "To the Nations of the World" address at the first Pan-African Conference held in London in 1900. In the famous quote now reproduced in the *Souls of Black Folk*, Du Bois (1996, 15) notes that the "problem of the twentieth century is the problem of the color-line, – the relation of the darker to the lighter races of men in Asia and Africa, in America and the islands of the sea." Tracing the "color line," the "life-line of imperialism," and the other lines that make and unmake the world in the twentieth century, Sukarno turns to the question of desire by stating that "conflict comes not from variety of skins, nor from variety of religion, but from variety of desires" (*Asia-Africa Speaks* 1955, 23).

Identifying desire as the basis of conflict, Sukarno reminds us of the need for multiple sites and fronts of mediation that could help develop a common, yet heterogeneous, ethic that interrupts the lifeline of imperialism. In part, this is because "the leaders who got together in Bandung came from a divided world." As Dipesh Chakrabarty (2010, 49) puts it, the leaders "were not of the same mind on questions of international politics, nor did they have the same understanding of what constituted imperialism." Chakrabarty even goes over Carlos Romulo's (the representative of the Philippines) and Roeslan Abdulgani's (Jakarta's ambassador to the United States) anxieties about Nehru's manner of relating with other delegates and his initial attitude towards the conference to illustrate that those gathered at Bandung "did not even necessarily like each other" (ibid.). But these desires could be reoriented and mobilized to craft a new world. As Sukarno goes on to remind the delegates, differences in the sense of community could become the basis of a community of sense based on the "common detestation of colonialism in whatever form it appears" and the "common detestation of racialism" as well as the "common determination to preserve and stabilize peace in the world" (ibid.).

However, the "shared anti-imperial ethic," and the desire to make a world in common that drew the delegates to the conference was also subject to the strictures of a world cut up along the geopolitical lines of the Cold War and colonialism. As such, Sukarno and the delegates sought to map the world differently and to narrate and craft themselves otherwise. Not only did they chart a "third way" that dis-identified with the common sense of Cold War political alignments, but they also presented a new political promise, which, if generalized, was meant to be a programme for world transformation. A programme to change world politics and history by presenting a different set of ethico-political commitments, different desires, and with it, other ways of relating.

FRAGMENT 4: SUKARNO'S GEOPOETICS

To fully appreciate the significance of the promise and programme of Bandung, it will be useful for us to pay attention to the narrative style and claims of commonality, hope and newness that Sukarno mobilizes in his speech. Through a skilful play on geographical and historical referents, he shifts the gaze of the delegates to the significance of the Bandung event. For instance, he points out the sacrifice and history of struggle that made it possible for the meeting of the "highest representatives of independent and sovereign nations from two of the biggest continents of the globe" to take place. The historical significance of the meeting is amplified by reminding us of the location of the Bandung Conference. That is, unlike the conference of the "League Against Imperialism and Colonialism" which had been held in Brussels in 1927 or the first five Pan-African Conferences held in London, Paris, New York and Manchester, the Bandung Conference marked a "new departure in the history of the world" given that "leaders of Asian and African peoples" did not have to meet in Europe or the United States and could meet "together in their own countries to discuss and deliberate upon matters of common concern" (*Asia-Africa Speaks* 1955, 28).

The significance of the venue of the conference is highlighted in the attention it drew, the anxieties it generated and the pride arising from the very fact that it managed to take place. Nowhere are these anxieties clearer than in Nehru's letter to Badr Tyabji, the then Indian ambassador to Indonesia, where he outlines his concerns about the conference. Dated 20 February 1955, a mere three months before the conference, Nehru remained uncertain about Indonesia's preparedness to host such a historically significant conference. Not only was he concerned that the whole world would be watching, he was also aware that inattentiveness to "trivial matters" such as different senses of hygiene and privacy would make it difficult to attend to bigger issues:

> I am rather anxious about this Asian-African Conference and, more especially, about the arrangements. I wonder if the people in Indonesia have any full reali-sation of what this Conference is going to be. All the world's eyes will be turned

upon it. ... The Conference will represent a historic event of great significance and might well mould the future of Asia and Africa. ... It will be a tragedy if the arrangements are feeble and a break-down occurs. ... I have learnt that it is proposed to crowd numbers of people in single rooms. It is difficult for me to say much from here, but the Indonesian Government or your Joint Secretariat will not get much praise from anybody if delegations are herded up like cattle. As I said when I was in Djakarta, we put up thousands of people for our Congress session in temporary huts or tents. ... Above all, one fact should be remembered, and this is usually forgotten in Indonesia. This fact is an adequate provision of bathrooms and lavatories, etc. People can do without drawing rooms, but they cannot do without bathrooms and lavatories. ... I am writing about what might be considered trivial matters. But these trivial matters upset people and frayed tempers are no good when we consider important problems. (Nehru 2001)

Nehru invokes the senses to underline the significance of the conference. The call for pre-conference preparations that is attentive to details like bathrooms and lavatories so that trivial matters do not stand in the way of discussing important problems illustrates that toilets are no trivial matter. By putting the "excremental habitus" on the table, Nehru remaps the diplomatic body and the sense of community and hospitality. Diplomacy here is not only about sanitized diplomatic talk and shared ideals by the *corps diplomatique*; it is also about making difficult arrangements about bodies that eat, sleep, smell and shit. The anti-colonial diplomatic body, as a community of sense, does not only attend to the consensual diplomatic subject, it also attends to that which is abject and often disavowed. Diplomacy involves attentiveness to the other's ablution and evacuation habits; to that which is central to the health, comfort and constitution of others – their shit. That which is intimate, yet colossal.

Like Nehru, Sukarno also turns to the senses, more so the painful experience of colonialism, in order to present a situated idea of the past that interrupts revisionist histories of colonialism that proclaim its premature demise or locate it in a distant past that should be beyond our concern. The conceptual, political and theoretical purchase of the way Sukarno narrates the colonial present is immense. This is especially so when he asks how it is "possible to be disinterested about colonialism" when it "is not something far and distant" when you or your contemporaries have "known it in all its ruthlessness" and "the heritage it leaves behind" (*Asia-Africa Speaks* 1955, 23). Here, he invites us to also look at ongoing forms of colonialism in "its modern dress, in the form of economic control, intellectual control, actual physical control by a small but alien community within a nation."

As if performing a chrysopoetic act that turns the base into the noble, Sukarno's speech turns the geographical lifeline of imperialism into a historical line of anti-colonial and Afro-Asian solidarities. A new line that inaugurates the promise and programme of Bandung in a manner that acknowledges the numerous relations that exceed colonial and nation-state relations. A new neighbourliness that proclaims the extension of what was an Asian affair into an Afro-Asian, and ultimately, a human affair:

> Relatively speaking, all of us gathered here today are neighbours. Almost all of us have ties of common experience, the experience of colonialism. Many of us have a common religion. Many of us have common cultural roots. Many of us, the so-called "underdeveloped" nations, have more or less similar economic problems, ... and I think I may say that we all hold dear the ideals of national independence and freedom. *Yes, we have so much in common. And yet we know so little of each other.* (ibid., italics mine)

Sukarno's narrative and its ability to frame how we sense and make sense of the past and possible futures is not to be taken for granted. Against the imperial dictates that colonized peoples' futures were "mortgaged to an alien system," he presents a narrative of colonial past, anti-colonial present, and sovereign futures that is not limited to the promise of "national independence and freedom." The programme of anti-imperialism also points to a third way that could craft a new Asia, a new Africa, and a new man. However, to realize this, we must also know others and know otherwise. As Sukarno goes on to proclaim:

> If this Conference succeeds in making the peoples of the East whose representatives are gathered here understand each other a little more, appreciate each other a little more, sympathise with each other's problems a little more. ... I hope that this Conference will give guidance to mankind, will point out to mankind the way which it must take to attain safety and peace. I hope that it will give evidence that Asia and Africa have been reborn, nay, that a New Asia and a New Africa have been born! (ibid.)

In many ways, Sukarno's maps of knowledge and relation holds a Bandung promise that exceeds the programme of national self-determination. It points to the possibility of what Walter Mignolo (2000, 745) has called a critical cosmopolitanism: a project that "connects the diverse subaltern satellites appropriating and transforming Western global designs" thus creating a "pluricentric world built on the ruins of ancient, non-Western cultures and civilizations with the debris of Western civilization."

FRAGMENT 5: CONSCRIPTS, INVENTIONS AND THE BANDUNG INSTRUCTION

How then are we to read the anti-colonial stories arising from the legacies of the Bandung Conference without reducing them to *romance* narratives of "overcoming, vindication, salvation and redemption" or forms of *tragedy* that focus on the contingent, the ambiguous and the paradoxical? (Scott 2004, 11) Which stories of Afro-Asian relations would enable us to realize the Bandung promise or energize its programme? In a long meditation on the "Bandung Instruction" in his *On African Fault Lines*, V. Y. Mudimbe (2013) offers a reading of the legacy of Bandung that cannot be reduced into the romance-versus-tragedy dichotomy. Beginning with the "critical indifference principle" that Jawaharlal Nehru invokes as the basis of assigning the "same suspicion" to the then existing world that had been divided by the capitalist and communist political projects, Mudimbe illustrates how Nehru's narrative provides a philo-sophical and political basis for non-alignment and world making (ibid., 335). Quoting from Nehru's 22 April 1955 speech "World Peace and Cooperation" that was presented in the closed session of the Bandung Conference, Mudimbe notes that Nehru's advocacy for the concept of peaceful coexistence and a departure from dominant ideologies is positive rather than merely reactive.[2]

It is worth quoting Nehru at length to fully appreciate Mudimbe's analysis of the Bandung instruction (non-alignment) derived from his speech and its implication for international and other relations:

> So I submit, let us consider these matters practically, leaving out ideologies. Many members present here do not obviously accept the communist ideology, while some of them do. For my part I do not. I am a positive person, not an "anti" person. I want positive good for my country and the world. Therefore, are we, the countries of Asia and Africa, devoid of any positive position except being pro-communist or anti-communist? Has it come to this, that the leaders of thought who have given religions and all kinds of things to the world have to tag on to this kind of group or that and be hangers on of this party or the other car-rying out their wishes and occasionally giving an idea? It is most degrading and humiliating to any self-respecting people or nation. It is an intolerable thought to me that the great countries of Asia and Africa should come out of bondage into freedom only to degrade themselves or humiliate themselves in this way. (Nehru 1955, also quoted in Mudimbe 2013, 339)

According to Mudimbe (2013), Nehru's discourse supplies us with a politi-cal philosophy of alterity, a moral subjectivity and an ethical mandate. He also identifies "a willed message in the way that Nehru posited such a novel project and conveyed the identity of a self-defined newly liberated subject ... conceived as a 'we-organism'" (ibid., 336). Tracing the foundational principles of Non-Aligned Movement (NAM) to the *Panchsheel* – the five principles of peaceful coexistence that were constitutive of Sino-Indian relations – Mudimbe notes that Nehru was "conscious of being a moral subject whose pronounce-ments were, as a matter of principle, to face the test of generalizability" (ibid., 337). When the five principles of mutual respect for each other's territorial integrity and sovereignty; mutual non-aggression; mutual non-interference;

equality and mutual benefit; and peaceful coexistence were incorporated into the Bandung principles in 1955 and adopted by the United Nations General Assembly on 14 December 1957, we witness the extension of an ambitious "regional transformation" project into "a praxis building of the world" (ibid.).

But the generalizability of these principles was not devoid of complications arising from the institutional forms it endorsed or those that sought to withhold the principles. Writing about Bandung and the "invention of sovereignty," Mudimbe presents a more tragic story that illustrates how the principle of self-determination and right to political autonomy (in Africa) affirmed the "more or less compact geographical and socio-cultural units organized by the colonial authority and structured kingdoms" and turned them into "administrative ensembles" that became the "new order of things." In the postcolonial era, these entities were recognized and endowed with rights of sovereignty that did not create a discontinuity with the logics of colonial rule or the colonial library (ibid.).

At the heart of the tension between the promise and the programme of Bandung or its instruction and inventions, are two versions of the anticolonial story and their related maps of relation. From Sukarno's speech, we see a committed effort to challenge and undo colonialism's ideological form and texture, and a gesture towards presenting a different institutional form or a form of institution similar to the colonial one but predicated on a different ideological and ethical script. Unfortunately, the inter-articulation of the anticolonial promise (and non-alignment) and the Bandung programme (national sovereignty), sometimes created a state-form that is haunted by the colonial legacy and its instructions insofar as the definition of peoples, collective anxieties and the modalities of rule are concerned. It is precisely these dynamics of defining and ruling that Mahmood Mamdani attends to in his analysis of the colonial institutional form and its legacy in Africa.

According to Mamdani (2001), the legacy of colonialism in Africa manifests itself in the colonial state's definition, division/aggregation and ruling of the population according to the distinction between ethnicities (governed by customary law) and races (governed by civil law). A distinction that meant that the population of the colony lived and was ruled under two different legal universes that created distinctions between peoples that could not be reduced to the simple categories of the colonizer and the colonized. As such, the move to decolonize most African societies might have transformed the relations between the colonizer and colonized while maintaining or creating a new regime of rule between different categories of the colonized, and it is this internal/institutional formation that is in need of further decolonization. As Mamdani puts it:

> The hierarchy of races included both colonizers and colonized. Similarly, the colonized divided into those indigenous and those not; in other words, whereas

all natives were colonized, not all nonnatives were colonizers. The hierarchy
of race included master races and subject races. Who were the subject races of
indirect-rule Africa? They were the Indians of East, Central and Southern Africa,
the Arabs of Zanzibar, the Tutsi of Rwanda and Burundi, and the "Coloureds"
of Southern Africa. ... In contrast, subject ethnicities were indigenous. Finally,
subject races usually performed a middleman function, in either the state or
the market, and their position was marked by petty privilege economically and
preferential treatment legally. (ibid., 656–657)

Whereas expert analyses of postcolonial politics often turn to narratives of
state collapse in an attempt to make sense of the changes in the postcolony,
Mamdani invites us to ask, "Which state is failing?" For it is often "what
remains of the colonial state in Africa that is collapsing" complete with the
institutions of colonial rule, some of which were inherited by the decolonized
states at Bandung and then given a form and legitimacy that was concretized
and moralized as the model for postcolonial polities (ibid., 652–653). Simply
put, reading Bandung critically (its failures, successes and aporias) tells us
more about the modern/colonial world than about the states of mind of the
Third World heads of state or the "nature" of previously colonized peoples.

From this critical vantage point we would be forced to ask what else
emerged institutionally and relationally from the way the ideological commitments to questions of human rights, sovereignty and territorial integrity
of all nations; the equality of all races; and the resistance to colonialism was
framed at Bandung? Tragic as some of the stories of the leaders and states
that participated at Bandung may be, their stories and politics highlight a
status that transgresses the *corpus* of modern knowledge that dictates how
and where political life must take place, its proper form and the principles
that remain non-negotiable as well as the categories and lives that they create
or negate. While some hagiographic narratives of Bandung may present the
state as something open to the possession of an individual or a group, reading the multiple lines, promises, programmes and inventions reveals that the
postcolonial state, or the state in general, can be a *status* that possesses us.

FRAGMENT 6: MERDEKA WALK,
A SHORT WALK TO FREEDOM

So much for the "Bandung talk," how about the walk?
Besides the great declarations of the 1955 Bandung Conference, few
images of African-Asian solidarity mark the "Bandung event" more than the
short walk along Jalan Asia Afrika made by Jawaharlal Nehru (accompanied
by his daughter Indira Gandhi), Gamel Abdel Nasser, Sir John Kotelawala
of Ceylon, Prince Norodom Sihanouk of Cambodia, U Nu of Burma,

Muhammed Ali of Pakistan and Zhou Enlai of China among other delegates at the conference. Not only does the parade of nations on the Bandung "Merdeka Walk" (Freedom Walk) from Hotel Savoy Homann or Grand Hotel Preanger to the plenary session at the Gedung Merdeka hold a symbolic and ritual significance, it is also a performance, popularization and enactment of the leaders' commitment to decolonization, the third way and the ten points of the Bandung Declaration (Dasasila Bandung) by taking the spirit of the conference to a realm beyond that of diplomatic summitry by presenting an opportunity for the leaders to interact with "the people" (Shimazu 2011, 15).

This short walk, an event that has imprinted itself on the imagination of former colonized people was re-enacted by Kofi Annan during the fiftieth anniversary of the Bandung Conference in 2005 and was performed again during the sixtieth anniversary of the conference in 2015 by presidents Joko Widodo of Indonesia and Xi Jinping of China among other world leaders. Taking place against the backdrop of colourful images of the leaders from the 1955 conference, we are reminded of the promise of Bandung. However, one cannot fail to notice the difference in rhythm and political effect between the 1955 walk and the more recent walks. Not only do you have more delegates today, they are also drawn from a more diverse world. One where some of the walkers from what was then the "wretched of the earth" have become some of the most powerful figures in the world while other walkers, in their commitment to sovereignty projects, reproduce wretchedness and make exiles and perambulators of the people they represent.

FRAGMENT 7: EXILIC DISPATCHES, DISSENSUS AND SONGS OF FREEDOM

"Yes, we have so much in common. And yet we know so little of each other." What would it mean to take Sukarno's challenge seriously today? Beyond revisiting and rehearsing Bandung talk or re-enacting the Merdeka walk, what kinds of inventions, attention and senses can one invoke in order to make sense of Afro-Asian relations in a way that is life-affirming while opening up to a world beyond Bandung?

I feel compelled to conclude with a story of Afro-Asian relations and entanglements from another place or even from another time. From those other lives that consider themselves to be the tragic conscripts of Bandung but can turn to other knowledges and times to reveal the multiplicity and depth of Afro-Asian relations through the numerous things, practices, senses and meanings that have connected these worlds.

Like Nehru's pre-conference dispatches articulating anxiety about the 1955 conference and the need to recognize its symbolic and strategic significance, another statement was making the rounds a few days before the beginning of the sixtieth anniversary of the conference. Signed by Octovianus Yoakim Mote, Benny Wenda, Jacob Rumbiak, Leoni Tanggahma and Rex Rumakiek, the statement from the United Liberation Movement for West Papua (ULMWP) called on the world and Bandung Conference delegates to re-evaluate the narrative and promise of Bandung. Unlike most celebratory statements, the ULMWP statement sought to highlight the plight of the people of West Papua who remained unfree sixty years after the Bandung Conference. Invoking the Bandung spirit of ending colonialism in all its forms, the ULMWP reminds the world, and the people planning to attend the conference, of the era of Dutch colonialism over the Dutch East Indies and Indonesia's sovereign claims that maintains the same colonial cartography. Significant here is how the quest for West Papua's freedom reveals the violence of Indonesia's sovereign claims which are manifested through "the power of awe and only becomes effective in an action of killing and injuring" (Hernawan 2015, 199). Against these colonial imaginaries, the Papuan state asserts its sovereignty over former Dutch New Guinea and West Papua's Melanesian rather than Indonesian identity.

In addition to addressing the silences and violence arising from national and sovereigntist narratives, the statement restores forms of politics and mediation that have been suppressed or glossed over by some of Bandung's official discourses by reminding us of its promise of freedom and solidarity:

> International support never ceased. Numerous African countries, for instance, declined to support the Indonesian claim to have annexed West Papua in an "act of free choice" in 1969. On the 60th anniversary of the Bandung conference, it is time for human rights violations in West Papua to end. More than that, it is time for the inalienable right to self-determination of the People of West Papua to be recognized, respected and implemented, at last.

Alongside the written statements appealing to the world and the Bandung Conference delegates, a more popular rhythm is also at play. In February 2015, members of Lucky Dube's One People Band announced that they were recording the song "Free West Papua" in collaboration with Benny Wenda, the ULMWP spokesman. This musician-politician-activist collaboration ties the West Papuan struggle today to the South African struggle to end apartheid. It creates an artistic "dissensual community" with the capacity for "creating a new community between human beings, a new political people" (Rancière 2008, 5). A community of people that negotiates, and even agitates for, or inhabits the "tension between 'being apart' and 'being together'" – the tension between arts of the community of sovereign states and the quest for a different status that renews the world through sonic connections that call for "disconnection" (ibid.).

Given the popularity of Lucky Dube's music in West Papua where his songs are usually played during public rallies, the dissensual aesthetic community built around freedom songs of the exiled/ex-communicated spokesman also provides another register of diplomatic communication and communion. These songs of freedom point to other rhythms of solidarity that energize the long walk to freedom and call forth a much more extensive world of politics. A world where subjugated peoples' voices count as more than mere noise. A voice and message of hope that "we" must heed in the spirit of Bandung. As Phuma Maduna of the One People Band puts it in her message to West Papua: "One day West Papua will be free and we'll be there to celebrate with you, marching and saying we are free and freedom is ours! I wish you good, good, good luck. Jah bless!"[3]

While recognizing the significance of the Bandung instruction and its political programme, the haptic, auditory and olfactory senses that the above Bandung-inspired fragments and entanglements map acknowledge that "life is too complex to be seized in its entirety." Read together, they seek to interrupt colonial logics and the postcolonial common sense of sovereign nation-states and their ideals of consensual community. Ultimately, attentiveness to other senses of Bandung, and other communities of sense, can retrieve critical and life-affirming elements of Afro-Asian relations that recognize, yet go beyond the shared experience of colonial *thingification*, the promise of a shared future (the third way), or a future of broken promises.

ACKNOWLEDGEMENT

This piece is inspired by conversations with Patricia-Pia Célérier and Abdourahman Waberi on the art of the fragment. I would like to thank Quỳnh N. Phạm and Robbie Shilliam for inviting me to contribute to the collection on *Meanings of Bandung* and for their patience and critical comments to earlier drafts of the chapter.

NOTES

1. For more on the tension between a consensual community and the dissensual community of sense that stages a "conflict between two regimes of sense, two sensory worlds," see Rancière 2008, 4–5. For a decolonial reading of a conflict between regimes of senses, see Walter Mignolo and Rolando Vasquez's treatment of the tension between Eurocentred aestheTics and decolonial aestheSis. Attentive to the way "AestheTics became Eurocentered in the eighteenth-century Europe when it was taken as the key concept for a theory of sensibility, sentiment, sensation, and briefly emotions," they go forth to illustrate how decolonial

aestheSis stages a confrontation with modern aestheTics in its attempt to "decolonize the regulation of sensing of all the sensations to which our bodies respond" (Mignolo and Vasquez 2013).

2. Jawaharlal Nehru, speech in the closed session of the Asian-African Conference, Bandung, 22 April 1955. File No. Sl/162/9/64-MEA.

3. A message from Lucky Dube's band to the people of West Papua, http://freewestpapua.org/2015/03/02/a-message-from-lucky-dubes-band-to-the-people-of-west-papua/. Also see One People Band's "Free West Papua" Video available at: https://www.youtube.com/watch?v=ysA_LlmX5Hg.

Chapter 4

De-islanding

Narendran Kumarakulasingam

INTRODUCTION

Writing about the revival of Bandung in both academic and non-academic works, Robert Vitalis (2013, 263) laments the inability of these writings to get right the line-up at the conference, let alone the politics. Privileging popular memory over the historical record and rooted in belief rather than in reality, these works, he argues, mistakenly posit Bandung as the birthplace of a race-based global identity as well as of the Non-Aligned Movement (NAM). Scrupulously poring over the first-hand accounts of observers, Vitalis finds that a lack of unanimity and ideological coherence among the gathering limits the materialization of anti-colonial desire into tangible success. The prevalence of "competitive state-building projects" and "regional state systemic logics" (ibid., 271) works to prevent the formation of a coherent movement of states demanding decolonization in the international sphere, or of a unified colour consciousness. Ultimately, he argues, unanimity at Bandung was restricted to support for ongoing anti-colonial struggles, calls for strengthening "Third World" presence in the United Nations (especially in the Security Council), appeals for disarmament, and the building of economic cooperation and cultural exchange between each other (ibid., 265). On the basis of this, the reader is urged to accept a more sober reading of Bandung – as a valiant but largely unsuccessful attempt to transform international relations.

In such a reading, the core problem is assumed to be one of poor historiography, itself a result of inaccuracy concerning the bedrock of history, evidence. Shoddy historiography in turn leads to incorrect assessments about ideological coherence and unity, which then result in an overstatement about the significance of Bandung. But I wonder if the new accounts are concerned primarily with producing a historical account of Bandung. After all, even though not many people might be able to live entirely outside of history in an era marked by the increasing reach of the nation-state, millions and maybe even billions don't always live by history alone. Or to put it differently, the historical does not exhaust all possible worlds for many of us. Not only does the historical not exhaust our worlds, but history itself was administered to the majority of the world as a means of getting them to accept their subjugation to the White Master (Guha 2002; Nandy 2009). History taught much of the world's inhabitants to look at their rich and diverse pasts and see only inferiority, thereby reorienting their cultural priorities as well as relationship to time. "Handcuffed to history" (Udayakumar cited in Devare 2001, 2), anti-colonial dissent itself began to be expressed in the idiom of history (Devare 2011). Given this deployment of History as a means of inferiorization, one has to wonder about the continued anxiety about being faithful to it. Why be faithful to that which ineluctably degrades and dehumanizes much of the world's inhabitants? Why collude in the inferiorization of parts of oneself?

Perhaps what to the historically minded appears to be shoddy historiography is but a form of dissent against the historical. Perhaps the over-reliance on memory and belief is not an empirical oversight but a testament to a creativity that refuses to be arrested by past and present colonialism. If so, what might it mean to read it as an incitement to uncuff ourselves?

ISLANDED

History is largely sustained by the faith that its understanding of the past will be borne out by the past. And integral to such faith is the separation between past, present and future. Myth, in contrast, is not concerned with getting the past right. Instead it freely traverses between past, present and future and works thereby to keep open the possibility of intervening in, reinterpreting and re-enacting the past (Nandy 2009, 55–63). Myth messes up history's linear temporality and refuses to be adjudicated on the basis of verifiable experience. Myths can be challenged only by other myths and become dislodged only when their hold on the public imagination is superseded by something else. Leaving aside for the moment the implications that the differences in adjudication may have for considerations of democracy, I want to foreground another crucial difference between history and myth, highlighted by the anthropologist Valentine Daniel. History, Daniel (1997, 50) notes, "provides a way of seeing the world," while myth "provides a people with a way of being in the world." Key to this additional distinction is that myth is inter-subjective – it is embodied; whereas history depends on a subject removed from the world. If this is the case, then fables are the provenance not just of myth but also of history. The difference between the two lies in something like the following: the latter has to deny that fable is constitutive of it, while the distinction between fable and truth does not in the least concern the former. Moreover, Daniel's discussion of myth as a way of being in the world reminds us that it is an important mode through which everyday life and reality are constituted for many people. Ultimately, what is at stake in the contest between the historical and the mythic is the degree of human freedom. Myth, because of its open-ended stance towards time, allows for creative reworking of the past, which in turn allows for a remaking of the present.

I am not entirely sure when or how history first failed to resonate with me. Perhaps it occurred during those social studies lessons beginning in sixth grade, when I gradually learnt that studying history had nothing much to offer a minority such as myself except a good grade at the examination. Studying history (which was part of the social studies curriculum, not a separate subject) in Sri Lanka meant learning that Tamils like myself were minorities who could belong in postcolonial Sri Lanka only as second-class citizens. But I didn't need this classroom history to be made conscious of my minority status. That had already been accomplished through a number of quotidian and somewhat extraordinary experiences in the 1980s. My body had already been minoritized by the time I opened my first social studies book. History lessons only reinforced what taunts, insults, slights, and intimidation had already taught me – that minorities needed to know their place in the "national order of things" (Malkki 1995). If they didn't, they would be punished.

Or perhaps my alienation from history resulted from the joke that was "archaeological fever." For a while, in the 1980s, there was a feverish round of digging up going on in order to substantiate the belief that Sri Lanka had been and would continue to be a Sinhala Buddhist nation-state. Predictably, the digging produced results that substantiated belief. Artefact after artefact was found and proclamation after proclamation issued by various government authorities. This archaeological turn was compelled by the vagaries of economic liberalization and Tamil separatism. The opening up of borders to foreign goods, alien ideas of individualism and unrestrained accumulation, and images all in the hope of emulating Singapore triggered an identity crisis for a nation whose foundation lay in Buddhist values. At the same time, increasingly assertive Tamil militants were attacking police stations, banks, military encampments, bombing public places and causing uncertainty in the majoritarian psyche about their right to govern the minorities. The state in turn responded with counter-terror and archaeology. Unable to make fun of the former, many of us, majority and minority alike, could not help but laugh derisively at the sudden coincidental finding of artefact upon artefact that once again proclaimed that the entire island belonged to the Sinhala Buddhist. The laughter was not occasioned by belief or disbelief about the island's true past but by the clumsy deployment of history itself. It was as if the postcolonial state itself could not be bothered engaging in a serious or sophisticated manner with history. Instead it seemed to be going through the motions in resurrecting and materializing history. It seemed that even those who killed in the name of history seemed to not believe in it. The conclusion to be drawn was simple: history, if anything, was a deadly farce, a killer joke.

Bandung was never available as history to me. It is not that I was entirely ignorant of Bandung. Growing up in Colombo, my knowledge of it was similar to the knowledge I possessed about some of the many relatives that I was introduced to as a child. That "Thalaiyar annai" was a close relative on my father's side was something I understood, but the knowledge of how specifically he was related to me remained elusive. For not only was Bandung not part of the government-mandated curriculum, but there were also no visible reminders of it in Colombo. For example, none of the streets in Colombo were named after Nehru or Nasser; instead most of them were named after various colonial masters, of whom there were many. The only counter-memorial to this absence was the magnificent Bandaranaike Memorial International Conference Hall on Bauddhaloka Mawatha that had hosted the NAM summit in 1976.

Ignorance, historians of science (Proctor and Schiebinger 2008) and philosophers (Sullivan and Tuana 2007) point out, is not a natural state but a product of power. By the time I was learning history, through social studies mind you, Bandung had already passed its expiration date, like the Kraft cheese tins that were being imported from New Zealand. I suppose it was an inconvenient memory best left behind as the Sri Lankan state pursued a wholesale programme of economic liberalization designed to make it the next Singapore. Thus I was completely unaware not only of Colombo's role in the organization of the meeting, but also of Sri Lanka's subsequent advocacy of Third World solidarity and non-alignment. Memories of Ms Sirimavo Banadaranike's standing up to the US militarization of Diego Garcia and demanding that the Indian Ocean be declared a "zone of peace" had already been replaced with cosy relations with the Americans, the British, the International Monetary Fund and the World Bank (Dhanapala 2010). Memories of special relations with China and India were forgotten as Sri Lanka distinguished itself by being one of only twelve UN members to side with the British during the passage of the General Assembly's resolution on the Malvinas conflict.

Reading (and listening to presentations) about Bandung over the last few years, I wonder how and whether Bandung would have resonated with me if I had encountered it between those yellowed well-worn textbook pages. Those government-printed pages taught me that history consisted of a glorious monolithic hydraulic civilization centred around (Buddhist) temple, (water) tank and (paddy) field, whose decline allowed it to be conquered by various masters for 400 years. This postcolonial history is but a child of the complex of processes that the historian Sujit Sivasundaram (2013) calls islanding and partitioning. While aware that the term "partition" has come to denote the bloodshed and displacement associated with the creation of the Indian and Pakistani nation-states, Sivasundaram nevertheless shows that the first set of partitioning processes in South Asia occurred with the British establishment of Ceylon as a crown colony following their defeat of the Kandyan Kingdom. Prior to its capitulation, the Kandyan kingdom not only had a "Tamil" king from the Nayakar dynasty from southern India ruling as a Buddhist king, but was also part of a larger political, cultural and economic geography that encompassed the Indian Ocean and parts of the mainland. However, owing to disputes between the Crown and the British East India Company, Ceylon was islanded from the mainland and administered as a separate unit. This process would ultimately lead to the island being imagined as a territorial entity of its own separate from the mainland. Crucial to this process was the policing of the movement of peoples, goods and ideas between mainland and island, and the "fabrication" (Fanon 2004, 2) of some people into "natives" and others into "foreigners." Anticipating the ideology of indirect rule (Mamdani 2012), the creation of a colony depended upon the theory and practice of nativism. Nativism created a Manichean world between colonizer and native, wherein the former would be defined in terms of history and the latter in terms of geography. Nativism brought into existence (imagined) a native subject that was defined by his being rooted to/in a particular place. The native, unlike the colonizer, was fixed to a place, partitioned and islanded from the rest, and this fixity in turn defined the native. Thus to be native was to be tied inextricably to a particular place and defined in terms of geographical particularity and isolation.

In Ceylon, the British practice of nativism resulted in the categoriza-tion of "Malabars" as immigrants and "Sinhalese" as "natives." While the British likely did not invent these categories out of thin air, they politicized and hardened what had been previously fluid identifications. As a result the island would be seen as belonging to the Sinhalese with the Malabars, later identified as "Tamils," becoming foreigners. Later on, as liberal reforms were introduced to the colony, the question of "who belongs?" was replaced by that of "who represents?" While the question changed, the terms of the answer remained the same. Representation to the colonial legislature was configured on racial/ethnic terms in line with the understanding that the native could represent only particular rather than universal interests.

If islanding began as a colonial administrative process, it continues today as a psychological make-up that sees the island as a distinct entity moving through time. Crucially, islanding severs the possibility of remembering past kinship and sociality with natives across the waters of the Palk Straits and the mighty Indian Ocean. It is against such a severing that Bandung materializes for me.

"WORLDS WERE BEING BORN" OR DE-ISLANDING

"[W]orlds were being born and worlds were dying," muses Richard Wright (1956, 17), upon reading of the upcoming gathering of twenty-nine newly independent Asian and African countries to discuss issues of racialism and colonialism. While recognizing that he represented no government, Wright nevertheless feels compelled to attend the conference. He feels compelled to do so because the gathering for him was not so much about newly independent states negotiating a new international order, but rather something more ele-mental and more universal. Wright recognizes that the meeting's significance lay not in the realm of ideology, but something more elemental. "It smacked of tidal waves, of natural forces ...," he says (ibid., 12). For him the signifi-cance of Bandung lay not in the ability to produce a coherent movement but in the opportunity it presented to engage with other human beings on the basis of emotions and experiences forged through colonial and racial subordination.

Responding to Ellen Poplar Wright's question about what he would report on, Wright (ibid., 13) says:

> I don't know. But I feel that my life has given me some keys to what they would say or do. I'm an American Negro; as such I've had a burden of race conscious-ness. So have these people. I worked in my youth as a common labourer, and I've had class consciousness. So have these people. I grew up in the Methodist and Seventh Day Adventist churches ... and these people are religious ... these emotions are my instruments.

What is striking about this response is that it is experience rather than ide-ology that is central to solidarity. One's experiences of racial and colonial subordination enable the possibility of engaging other similarly subordinated beings on the grounds of particularity. Wright does not presume a common colour or class or religious consciousness, let alone shared interests. Rather, what is articulated here is the ability to listen, on the basis of one's particular-ity, to the other's particularity. Wright's words mark for me the possibility of affective anti-colonial solidarities.

Reading Wright's reading of Bandung, it is not the meetings held on the island of Java that come to mind, but that of another Bandung before Bandung, the recursive journeys taken by another islanded native, the n_ of Césaire's *Notebook of a Return to the Native Land* (2001). Prostrated, silenced, islanded and enervated by the subtle as well as overt violences of the master, the n_ does not acquiesce to being islanded. Instead, he undertakes a journey of radical self-founding, an expulsion of the colonizer within. And central to this self-founding is the imaginative solidarities sung into existence by the decolonizing subject. Let us listen to the prose-poetry of de-islanding:

As there are hyena-men and panther-men, I would be a jew-man
A Kaffir-man
A Hindu-man-from-Calcutta
A Harlem-man-who-doesn't-vote (ibid., 11)

Aching, longing, and reaching out, the song sings into existence a world "not tinted with the arbitrary colors of scholars" (ibid., 43), a world not bounded by "the chancelleries" of nation-states (ibid., 29), but instead a consanguineous world created by the solidarity of having to endure servitude. As the song continues the world turns. That insignificant "calabash of an island" (ibid., 15), that "little ellipsoidal nothing" (ibid., 14) claims consanguinity with those defying the "white screams of white death" (ibid., 16). "Virginia, Tennessee, Georgia, Alabama, … Toussaint" (ibid.).

For Césaire, like for Wright, solidarity does not depend upon shared ideology but instead upon relatable experience. Crucially for Césaire, this kind of experience forges a new universality, not through the emptying out of particularity, but instead through a deepening of it. How might we begin to even contemplate such a possibility and its implications?

INCLINING TO LISTEN

Solidarity is all too often presumed or judged on the basis of univocity. There is an assumption that solidarity is predicated on a uniformity of thought and action. What is often forgotten in this way of thinking is that a more fundamental condition of solidarity is the ability to speak and listen without denying the presence of power/difference. It may be that what is important in solidarity is not so much the creation of new outcomes or the crafting of a uniform voice/strategy, but the honing of the ability, especially among the powerful, to listen and hear others. Ranajit Guha (2004, 9) addressing what he calls the "small voice of history" within the Telangana movement, with a nod to Martin Heidegger, reminds us that "to listen is to be open to and existentially disposed towards: one inclines a little on one side in order to listen." Solidarity, Guha teaches us, corresponds to listening and inclining towards the small voice, often speaking in an undertone, as if in pain, against the commanding discourse of the powerful.

Modern colonialism's privative modes of non-listening are many. They are all made possible by the arrogation on the part of the colonizer that he knows what is best. From this, it follows that politics is but a matter of pedagogy (Chakrabarty 2010) – of teaching inferior others to either know their place or learn the appropriate lessons that will (putatively) allow them to overcome their inferiority. As Wright's interviews in Paris as well as Anglo-American responses to the conference revealed, the response of the master was to turn a deaf ear, to not-listen. The response of the *New York Times* to the Sri Lankan premier's pointed questioning about Soviet colonialism provides an excellent illustration. As Appadorai (1955, 19) and others (Kahin 1956, 18–19) have commented, Sir John Kotelawala created quite a stir by unexpectedly raising the question of "Soviet colonialism." Wondering if the communist satellite states of Central and Eastern Europe – such as Albania, Bulgaria and Hungary – were not colonies, he asked if the gathering should censure Soviet colonialism as well as Western imperialism. The *New York Times*, reporting this, editorialized his remarks as finally putting the question of colonialism in the "correct perspective." If this move on the part of the *Times* reflected the colonial move of the arrogation of propriety (Muppidi 2012, 72), the response to the speech on the part of the Bandung participants was noteworthy for its absence. Tellingly, there were no lectures or musings forthcoming from any party about what a *proper* perspective on colonialism entailed. While there was of course a lot of disagreement among those present, none of the more powerful members, at least to my knowledge, are on record telling Colombo how it should think about colonialism. There was no arrogation of propriety – of how to think properly about colonialism.

Another instance of listening on the part of the powerful can be gleaned from the response of the prime minister of China Zhou Enlai to the opening day speeches. Responding to the fears of Chinese domination expressed by some of the members, especially Cambodia and Thailand, Zhou begins by stating China's belief in communism. However, he did not go on to insist on ideological uniformity, or that the militarily less powerful adopt the positions of the more powerful:

> [W]e should seek common ground among us, while keeping our differences. As to our common ground, the Conference should affirm all our common desires and demands. This our main task here. As to our differences, none of us is asked to give up his own views, because difference in viewpoints is an objective reality. But we should not let our differences hinder us from achieving agreement as far as our main task is concerned. (cited in Kahin 1956, 53)

In the acceptance of different ideologies and social systems is a stance that does not define the self exclusively in ideological terms. Nor does such a stance see the presence of competing ideologies as a fatal contradiction. Modern colonialism was premised upon an inferiorization of difference. Millions of people were cast as backward because they did not subscribe to the correct ideology, or did not seem to have a coherent ideology. Might it have been the experience of such inferiorization that enabled Zhou to be able to adopt such a position rather than seeing the gathering at Bandung exclusively through ideological terms?

It might be that such small voices and small acts of listening remain illegible to some. This is the message that one finds in Vijay Prashad's (2007) moving part-elegy, part-inquest of the Third World Project. For Prashad, anti-colonial desires are doomed to be circumscribed to the local unless they are writ large as a single movement and ideology. I am not entirely unsympathetic to Prashad's line of thinking, but I wonder for whom anti-colonial desire needs to manifest as ideology/movement in order to be apprehensible. Instead of bemoaning the Third World's failure to produce a coherent ideological project, we might think about the "Third World" in terms other than ideology or as something more than a project. Keeping in mind Ashis Nandy's caution, "[t]heories of salvation do not save. At best they reshape our consciousness" (2004, 440), can we think of the lack of univocity and coherent ideology as a testament to the limits of both colonialism and other theories and programmes of salvation when thinking about human liberation? Can we conceive of the expression of anti-colonial desire itself as a sign of the failure of the historical to monopolize our life-worlds?

BANDUNG BEYOND BANDUNG?

I see/sense Bandung being recreated and restaged in all kinds of unlikely instances. Let me close with one such instance. The instance in question concerns a story pertaining to the end of the war in Sri Lanka in May 2009. It concerns a young fighter with the Liberation Tigers of Tamil Eelam (LTTE) during the organization's last stand at Mullivaikal. While the story is part of a larger archive being assembled to testify to the war crimes and crimes against humanity perpetrated during the last stages of the war, I want to focus on a small instance within the account where I see the ability to listen across difference materializing.

The instance in question occurs during our young man's extended incarceration, marked by frequent bouts of torture, in one of the "welfare" camps. The young man had been brought to the camp when he crossed over to the military-controlled area after being ordered to surrender by the LTTE hierarchy. During each torture session, the prisoner is blindfolded so that he will not be able to identify his tormentors. However, during one of these sessions, he recognizes the voice of one of his torturers as belonging to a young man whom he had known from his village. During "breaks" in the sessions, the two villagers begin secretly conversing.

The account, because of its focus on the violation of human rights, does not dwell on, or accord any significance to, what exactly passed between the two villagers. Yet I find myself captivated by this clandestine exchange. If torture is meant to shatter the world of the victim (Scarry 1985), to reduce the victim to something less than human, why does the torturer engage in conversation with his victim? And why would the tortured converse with his tormentor? Is this exchange a testament to the survival of certain forms of sociality despite ideological differences? Are the torturer and the tortured intimating to us that while ideology may divide us, it is imperative that we not take such ideology too seriously?

I suspect that many Third Worlders and villagers, whether from the Global South or the Global North, will not be surprised by this story. In fact, I am almost certain that it will trigger similar stories in many of them, even if these are considered something of an embarrassment in the over-professionalized circuits of Political Science and International Relations. For the historically minded, Bandung signifies a valiant but ultimately doomed Cold War era attempt on the part of ex-colonial states to mount an ideologically coherent and transformative movement to reshape international relations. For them, dissent, to be counted as proper dissent, must be written in the language of the master. But villagers, even if they are not able to entirely escape the language of the master, are nevertheless not bereft of other more mellifluous languages. So, they imagine, conjure, sing, speak of, and live in worlds not yet buried by the master, chancellery, or science. Do you/I have the ears to listen? The heart to respond? The courage to join?

ACKNOWLEDGEMENT

I am very grateful to Quỳnh N. Phạm, Robbie Shilliam, Reina Neufeldt and Himadeep Muppidi for their painstaking readings, inspiring suggestions and generous comments.

Chapter 5

A Meaning of Bandung

An Afro-Asian Tune without Lyrics

Khadija El Alaoui

We'll sing and we'll always sing
We'll bring good news and raise the hopes ...
The street is our home and our song ...
From the tunes of the street come our words
In tune with the street we'll sing ...

—(Ahmed Fuad Negm, "We'll Sing," 1974[1])

THE PROMISE OF BANDUNG

In Bandung, Indonesia, in 1955, representatives from twenty-nine newly independent nations from Africa and Asia gathered to practice a politics whose agenda and subject matter, as Richard Wright aptly recognizes, "had been written for centuries in the blood and bones of the participants" (1956, 14). The blood and bones of Bandung are constituted by the struggles against the ravages of the slave trade, colonialism and all other manifestations of European violence. The gathering of African and Asian nations also meant conversations across cultures and traditions that promised the revitalization of ways of being and knowing that transcend the Western lethal imagination. As such, Bandung raised the hopes of so many hearts beating on the African and Asian continents and probably beyond wherever colonialism, oppression and injustice were. Egyptian poet Fuad Haddad, for whom his craft had to serve the cause of justice and equality, thus witnessed this moment in his poem "Joy":

I said to the bricks: Are you happy? They said: Listen
To the white dove from Bandung speaking in rhyme (cited in Radwan 2012, 84)

61

Not surprisingly, Bandung was closely followed by the worried eyes of Western powers led by the United States. Indeed, true to its imperial commitments, Washington would try its best to thwart the gathering of the twenty-nine African and Asian nations. Journalist Mohammed Hassanein Heikal (1976, 342–43), who accompanied President Jamal Abdel Nasser to Bandung, writes that the Western countries made desperate efforts to prevent Egypt from attending the Afro-Asian Conference. According to him, Kermit Roosevelt, chief of the CIA's Middle East operations, met with Abdel Nasser in Cairo and showed him a report in which Washington claimed to have some information that the Muslim brothers were planning to assassinate the Egyptian president during his stay in Indonesia. It is important to recall that Roosevelt, who was supposedly worried about the Egyptian president's life, dealt a fatal blow to the democratic experience in Iran through the overthrow of the democratically elected Mohammad Mossadegh on 19 August 1953. The Iranians' guilt was nationalizing their oil so that they could benefit from their own resources! In fact, the operations Roosevelt was conducting in the Middle East for the Eisenhower administration aimed at teaching the newly independent countries not to take their independence too seriously (Roosevelt 1979; Kinzer 2003). In the direct words of the *New York Times* editorial on 6 August 1954: "Underdeveloped countries with rich resources now have an object lesson in the heavy cost that must be paid by one of their members [Mossadegh] which goes berserk with fanatical nationalism" (cited in Chomsky 1992, 50).

However, as far as the Western countries were concerned, the lesson they sought to teach "underdeveloped countries" went unheeded. In less than two years after the toppling of one Mossadegh, they had to deal with so many defiant Mossadeghs banding together to speak of ways of living peacefully on this planet, despite the colonizers' desire to hold on to its macabre vision. Abdel Rahman Al-Sharqawi, Egyptian poet, novelist, playwright, scholar and secretary general of the Afro-Asian People's Solidarity Organization from 1979 to 1987, was surely conveying the feelings of many people when he wrote his poem "A Message to President Truman from an Egyptian Father" in 1953:

Are you reading these words?
If you collapse over food
Then gulp down the oil of the Prophet's land to flavor
    some of what you are swallowing
For some food is rock-hard and resentful
Egypt and her neighbors are no more among the sweet easy bites
And Vietnam is in the throat like a thorn
And Western Europe tastes bitter and is too hot to cool
And Iran burns the throat of the god. ... You surely need a dose
From where ... if not from Makka?

At the end of the poem, Al-Sharqawi tells the US president:

You disguise all your treasons with the claim of regime and regime change
and the claim of [Soviet Union] attack
and many claims that are lame and incorrect
Let's quit this boring talk
Doesn't this dear world order rest on our hunger, our exploitation
and our humiliation?![2]

Al-Sharqawi's concerns and questions constituted some of the reasons that required an event in the magnitude of the Bandung Conference. The real threat to the West's "dear world order" is not simply "fanatical nationalism," that is, a Mossadegh, but a different globality altogether, that is, many defiant Mossadeghs *banding together*. Drawing on the political thought of Algerian thinker Malek Bennabi, dissidents' activism and people's poetry especially in the context of North Africa, I will discuss the significance of Bandung not simply as a formal diplomatic event but also as an opportunity for the political-ethical renewal of formerly colonized societies as well as a promise for neighbourly hospitality and human connection.

BANDUNG AND THE RENEWAL OF THE HUMAN SPIRIT

Malek Bennabi, one of the leading Arab intellectuals (1905–1973), argues that Arabs were successful in fighting colonialism but failed to free themselves from the very source that enabled colonialism, which he calls coloniability. Even though Malek Bennabi's main education was in French schools, he also attended Arabic schools in Tebessa and Constantine, Algeria. Later he went to Paris in 1930 to pursue his studies in l'Institut des Etudes Orientales. Yet, he was not admitted into the university of his choice because access for Algerian Muslims, Bennabi ([1966] 2015, 216) writes, "did not depend on scientific criteria but on political ones."[3] Moreover, because of his political activism in Paris, he was blocked from graduating from his electrical engineering studies, which made it impossible for him to find work in his field. In fact, what Bennabi calls the language of colonialism did not even allow him to travel to Makka, Saudi Arabia, where he wanted to settle. Bennabi was convinced that the embassy of the Egyptian Kingdom in Paris denied him the visa of transit under the instruction of the colonial masters (ibid., 352–53).

The humiliation inflicted by one's own to satisfy the desire of the colonizers constitutes an aspect of the concept of coloniability, for which Bennabi is best known. In *Vocation of Islam*, Bennabi argues that every story of colonialism is preceded by coloniability ([1954] 2006, 82). Colonialism in this line of thinking implicates not only the colonizers but also the colonized. A society becomes colonizable, Bennabi argues, when it abdicates its historical function and ceases carrying out its concerted actions in history. A society that no longer works for the very goal for which it was constituted becomes disoriented, morally weak and intellectually paralysed (ibid., 76–81). As a consequence of coloniability, Bennabi observes that a large number of the educated Muslims in France develop a consumerist attitude towards ideas and objects, which only leads to the trap of what he calls "heaping up" (ibid., 57–65). He points out that the intellectuals' import of various items of Western knowledge diverts them from engaging their societies' problems; that's why he compares the mentality of stockpiling to "the paradox of a captive who asks his jailor the keys of his cell" (ibid., 85). For Bennabi, even the Muslim scholars who led the reformist movement in the early twentieth century could not infuse their cultures with the much-needed energy to transform people and inspire them to become shapers of their destiny. He imputes their failure to aspects of coloniability: their dogmatism and their practising what he calls the despotism of words and forms through the godification of the Arabic language that was no longer allowed to grow and evolve (ibid., 43–56).

Colonialism, which Bennabi compares to a cursed whip that seeks to beat ways of lives to death, ends up operating a magical wand, as it urges, without its own volition, the colonized to resist both colonialism (what the colonizers do) and coloniability (what the colonized do to themselves) ([1956] 1981, 249). Resistance, triggered by the destructive forces of colonialism, would lead to the other important work of dealing with the interior destructive forces of coloniability. If in anti-colonial struggles, the colonized were fighting colonialism, the event of the Bandung Conference, Bennabi maintains, was an opportunity for self-renewal with ethical and educational dimensions, which are key elements to free societies that succumbed to coloniability (Naylor 2006, 135). In this context, Bennabi views decolonization as a complex phenomenon: it is about not only the freedom of land but also the freedom of the human spirit.

In his *L'Afro-Asiatisme*, published in French in 1956, Bennabi celebrates the Bandung Conference as the bearer of salvation for humanity through its reinvigoration of neighbourliness and its emphasis on peace, freedom and coexistence. He writes: "A new dialogue has begun in history, a dialogue in which the speaker to power is not another power of its own kind, leading the world to war according to the politics of the 'edge of the abyss.' This is a new kind of language, in which the speaker is not armed with nuclear weapons, but with new ethical and political laws, whose effectiveness and impact Gandhi has proven" (1981, 54). Hearkening to the Bandung language, Bennabi describes it as exuding breaths of Gandhian and Tagorian principles, which besides the input of African and Asian leaders, articulate a vision of salvation for both what he calls the Tangier-Jakarta axis that suffers from colonialism and coloniability as well as the Washington-Moscow axis that is addicted to control and power.

Even as Bennabi recognized that Europe suffered from a double psychosis – sense of guilt and addiction to power – both of which urged Europe to fanatically cling to the conviction that it could not have security without domination and control, he remained hopeful that Europe (and more broadly the Washington-Moscow axis) would have to embrace the Bandung idea (ibid., 250–51). He envisioned that the Bandung principles of peace and coexistence offered the colonizer the chance to regain their soul and the colonized their dignity. Bennabi writes that "the loss in the realm of control equals gains in the realm of human connection" (ibid., 173). Significantly, African American writer Richard Wright also envisioned the possibility of gaining in the realm of human connection, if the Western nations relinquished the addiction to dispossessing and subjugating peoples and learnt to live according to their means instead. Wright (1956, 203) suggests: "to have an ordered, rational world in which we all can share, I suppose that the average white Westerner will have to accept [a more equitable distribution of global wealth] ultimately; either he accepts it or he will have to seek for ways and means of resubjugating these newly freed hundreds of millions of brown and yellow and black people. If he does accept it, he will also have to accept, for an unspecified length of time, a much, much lower standard of living." Yet, the Western world's continuing aggressions through invasions and coups besides the neo-liberal policies of the 1980s onwards reveal that the addiction to subjugating others is almost incurable.

Bennabi's embrace of what he calls the Bandung idea, that is, the confirmation of the human connection through the practice of neighbourliness, is inscribed in the prophetic tradition. Bennabi reminds us of the importance of the neighbour in Islamic tradition that gave him or her many rights until the Prophet Mohammad's companions thought that he or she would be entitled to inheritance as well. Expanding the meaning of the term neighbour, Bennabi writes: "If the neighbor is the one seen and heard everyday, in today's world we hear and see people thousands of miles away. Our neighborhood then is not confined to our street or city or even country. It exists everywhere, wherever others are" (1981, 242). Hence the importance of Bandung in Bennabi's eyes: if the Asian and African participants were embodying the idea of neighbourliness by grounding together and thinking together about their future, their call for peace and coexistence was broadening the dimensions of neighbourliness to include all humanity.

Additionally, Bennabi's attachment to the idea of human connection has its roots in his own experiences in Algeria. He recounts in his *Memoirs of a Witness of a Century* that when he worked as a juristic assistant around 1925, his main duty was to travel with his superior to small towns and villages to deliver the court's verdicts. He recalls with admiration how almost every time when they approached the dwelling of the peasant whom they wanted to deliver the verdict to and who knew well the purpose of their visit, he would hurry up to greet them and insist on offering coffee first. Later, after they dealt with the legal measures, the host, despite his grievances, would insist on their staying for lunch, during which he would not mention the issue of the court at all. Bennabi writes that for the peasant the execution of judgment is a fleeting event while hospitality that confirms the human bond is vital. Bennabi describes this disposition as "the hospitality call of the Algerian peasant" (2015, 166).

He himself extends this hospitality towards Europe which "has annihilated nations and even went to the impossible extent of demonizing humanity" (1981, 227). By doing this, Bennabi allows us a glimpse into the generosity of the colonized that keeps inviting Europe to shed the burdens of control and power and be otherwise. For Bennabi, as scholar Jamel Al-Hamri (2016) points out, the victory of humanity cannot be achieved at the expense of othering people; it can be achieved only if it includes the others, who must, therefore, never be turned to total enemy. It should be pointed out that Al-Hamri embraces and embodies Bennabi's thought of inclusion today while his country, France, persists in maintaining the old structural exclusion of many of its own citizens, inheritors of immigration and colonization, through the continuing reinvigoration of racist and Islamophobic discourses.

In a lecture he delivered in Aleppo, Syria, in 1960, Bennabi admitted that colonialism was trying its best to kill the Bandung idea by all means; yet, his critique understandably pored on the Afro-Asian solidarity movement that was investing more in reacting to what he calls the problems of power created by the Washington-Moscow axis, rather than on the problems of survival that permeate the Tangier-Jakarta axis (2012, 116–17). Instead of dancing to Washington-Moscow's tunes, Asian and African nations, Bennabi insists, need to work on the social and political problems that beset their societies. What if instead of obsessively worrying about the schemes of Britain and the United States to keep Egypt on the leash, President Abdel Nasser worked together with his people and neighbours to put in place structures that would guarantee political participation and social justice? What if instead of muting the poets' voices by long sentences in prison for offering their hearts and words to the *ghalaba* (the poor), Abdel Nasser invited them to draft the country's constitution? If Abdel Nasser and other leaders understood well the priorities, no foreign power could stop them. Yet, their failure to do so signalled traces of coloniability.

Signs of coloniability abounded as Bennabi cynically remarked in his second introduction to *L' Afro-Asiatisme* in 1971: "Precautions were taken inside the third world and outside so that the Bandung spark does not catch fire" (1981, 12). He points out that one of the decisions made by the Cairo Conference in 1957 was to establish an Afro-Asian literary award. Nevertheless, this very simple decision did not materialize until 1969 (ibid., 13). Small wonder that the conference on "Vision of Bandung after 50 years: Confronting the New Challenges," hosted by the Afro-Asian Peoples' Solidarity Organization in Cairo in 2005, concluded that the main obstacle that disabled the Bandung vision was the dictatorship practised by many governments in the very countries of the Non-Aligned Movement (NAM) ("Vision of Bandung" 2005, 207–08). According to their own findings, the challenges then are not new. They are the same stinking old wound: internal tyranny. In this sense, although the term coloniability risks some civilization-mission overtones that legitimize colonialism, it does alert colonized peoples to a grave danger: When a society succumbs to internal injustices, it renders itself vulnerable to external forces of tyranny that employ the situation as an obscene pretext to save the society from itself. Then things fall apart, as Chinua Achebe reminds us, unless dissident activists, storytellers and poets piece together the parts leading up to the Bandung promise.

BANDUNG AND DISSIDENT RHYME

The 1950s were certainly a very promising decade: the brutality of the colonial rule was on the wane, while self-determination and dignity were on the rise and international events such as the Bandung Conference and the NAM gave a platform to forge solidarity with those who suffered the same fate by the hands of Western or Eastern colonial powers. In the context of Egypt, Abdel Nasser's popularity in the Arab world and beyond rested on his recognition that colonialism has been eating away at people's pride and dignity, which he promised to restore by putting power in the hands of the people (Heikal 1976, 144–45). Yet, what pride and dignity could be restored if during Abdel Nasser's rule, thousands of political prisoners, especially communists and Islamists, filled Egyptian jails? If the premise of justice is neglected, even if with the best intentions, then the new rule becomes a new tyranny that replaces the older one. Instead of the promise of freedom and dignity, there is only entrapment and tonguelessness, as Syrian poet Nizzar Qabbani put it in his 1967 "Footnotes to the Book of the Setback" addressed to President Abdel Nasser:

Sultan
Half of our people are without tongues

What's the use of a people without tongues?
Half of our people
Are trapped like ants and rats
Between walls. (cited in Al-Udhari 1986, 120–21)

Egyptian poet Fuad Haddad, who had celebrated Bandung and heralded
Abdel Nasser as the hero of the poor, spent many years of his life in prison
from 1953 to 1956 and again from 1959 to 1964, that is, whenever relations
tightened between the Egyptian government and the communists (Saleh
2007). Another Egyptian poet, Hashem Al-Refa'i left behind him a large collection of poems even though he was assassinated at the age of twenty-seven
in 1959. Unlike Haddad, Al-Refa'i acknowledged the historical significance
of Bandung, but condemned President Abdel Nasser's participation in it. In
"Jamal ... Comes Back from Bandung," which he wrote in May 1955, the
poet cautioned against misguided celebrations:

O, my people!! Why are you cheering?
And for whom have you raised these flags?
For which festival have you set up the procession
in which I saw warmth and multitudes (Al-Refa'i 1985, 404)[4]

Al-Refa'i's first lines in "Jamal ... Comes Back from Bandung" probably
best chronicled the popularity of the Bandung Conference; yet, the poet chose
to go against the current and warned people of what was in store for them.
He wrote:

Who came back from Bandung, O my people,
But the one who doles out humiliation and pain to us
He was in conferences expressing his opinion
and planned a strategy for the squandered peace
He let out a cry from the podiums
Which will prove to be but ... words. (ibid., 405)

The poet even critiqued Jawaharlal Nehru, whom he considered a true
revolutionary, for allowing the Egyptian president to be part of the Bandung
Conference. For Al-Refa'i, the conference was meant for those who wanted
the good for their peoples, while the Egyptian president who used prisons
and torture to silence his critics cannot possibly mean well for his. Even
though Al-Refa'i's voice must have belonged to a minority in Egypt, and the
broader Arab-speaking world, especially in the 1950s and early 1960s, more
poets later came to realize some truth in his uncompromising position. Abdel
Rahman Al-Abnudi (2002), known as the Poet of the Dawn, comments on
that era: "The [Egyptian] Revolution ... concentrated on national liberation

movements, joining the NAM and making significant achievements on that front. Internally, however, we were always followed, there was always someone trailing our steps on the pavement and looking over our shoulders as we had our morning coffee. For my part, my voice did not find free expression until 1967 defeat, which took place less than two months after I came out of prison." What kind of a revolution is this in which poets find their voice only when it is defeated? Tyranny aborted the revolution, despite the promising dawn of anti-colonial nationalist movements and gatherings such as the Bandung Conference. There can be no anti-imperialism abroad and tyranny at home simultaneously.

The story of Egyptian feminist Duriyya Shafiq clues us into another relationship between the battle against colonialism, Bandung and the broader struggle for justice. Educated in French schools in Tanta and Alexandria, Shafiq later received her PhD in philosophy from the Sorbonne University in Paris in 1940. Back in her country, Shafiq founded and edited the *Bint al-Nil* journal (Daughter of the Nile), in which she called for women's participation in the national liberation struggle against the British. Besides writing to mobilize women, Shafiq also led a group of her colleagues from the Bint al-Nil military unit to "surround Barclay's bank and stop its activity for twenty-four hours" (Nelson 1996, 178–79).

Shafiq's demonstrations didn't target only humiliation perpetrated by Britain but also that by her own government. In 1951, she stormed the parliament demanding women's right to vote. In 1954, as she was disenchanted by the military rulers' continuing disregard for women's political rights, she and several other women went on hunger strike and were able to wrench the promise that the new constitution would grant women's full political rights. Yet, growing increasingly disappointed with her government, Shafiq left Egypt for a while and toured many countries in the Global North as well as Global South to engage in conversation with the neighbours. In India, which she called "the land of Gandhi! My Master! *Satyagraha*, power of truth, non-violence," she interviewed Prime Minister Nehru (ibid., 222). On 6 February 1957, Shafiq sought refuge in the Indian embassy in Cairo where she wanted to go on a hunger strike unto death to protest Israeli occupation and Abdel Nasser's increasingly authoritarian regime. In a letter she dispatched to President Abdel Nasser and UN Secretary General Dag Hammarskjöld, Shafiq stated:

As an Egyptian and as an Arab, I demand that the international authorities compel the Israeli forces to withdraw immediately from Egyptian lands and reach a just and final solution to the problem of the Arab refugees. Second I demand that the Egyptian authorities give back total freedom to Egyptians, whether male or female, and put an end to the dictatorial rule that is driving our country towards bankruptcy and chaos. (cited in ibid., 238)

Shafiq explained that her choice of the Indian embassy rested on India's neutrality. Could it be that Shafiq was hoping that the Bandung spirit would convince one of its very nurturers that her demands were at the heart of what he was calling for on the international scene? Vijay Prashad spells out the implications of the Bandung spirit: "The colonized world had now emerged to claim its space in world affairs, no just as an adjunct of the First or Second Worlds, but as a player in its own right" (2007, 45). Shafiq's writings and activism indicate that the Bandung spirit could not hold until it included men and women and addressed all forms of injustices, whether committed by foreign occupiers or one's own government. Similarly, Shafiq' choice of the Indian embassy could reflect her taking seriously the neighbourliness to which many African and Asian leaders appealed in their addresses in Bandung. Shafiq was probably also politicizing the local cultural code of seeking help from the neighbours in times of crisis. Even now, there are many people, especially in densely populated areas, who would seek help in cases of abuse from their neighbours instead of the police.

However, Shafiq's knocking on the door of the neighbour came with a heavy cost: she was sentenced to house arrest while even her ideas had to be arrested and thrown into oblivion. The state confiscated her publications and instructed the newspapers not to mention her name again. Although many of even Shafiq's friends chose to withdraw their support on account of their disagreement with her act, and many others considered her "a traitor to the revolution," the story of Shafiq is instructive in at least two ways. The first is more obvious: The very champion of Arab nationalism, who demanded the translation of Sardar K. M. Panikkar's *Asia and Western Domination* and made it required reading to all officers, reproduced devastating forms of oppression and denied dignity to his own people, especially women. Second, Shafiq's visit to neighbouring countries and knocking on the door of the Indian embassy tells us that the politics and ethics of neighbourliness, what Bennabi learns from "the hospitality call of the Algerian peasant," remains one of Bandung's greatest promises.

THE BANDUNG OF NEIGHBOURS

It is not only politicians that many a time fail to practice neighbourliness beyond speech, but also intellectuals, including Bennabi. If Bennabi's writings subscribe to the vision of cementing solidarity between Africans and Asians through learning more about each other's cultures, his ears and eyes remained more tuned to the theories coming from the Northern neighbours. Where are the African and Asian voices, stories, and theories in his prolific writings? His inadequacy in grounding with his neighbours was likely reflective of the messiness of many Arab intellectuals schooled in the West: they understood the importance of engaging the neighbours but their produced knowledge remained heavily focused on their immediate context and on the West as interlocutors.

However, if leaders and even leading intellectuals fail to seriously build bridges and strengthen connections with their neighbours southwards and eastwards, many poets embody Bandung in their conversations across cultures and traditions. Poets are steeped in these conversations because they are in the forefront battling all forms of injustices and rushing the break of dawn. The great Turkish poet Nazim Hikmet (1962) reminds his Asian and African sisters and brothers that:

> our poems yoked to the skinny ox should be able to till the land
> our poems knee deep in mud should enter the rice fields
> our poems should be able to ask all the questions
> our poems should be able to gather all the lights
> our poems like the milestones
> should be able to stand at the crossroads
> see the approaching enemy before anyone else
> beat the tom-toms in the jungles
> and until on this earth not a single slave country or slave
> not a single atomic cloud remain.

Salah Jahin, whose poems in colloquial Egyptian Arabic stand solidly at the crossroads, declares in "I Can't Forget People" in his 1955 collection *The Word Peace* (cited in Radwan 2012, 121–22):

> I cannot forget about people doled out as spoils
> between Dulles the thief, and Churchill the crook,
> and describe the beauty of sunset with the sun bleeding into the clouds
> I am committed to feel pain and bleed poems of fire
> to see future days of youth beaming at us in the distance.

With their commitment to feel pain and bleed poems of fire, poets are bound to cross-national, linguistic and ideological borders and make many Bandungs. In "Until We Meet," an elegy for Pablo Neruda, who was known as the people's poet, Jahin portrays the poets' devotion to the cause of peace and justice as eternal, since it follows them even in the other world. Jahin talks of Neruda being nursed by poet Federico Lorca (1898–1936), who would ask whether there are still people who "point their rifle towards innocents, towards love, towards dream, towards truth and towards growth." Of poets and poetry, Jahin writes (cited in Radwan 2012, 55):

> Poetry has always been a single path
> A single song with no end

A single lullaby without a birth
A single elegy without tears
A moment of happiness, at a costly price
Pushkin and Abu al-Ala' can tell you.
Poetry has always been an obscure charge
And for every poet there is a penalty.

Poets are always already practitioners of an alternative international relations. That's why they celebrate Bandung as the crowning of anti-colonial struggles and the beginning of a new politics that foregrounds the voices of the oppressed and promises to prioritize their demands for peace and justice. Fuad Haddad's "Joy" captured the great expectations of the time, in which even the bricks were happy because they could hear "the white dove from Bandung speaking in rhyme." Unlike the cacophonous politics of the colonizers, leaders of African and Asian nations would be composing politics in rhyme with the heartbeats of their peoples.

One of the poems of fire that was written to commemorate the first anniversary of the Bandung Conference was Taj al-Sir Al-Hassan's "Asia and Africa's Song" which was sung by musician Abdelkarim Al-Kabli. The Sudanese poet Al-Hassan, who spoke fluently Russian, Persian and English, besides his mother tongue Arabic in which he composed his poems, was known to have declined all honours bestowed on him by successive Sudanese governments. He maintained that his first and foremost commitment was to people, a promise he succeeded in keeping until he passed away in 2013. "Asia and Africa's Song" begins with the poet's recollection that the Asian-African ties are not new, as their relationships have been chronicled in old songs. Al-Hassan chants:

When I play, O heart, the old songs
And dawn overlooks my heart on
The wings of a cloud
I will sing the last stanza to the intimate land
To the blue shadows in Kenya's forests
And Malaya
To my companions in the Asian countries
To the Malaya and to the young Bandung
To the green nights of joy in new China
…
O my companions, makers of glory to the people
O candles whose green light is my heart
…
I don't know, O companions, for I have neither visited Indonesia
The land of Sukarno, nor have I seen Russia
Yet, now that radiance is in the heart of New Africa
And darkness drinks from the light of faraway little stars

I have seen the people in the heart of Malaya
The way I saw Jomo.
I have seen Jomo
Stretching like the light of dawn in a day
Egypt, O my country's sister, full sister
...
Egypt, O Jamal's mother and Saber's mother
You fill my soul, you, O, my country's sister
We will uproot the enemies from the valley
Friendly hands have been extended to us
The face of Gandhi and the echo of deep India
The voice of Tagore, who sings
With two wings of poetry on an art garden
O Damascus
Our dawn is about to break and our hopes lie in the East.[5]

"Asia and Africa's Song" taps into the expectations filling the hearts of the majority of people in the Asian and African continents: the East is where the new dawn and hope lie, in contrast to the West from where a long night of colonialism and despair has come. Bandung's significance lies in allowing the neighbours to put their hands together, support each other in uprooting the remaining colonizers and stand together against the emerging neo-colonialism. So much was pinned on the African and Asian solidarity, as it would generate what Bennabi calls the language of new ethical and political laws to push against the greed of the colonizers and create a political platform to tackle the urgent issues of freedom and social justice. Al-Hassan also leaves us an important hint: Africa and Asia can be a song only if they include all their peoples. Significantly, his poem pays tribute to not only visionary leaders such as Gandhi, Jomo and Sukarno but also poets such as Tagore and everyday anti-colonial fighters, such as Um Saber, a mother who used to deliver ammunition to the Egyptian revolutionaries.

CONCLUSION

With eyes that never look away from the sites of pain while their words envision the possibility of another world, poets are bound to practice neighbourliness as it was promised by Bandung. Egyptian vernacular poet Ahmed Fuad Negm, known as *'Am* (uncle) Negm, carried the tradition of having conversations across cultures. For instance, his "Guevara Is Dead" (1967), "Ho Chi Minh" (1969) and "Pablo Neruda" (1973) teach the heroism of the neighbours, whose death does not mean the end of the cause: justice. Similarly, Palestinian-Egyptian poet Tamim Al-Barghouti, whose poetry today travels like wind in the Arab world, articulates injustice as a nationality, thereby broadening solidarities to include all the oppressed. Another example is Corinne Kumar whose activism led to the foundation of the World Courts of Women. In "From a Corner on the Arab Street," she collects the stories of Iraqi people savaged by US war crimes with the complicity of the United Nations, in order to "keep alive our collective memories" (Kumar 2004). The collective here is not confined to any particular nationality or ideology but refers to a political imaginary rooted in global suffering and the ongoing quest(ions) for justice (Kumar 2011). Collected stories from the Arab streets interweave with stories from the US streets that stand in solidarity with the oppressed within and without. No wonder that some of the Arab poetry travelled to other sites of protest, such as Zuccotti park in New York, where activist and musician Stephan Said chants Ahmed Rami's iconic "I love the life of freedom like the birds singing in the trees/As long as I am surrounded by all of my beloved people/ all countries are my home" (1937). Said (2011) explains that the poem/song "I love the life of freedom" is an anthem to global unity, equality and justice. The Bandung promise has remained alive in the streets and far exceeded the conference. Street Bandung is where neighbourliness is practised, new ways of doing justice are imagined and the hospitality call is amplified. In this way, Street Bandung is truly a song whose lyrics are written in the skins and memories of all those who struggle for the promise of neighbourliness and freedom.

ACKNOWLEDGEMENT

I am very grateful to Quỳnh-ji Phạm and brother Robbie Shilliam for the idea, the invitation and the generous filling of my cup, which made writing feel like a gathering around a tray of tea and sweets at home. I am also always grateful to my fellow villagers who grounded once in Poughkeepsie, especially our Acharya. Our conversations then meander through all my pieces of writings. I am thankful to Houda Debbabi, the defiant poet who unearthed many Bandung poems for me and to Haifa Al-Owain and Anfal Hammad, the nurturers of Kalimat-Nour and our wadis in Al-Khobar. Your fighting spirit is contagious.

NOTES

1. Translated from Arabic by the author, audio recording available at: https://www.youtube.com/watch?v=g7yHjTvg2xg (Accessed 13 April 2016).

2. Translated from Arabic by the author.

3. Henceforth, all quotes from Bennabi's writings are translated from Arabic by the author.

4. Translated from Arabic by the author.

5. Translated from Arabic by the author, audio recording available at: http://www.sm3na.com/audio/87a5394a9c3d (Accessed 26 March 2016).

Chapter 6

From Che to Guantanamera

Decolonizing the Corporeality of the Displaced

Rachmi Diyah Larasati

It is a family trip in 1994. It is a reunion, as I have just returned from Hà Nội where I performed in an Indonesian cultural mission for war veterans, businesses, and the diplomatic corps in Sài Gòn. It was a cultural mission unusually filled with folk dances rather than court dances. The visit to the neighbouring country marked the Indonesian independence celebration, and also signalled Việt Nam's membership in the Association of South East Asian Nations (ASEAN).

This family trip revisits a site where my uncle was last seen by family members during the massacre era. It is the city of Batu Malang, in East Java, a place my aunt has always referred to as the leisure space for the Dutch white men. It is in a mountain valley, a site of beautiful topography with many temples and fruit stalls, full of fresh and colourful flowers. It bears colonial landmarks in the form of many houses architecturally distinct from the sur- rounding Javanese houses; distinct because they were strategically built with only the concern of facing the mountain view and tracing the volcano, but with little attention to the wind, the sun or native neighbours. This cityscape marks the contradiction between traditional households and the Dutch amte- naar *(officer) vacation houses. Furthermore, the traditional houses are often surrounded by cow farms for milk production, as in the old times we (the natives) were the ones who prepared milk for the Dutch military. My aunt, whose house is not far from the small river where all the cow manure and wastewater from the cow farm is dumped, starts to complain. Her storytelling is etched in my memory: "The cow shit smell and the dirty water flow towards the small river near us where I plant my Kemuning[1] flowers. The cow shit smell has become the daily smell that fights my Kemuning, and the thick dirty water is my scenery." This contradictory coexistence is intricately linked with the remembering of the identity of this place itself; it is connected not only*

75

with a big city, but also with the traces of alliances beyond East Java, and beyond even Indonesia entirely.

Batu Malang always reminds us – Indonesians – of the Dutch sanctuary of ages past, and it continues today as recreational villas for Indonesians to enjoy the nice cold weather of the mountain. Even now Batu Malang has the feeling of a postcolonial space; the mixed feeling somewhere between a trace and a hint of cosmopolitanism wherein the architectural designs of upper-middle-class houses along the road serve as markers of those who are considered successful economically. Although the spatial registry of the visitors has changed to one of native presence, especially after independence, these Indonesian bodies remain demographically marked, and the repeatedly changing bodies also resemble the massacre era during which prisoners from different regions arrived constantly. It seems sporadic and chaotic, this in and out of visitors, as if they inhabit the space between land dispossession, the corporate tourism industry and farming. For many European tourists, a visit to Batu Malang includes a volcano trip around the area. Yet the same geographical site can bear traces of different remembrances. One could be about entertaining the scenery of the town and the volcano, while the other could relate to the sustenance of livelihoods. An article on the issue of volcano lovers similarly reminds me of this fascination of traces that are remembered differently (Wood 2008). Volcanoes and ecological concerns often provide fascination as a form of neo-liberal desire that is evocative of the projects of the former colonial government.

I begin with this story of land, urban development, movement of bodies, and the demarcation of ecological beauty versus the cow manure and waste that my aunt refers to, as I want to use the reading of this spatial (de)colonization as a possible marker of the historicity of Bandung. This historicity in connection to Indonesia is crucial to my discussion of the song "Guantanamera" and Che. It speaks to the dualism of both commodification and memory as I often heard the song performed in the tourism spaces of that recreational town Batu. This dualism was also intimated by one *of the songs my dance troupe performed in Hà Nội in 1994. Indeed, its very name was suggestive: "Madu dan Racun" ("Honey and Poison"). Hundreds in the audience were dancing to "Honey and Poison," which apparently had already become popular in Việt Nam.*

Back in Batu, my family is seated on the patio of a restaurant and a group of young East Indonesians from Maluku/Mollucas (Ambonese) start singing in front of us as we wait, ready for our food to be served. The band chooses the song "Guantanamera," a very big hit back then in the 1950s, which existed in many different versions like keroncong *and* ndangdut, *popular forms with guitar and bass. The song became famous after Che Guevara first visited Indonesia.*

The type of restaurant that we are in, where this kind of song is played, is usually located in tourism areas with upper-middle-class service providers, places where travellers stop to rest from their driving. This one where we are seated has a funny name: "Ethok Ethok-e Dutch Tea House," loosely translatable as "Pretending to be a Dutch Tea House."

This patio and the song, along with the mountain view and the garden surrounding us, is the perfect site in my imagination. At the corner there is a poster of Che Guevara with the caption "Muerte al Invasion," *framed in a rustic old teak wood picture frame and next to it is an advertisement for a travel agency that provides tourist shuttles to Bandung. In the old times, Bandung often sparked the imagination as topographically similar to Batu, where we are seated now. In fact, many orientalists called it the "Paris de Java." In colonial times, Bandung was also a sanctuary for Dutch officers, and many accounts of forced labour in tea plantations and dispossessions mark the older relationship between the native and colonialism. That place also sparked cosmopolitanism in the form of technology and a certain hybridity; it is the birthplace of the Science Technology University (ITB), as well as a mixed race population (with lighter skin colour) that would later dominate the film and fashion industries in Indonesia.*

Returning to the patio of my family trip to Batu Malang, the Ambonese singer and the band are perhaps trying to understand who we are, as they keep asking my aunt to stand and sing with them. We laugh and tease my aunt about getting such an offer, which usually only upper-middle class people get in this kind of space – to sing together with a band. My aunt refuses, and points to her hijab and says, "I am from the village, I do not sing. Unless someone who looks like Che is in the audience." I begin to look at her closely, because this is her political statement, a catalyst. Her tactical words, "I do not sing, I am from the village," had been saving her life from political massacre from 1965 until the end of 1972 as she and most artists like her were banned and many even killed, especially when there was a link to a specific artist's organization.

The band sings very well, and they often play the song in Indonesian and in English, too.[2] While my cousin (whom my aunt named Tito Abdullah Mohammad) and I try to imitate them and sing together, my aunt starts to look upset. She keeps fixing her hijab, because the mountain wind is strong this late afternoon. Seated next to her is my grandmother. Sometimes she glances in the direction where my uncle was last seen, towards the military district office nearby. Suddenly both, almost at the same time, raise their right hand and say, "hidup pak Karno!" (Viva Mr Sukarno!).

Suddenly we are all quiet, and the song has ended. The song, "Guantanamera," has reminded us of the purpose of the trip itself, to this place, where we were trying to revisit the site of our family members' disappearance during the Indonesian massacres. One of them was a singer, last seen, in fact, not far from this restaurant, which is near the Military District Quarter that inherited many small prisons from the Dutch colonial offices. He was arrested at home, after a big performance of his, where he sang many different songs including "Guantanamera" with a Javanese pentatonic ensemble (gamelan) and incorporated words such as "berdikari" (creative and independent). Although we knew that he couldn't really speak English or Spanish, he nonetheless creatively incorporated a Javanese pentatonic ensemble and its instrumentation into his shadow puppetry. My aunt often accompanied him in opening the show with her dances, yet my uncle's disappearance has made her disclaim that aesthetic exchange and embodiment of his legacy. This family trip and the young Ambonese band performing for our family is like a surrealist catalyst, and my grandmother whispers, "one day we will find your uncle." It is a promise that we no longer remember.

The commodified form and circulation of song somehow proposes a different value of global alliances, imagination and what has become enmeshed in remembering those. This duality of commodification is the inspiration for this chapter, and is also the vulnerability of it, as it could be an invitation to open space for a romanticism that would again serve the neo-liberal and neo-colonial return. I also recognize a mix of references from listening to a singer paid to sing for me and my family, guests in a café that is somehow "lower" and marks itself as inferior by referring to itself as "*ethok ethok-e*" (pretending to be) Dutch, a colonial measurement that considers the European the highest supreme of being and "us" as less than that supreme European legacy. But the consistent pondering of image and memory of signs, such as the song "Guantanamera," Che and the slogan "*Muerte al Invasion*," also makes me wonder about the different registers of values in the commodification of an original image and its possibility, while it plays romantically in a setting of capitalist seduction – through materialized memory – in the form of tourism.

THE MACRO POLITICS OF EXCHANGE

I am particularly interested in how non-aligned countries form cultural alliances during and after the Bandung Conference through the spread of certain "internationalized" texts/songs (such as "Guantanamera") and plays containing certain spatial identity dialectics. The popularization enables the practitioners to dwell with communities with the reference of strong memories and alliances, and to also engage with the vulnerability of popular (globalized) culture as a form that expresses marginalized content in a mode of commodification.

My question then is how this dualistic role enables the memory of Bandung to stay present and maintains its positionality to inspire decolonization. I am aware of the non-homogenized memories of certain icons and art forms (like such songs) in communities where citizenship is attached to political identity (i.e. Indonesia). I look at layers of memory and experiences, each of which is a "witness" to dealing with this notion of becoming. Is it possible to hold the political value of the artistic form as an embodiment of memory and a decolonizing process while functioning in a neo-liberal spatial configuration?

In thinking about this decolonization I see a journey of thinking, a separation from dominant order, a resistance and rebuilding of strength, and a revisitation of the relationship with equal rights as a form of exchange. Decolonization as Sukarno offers also deals with producing a "counter narrative," a claim of the right to determine dignity because, as some scholars have argued, "colonialism did not end with formal independence" (Savigliano 1995).

Approaching the notion of "globalism from the peripheries" as a kind of power structure that maps the specific historicity of connectivity – of which one example could be artistic expression – is a form of social engagement. The song "Guantanamera" marks this historicity: although it has currently become marginalized memory, it was a marker of a "modern form of popular music," if compared to what most Indonesians listened to in that era. This study narrates the tension between contextualized value and local value, that is, the specifics of the cultural context as a language of resistance on the one hand, and a flexibility of identity marking a neo-liberal threat on the other hand. Although "Guantanamera" lies at the periphery of the globalization of the Euro-American popular form, it is considered popular in Indonesia and distinct from traditional songs. I wonder if by continuing to sing it, the community's embrace of the memory of a global past will be maintained, and if that will also cause the spirit of alliances to be sustained.

I also call attention to the reification of "traditions" (as disembodied objects) and their valorization when ready for mass consumption. Their value when identified with the postcolony is associated with rarity, making them worth keeping, collecting and transmitting. In these complex operations, "native" producers/practitioners of "traditions" become abstract labour, and "traditions" migrate – disembodied and appropriated by cosmopolitan artists – as sources of inspiration. Here I argue that specific politico-aesthetic tactics are employed by "native" artists of embodied "traditions" (dance, music, etc.) to interrupt this displaced recycling of Global South "traditions" and to partake in mobility in globalization as they reclaim a counter-exotic space in global culture where innovation and tradition can coexist.

The rhizomatic fashion in which the national narrative in song and dance is practised, and its appearance in literary projects, embraces a particular notion of postcolonialism to form an alliance between different "homes" that nonetheless share a similar genealogy of identity (marked by being free from war and newly independent, and located more in a periphery status within the international sphere, or so-called traditional aesthetics). As introduced earlier, the song enables us to think differently about how these exchanges become a form of resistance but are later commoditized.

Returning to the corner of the restaurant patio, where Che's picture and the ad on Bandung intermingle like neo-liberal expansion, I argue that in this space negotiation and resilience of memory still remain, while maintaining the political economy of time. Bandung in this context has many different entities/meanings, and for me is a very marked spatial and temporal recon-figuration of consciousness: not only the legacy of the 1955 event where Indonesia's first president Sukarno took the lead in a very crucial positioning in world politics, but also a cosmopolitan space of resemblance in memory and alliances of citizenship and their differences. A citizenship that is marked by global politics, and is radical in its persistent challenge to the power of the West. This alliance of citizenship (the Global South) is a highlight of the memory of togetherness in a globalized space that is still very peripheral.

Furthermore, Bandung is a place that marked my uncle's youth. Therefore, I bring you to a different kind of dialectic formation of events, and engage how Bandung reflects precisely that moment of unwanted radicalism and also the creation of erasure when popular culture took a lead in commemorating the moment through commodification and neo-liberal desire.

When Che and the song "Guantanamera" appear in a tourism setting, the produced aesthetics is reminiscent of an old longing. This longing harks back to the image of a garden with volcanic scenery in the writing of Stamford Raffles (1817), a lieutenant governor of British Java:

> Nothing can be conceived more beautiful to the eye, or more gratifying to the imagination, than the prospect of the rich variety of hill and dale, of rich plan-tation and fruits trees or forests, of natural streams and artificial currents ... it is difficult to say whether the admirer of the landscape, or the cultivator of the ground, will be most gratified by the view.
>
> The whole country, as seen from mountains, as seen from considerable eleva-tion, appears a rich, diversified and well watered garden. (cited in Wood 2008)

This writing clearly marks a colonial embodiment of the union between tourism and slavery preserved in the imagination of the Indonesian pres-ent. Raffles's desire to create a beautiful garden and economic centre is also a colonial enterprise (in mediating the takeover from the Dutch), as his expansion of desire also enables him to be more powerful, and his found-ing of Singapore reflects to many his policy of occupying Java. This trace of the colonially structural landscape is reserved today as policy, and often continues through tourism in Indonesia. The tourism sites embrace this dualism; the labour is both erased and kept in the narrative of antiquity. Just like the song "Guantanamera" that I heard on the family trip, Bandung in a tourist setting sparks a different meaning of this romantic longing for what was past and promises a more universal function of botanical beauty for the garden of Java and its volcanoes.

Such a cosmetic façade belies other memories of these volcanic areas. As we were walking around after our meal, my grandmother started mentioning names and events, as if at random, but I started to hear the pattern. There were the names of many foreigners, offices and events. This spatial knowledge was embodied through her walking, but its references were not translated to us. Sometimes she focused on beautiful things, like a tea ceremony held by a foreign family, and sometimes she switched to riots during the tea event. The area we walked is not far from Gedangan, where peasant movements since 1904, often categorized by colonial officers as riots, were blamed for forcing European communities into frenzies during times of rural unrest (Fernando 1999). This tension between labour and ownership during colonial times left its mark on some volcanic areas that have now become tourist destinations. This memory, and the continuing mechanism of pressure in agrarian politics, became a new wave of struggle in the post-independence era. The new state under Suharto incorporated the colonial machine's methods and reappeared as a new form of dominance over its own people.

With regard to the commodified circulation of the song "Guantanamera," since it has sparked worldwide interest, it has many versions, including differences in how to play the instruments, with variations and improvizations, marking how originality is erased within the shadow of popular music. As Peter Manuel (2002) reminds us, this kind of erasure occurs not only in the content, the memories and the values that are attached to such an artistic expression but also through the technicality of how the music is played, or how the song is sung, translated and changed to a more globalized aesthetic code.

Some ethno-musicologists have argued that different versions of "Guantanamera," as the song travels worldwide, possess technically different tonicities and arrangements. This particularity of technique has to do with certain ways of listening and responding to Latin American music that are common in the West. For instance, in discussing the making shorter of the playfulness of tonality in the Cuban song, Manuel suggests that the change in technique does not offer a similar or simplified version of the song, but rather generates a different interpretation of where the song should end. In fact, in many concerts, players from South America often comment that when the "Guantanamera" song is played there are protests where people say, "Oh no, don't do that – that's the gringo way of ending it!" (ibid.) However, these protests do not prevent commodification, but are faded in the glamorization of a popular form. I argue in this study that the widespread circulation of "Guantanamera" has displaced its historicity. However, in a different form of translation, the persistence of certain memories, such as those my aunt and grandmother refer to, enables the bringing back of locality and the particular.

CHE FROM BANDUNG TO THE BUDDHIST TEMPLE BOROBUDUR AND THE SULTAN'S ROAD (MALIOBORO) IN JAVA

Hundreds of vendor stalls sell T-shirts with Che's image, a famous picture with a black hat and a red star on the front. This image is everywhere. Hung like flags of a country named "Che," in many different colours and sizes, this materialized hint of alliances and traces is left as an empty promise – but spreads like rhizome. Many youths wear the T-shirt, and many villages and houses have a wall decoration of Che. But who could understand the trace? As the ambassador who arrived in Indonesia first after Cuban independence, Che had some agreement with Sukarno on international relations. Borobudur, a site of Buddhist civilization not far from the sultan's road Malioboro, hosted his arrival. It was a marker of hospitality that was not royal, but elegant. The trace of Che's post-Bandung presence in Indonesia is left in the current time with the T-shirt vendors, and sold for domestic and international tourists.

This image of Che is now sold as a tourist souvenir. Many foreigner tourists also search and consume the same materialized memory in the form of a replica that often erases the significance. I imagine the paradigm is different when the Euro-American tourist is looking at the materialized trace. I also think the pattern of unfamiliarity for them entangles with the idea of "Otherness" that Edward Said (1977) famously theorizes, and with the notion of seductive translation that I learn from Shaden Tageldin's work (2011). These images, texts and traces for us Indonesians are layered with a historicity of the Indonesian state in conjunction with the capitalist mode of what plays well in global alliances.

By looking at these texts/images as they appear in songs, pictures, movies and dances, I am interested in the corporeality of political narrative and the embodied memory of national struggle formed, reformed and transmitted in international alliances. This form, that was once radicalized, has enabled the reappearance of alliances and negotiation of borders. Yet in line with postmodern rejection of historical specificity, the new form of cultural commodity must conform to universalized standards to be popularized.

To conclude, I return to my aunt's story. *Although on the way home we recite the* "Guantanamera" *song again and again from many different genres of musical composition, including the one that my aunt suggested was famous during the Asian-African Conference led by Sukarno, there is something unsettled in our circle, the unspoken hopelessness of "finding." In fact, this disappointment is unspeakable, although it is expressed in laughter, when we the young members of the family tease her about having pretended that she does not sing. This affirmation of not singing, the disclaiming of that memory, is her survival tactic. Jokes and laughter are also strategic remembering free of the state apparatus of control. This playfulness of narrative in remembering, with special reference to Sukarno and "Guantanamera," and the disclaiming of any political reference in the broader sense, was surprisingly also undone by my aunt when she responded with her offer to sing if someone who looked like Che was in the audience.*

This mention of Che as a symbolic value of worth – to surrender our memory and its exchange – is a serious gesture on her part. But as Che's image is also very commoditized in Indonesia in multiple forms, such as films, media, T-shirts, posters and many artistic embodied forms, my aunt's words "seperti Che," or in English, "someone like Che," hint at the many metamorphoses of being/becoming and how they are like replica, the resemblance of images and patterns that are far away from their origin.

Bandung then offers an inspiration, sparked from quiet yet resilient collective memory, of clearly bringing a political consciousness to global alliances and solidarity. Although these spatial decolonizations are disrupted by vendor stalls in streets near the Sultan's palace in Java, and by singers at the corner of a coffee shop that calls itself "Pretending to be Dutch," these moments are also reminders of Sukarno's leadership. The question then is how the fragmented memory, in line with the capitalist mode of production and within the space of neo-liberal desire, can retain the pondering of meanings that go along with the decolonizing spirit. This chaotic fragmentation of Bandung, then, still shares the hope of interrogation of where its traces have fallen.

NOTES

1. Kemuning is the name of a flower that is often believed to create a good smell until far into the night. Kemuning is also believed to be a hint that there is a ghost, a non-proper death, because of political violence. It is a symbolic order of traces and hints in many traditional folk tales.

2. Since tourism has now become a part of their everyday, singing in many languages has become a tool to attract more consumers.

Chapter 7

Before Bandung

Pet Names in Telangana

Rahul Rao

INTRODUCTION

The history of the 1955 Bandung Conference cannot begin with the conference itself. And it cannot be told entirely as a history of states. Most accounts of the conference acknowledge its historical antecedents in prior gatherings of anti-colonial delegates such as the Pan-African Conferences, the Pan-Asian People's Conferences, and the Communist Internationals in the first half of the twentieth century. But despite convening decades before the achievement of independence by many of their participants, these antecedent gatherings tend to be viewed through the prism of statehood, the representatives of nationalist movements and parties that they brought together being seen to be animated principally by the aspiration to sovereignty. Yet if we take seriously the sense of Bandung offered by Quỳnh N. Phạm and Robbie Shilliam in the introduction as an "archive of sensibilities, desires as well as fears," or Mustapha Pasha's (2013) equally evocative account of it as "a 'structure of feeling' associated with the injuries and violence of colonialism," it behoves us to ask who had these feelings and how deep they ran. To do some of this work, I want to take a break from the ontology of statehood to offer an impressionistic social history of this archive of feeling by exploring sentiments of pan-Asianism as they expressed themselves in the everyday life of one family – mine – whose members had little to do with the formal development of an international imaginary for the emerging state of India.

The trouble with autobiographical family histories is that they are always in danger of lapsing into self-indulgent romanticism. Happily, the story I am about to tell has decidedly unromantic dimensions that stand in tension with the preoccupations of a postcolonial politics to which I have usually tethered myself. For one thing, to speak of the everyday is not necessarily to speak of the subaltern. This chapter is about the everyday lives of elites, albeit not *state* elites. So this is also the story of my elite origins and the histories of primitive accumulation on which my life prospects and those of my social class and caste were built. Second, the chapter focuses on pan-Asianism, one of the constituent discourses on which the Bandung moment was founded. But it reveals pan-Asianism in a different light from its usual presentation as a straightforwardly anti-imperialist discourse. Accustomed as we are to criticizing the exclusivist claims of nationalist movements – particularly in a subcontinental state system that emerged out of the blood-soaked experience of Partition – it can be tempting to welcome cosmopolitan solidarities as attenuating the exclusiveness of particularistic attachment. Yet as I will try to show, pan-Asianism, pan-Islamism and analogous structures of affect could serve *both* progressive and reactionary ends, often at the same time.

TOGO AND NOGI

My mother's maternal grandfather and his brother had Japanese names. Born in rural Telangana as N. V. Ramakrishna Reddi and N. V. Gopalakrishna Reddi, they would only ever be called Togo and Nogi respectively by all those close to them for the entirety of their lives. As children we were told that they had been named after two Japanese generals and we accepted this, as only children will, as the most unremarkable thing in the world despite a self-evident absence of any Japanese ancestry or other influence in our lives. It was only as a graduate student at Oxford reading Sumit Sarkar's *Swadeshi Movement in Bengal* (1973) that I realized that *many* nationalist Indian families had named their sons Togo and Nogi in honour of the Japanese generals who had played decisive roles in that country's defeat of Russia in 1905. Nobody in my family had explained to me that Togo and Nogi owed their names, not simply to an eccentric gesture by their father, but to a global outbreak of pan-Asianism.

Pankaj Mishra captures the enormity of this moment when he begins his book on pan-Asianism with the following claim:

> The contemporary world first began to assume its decisive shape over two days in May 1905 in the narrow waters of the Tsushima Strait. In what is now one of the busiest shipping lanes in the world, a small Japanese fleet commanded by Admiral Togo Heihachiro annihilated much of the Russian navy, which had sailed half way round the world to reach the Far East. Described by the German Kaiser as the most important naval battle since Trafalgar a century earlier, and by President Theodore Roosevelt as "the greatest phenomenon the world has ever seen," the Battle of Tsushima effectively terminated a war that had been rumbling on since February 1904, fought mainly to decide whether Russia or

Japan would control Korea and Manchuria. For the first time since the Middle Ages, a non-European country had vanquished a European power in a major war; and the news careened around a world that Western imperialists – and the invention of the telegraph – had closely knit together. (Mishra 2012, 1)

The excitement would have been palpable in those hotbeds of nationalist fervour – Bengal, Bombay and Madras – that the telegraph had reached. But how could any of this have mattered to a zamindar in Munagala – a principality measuring about one hundred square miles that stood outside, but was encircled by, the territories ruled by the Nizam of Hyderabad – in what is today the Nalgonda district of Telangana state, unreachable by train, a day's travel in a time of rudimentary transport from the nearest town Bezawada (Vijayawada) 72 miles away, and even further away from the city of Hyderabad. Upon digging deeper, I discovered that the pan-Asian interests of Raja Nayani Venkata Ranga Rao – father of Togo, Nogi, and four other children – extended beyond the pet names he had chosen for his two eldest sons.

NVR Rao was born in 1879, adopted in 1883 by the then zamindarni of Munagala, Latchamma, and educated at the Noble College in Masulipatnam (Machilipatnam) which was one of the first four educational institutions established by the British in India. In 1900, aged twenty-one, he took over the administration of the estate. A biographical note published in 1908 reports him as being a strict observer of the Swadeshi movement's boycott of foreign goods "long before the agitation of Bengal was conceived" (Vadivelu 1908, 304). As with the wider movement, the boycott was particularly emotive when it came to cloth – the commodity that was emblematic of the way in which British imperial tariffs had crushed native industry with the ferociously competitive products of the Industrial Revolution. We learn from this note that the zamindar of Munagala had many weavers on his estate, some of whom were sent to distant places at his cost to learn how to use modern flying shuttle looms. One had been dispatched to Japan to learn about weaving and dyeing at the Technical Institute of Kyoto. We are also told of his patronage of the arts, education and culture. Besides establishing a primary school on his estate and offering scholarships for higher education, he is credited with helping to establish the Sri Krishna Devaraya Andhra Bhasha Nilayam, the oldest non-governmental library in the erstwhile state of Andhra Pradesh and later a cradle of nationalist activity against the Nizam's rule. He also founded the Vignanachandrika Mandali, a literary association that would devote itself to publishing in Telugu. Among the many works that he commissioned were a life of Krishna Deva Raya, the sixteenth-century ruler of the Vijayanagar empire, and a history of Japan in Telugu. The note ends with the observation that the Munagala zamindari was remarkably free of disputes between landlord and tenants. It is difficult to know how seriously to treat this last observation. The writer of this note seems to have made something of a career for himself out of chronicling the lives of minor aristocracy, perhaps even being patronized by the very people he wrote about. So it isn't surprising that the tone of much of this account is hagiographical. In any case, 1908 was early in the career of NVR Rao, with later accounts being less flattering.

Between 1895 and 1928, NVR Rao's title to the estate was challenged by a set of rival claimants within the family alleging irregularities in the circumstances of his adoption. Tortuous even by Indian standards, the legal proceedings wound their way through courts in Warangal and Madras before reaching the Privy Council in London, which ruled in his favour (Raja Keesara Venkatappayya 1928), leaving him vindicated but financially drained. Determined to replenish his coffers, NVR Rao demonstrated more conventional zamindari resolve, raising taxes and squeezing his tenants by every means possible. Oral histories of his reign from this period onwards record a litany of abuses including bonded labour, the extraction of free services from artisans, extortionist money lending and punishment of recalcitrant tenants through land seizures, violence and social boycott (Rao 2013).

The political tide was beginning to turn against zamindars everywhere in the region, with the formation of *rytu sanghamulu* (peasant organizations) including in Munagala in 1930, and with elements of the nationalist movement promising to abolish zamindari land tenure. Unsurprisingly there was resistance to the zamindar, principally in the form of three satyagrahas in December 1938, June 1939 and May 1947, each of which was met with a wave of repression from the police and the zamindar's own employees. To all intents and purposes a Congressman, NVR Rao nonetheless cultivated a highly opportunistic relationship with the party: in the 1937 Madras Provincial Assembly elections, he is said to have struck a deal with the Congress, offering to mobilize people in his pargana to vote for the party in return for their promising not to propagate a left-wing agenda in the area. But the Congress was itself a divided house, formally withdrawing from the local satyagrahas, even as many party members remained in the *rytu sanghamu*. The communists were more categorical and consistent in their opposition to the zamindar. EK Rao (2013, 151) estimates that forty-two peasants, most of whom were members of the Communist Party of India (CPI), were killed in the unrest in Munagala between 1947 and 1951. Indeed Nalgonda district would become the epicentre of the communist insurgency that erupted in this region.

Against the backdrop of these turbulent agrarian relations, NVR Rao's interest in Japan appears in a different light. Notwithstanding the resonance of 1905 for nationalists across the ideological spectrum, for conservative elites, the Meiji Restoration offered an attractive example of modernization through reform from above that had *not* unwittingly unleashed revolution from below, as it had in Russia and as it would in China. Of course this had much to do with the peculiar social structure of Japan, specifically the bifurcation of political and economic power, which left the landed upper classes unable to scupper the Meiji reform agenda (Skocpol 1979, 100). These profound differences may not have been apparent enough to dampen the hopes of conservative modernizers that Japan's example could be emulated. By 1915, when Tagore (1917) was delivering his famous critique of nationalism at lectures in Japan, the love affair with that country had already begun to wane in progressive Indian circles as Japanese militarism and imperial ambition increasingly came into view. In more reactionary quarters however, admiration of Japan and its promise of modernity with order remained firm.

KEMAL PASHA, ATATÜRK AND DURRUSHEHVAR

Togo's eldest daughter Rukmini (my grandmother) married Madhusudan, who had a lifelong passion for horses: he would name three of his horses Kemal Pasha, Atatürk and Durrushehvar. To understand these naming decisions and their evocation of a different pan-Asianism, we have to shift scene from rural Telangana to the city of Hyderabad, capital of the princely state ruled by the Nizam. Madhusudan's father S. N. Reddy had been educated at Deccan College, Pune, and Cambridge, after which he qualified as a barrister and then began training under a number of different police services in the United Kingdom. Upon returning to Hyderabad in 1925 he was appointed an assistant commissioner of police, eventually rising to head the Nizam's transport authority (Mudiraj 1934, 553–6). Madhusudan's early life was immersed in the world of the military: he was educated at the Shivaji Military School and Wadia College, Pune, and the Indian Military Academy, Dehradun, where he received his commission in 1947. After a stint in the army, he would spend the rest of his life working with horses, as an official in race clubs and later as a breeder on a farm that he set up near Bangalore.

It is not difficult to see how someone of this background might have been impressed by the military exploits of Mustafa Kemal in faraway Turkey. Having fought on the "wrong" side of the First World War, the Ottoman Empire had been devastated by the Treaty of Sèvres (1920), losing all of its non-Turkish lands and control of its finances besides also conceding British, French, Greek and Italian zones of influence (Fromkin 1990). Spurred by the humiliation of this defeat, Kemal mobilized his followers in an astonishing military turnaround that succeeded in winning back territories lost to Greece, expelling foreign troops, cancelling privileges enjoyed by the Western powers, and establishing the boundaries of modern Turkey under the 1923 Treaty of Lausanne. Here is Mishra again on the reverberations of this moment:

It is hard to exaggerate the impact of Atatürk's success on opinion across Asia – the greatest victory of the East since the Battle of Tsushima. "The truth,"

Muhammad Iqbal wrote, "is that among the Muslims nations of today, Turkey alone has shaken off its dogmatic slumber, and attained to self-consciousness." (Mishra 2012, 204)

For modernizing elites in Hyderabad, Atatürk's relentless secularization of Turkey might have evoked additional admiration because it seemed to augur a way forward for their own state whose ruler Osman Ali Khan – infamous as much for his prodigious wealth and miserliness as for his numberless concubines and offspring – epitomized the decadence of the Indian aristocracy. And yet the extraordinarily cosmopolitan communal mix of Hyderabad's ruling elites meant that reactions to Kemal's military and political exploits were bound to be complex and contradictory.

Perhaps the greatest symbolic gesture in Kemal's modernization of Turkey lay in his abolition of the Ottoman sultanate. But the position of the emperor did not disappear in one stroke. In November 1922, Turkey's Grand National Assembly effectively separated the political and spiritual authority of the office, appointing Abdülmecid II, the cousin of the deposed sultan Mehmed VI, as the caliph in an attempt to give the new republican government a veneer of Islamic legitimacy. In March 1924, fearing that Turkish monarchists would use Abdülmecid to revive the sultanate, Kemal had the National Assembly abolish the caliphate as well. Abdülmecid and his family beat a hasty retreat aboard the Orient Express, to begin a life in exile in Switzerland in greatly reduced financial circumstances (Zubrzycki 2006, 133–8). With the collapse of the Ottoman Empire, Hyderabad was now one of the most significant Muslim states, its ruler believed to possess the largest private estate in the world. That same year, one of the Nizam's key advisers suggested that he offer financial support to the hard-pressed Abdülmecid as a way of enhancing his own stature in the Muslim world. The suggestion appealed to Osman Ali Khan, in part because it offered a form of atonement for his support to the British (always the only guarantee of his own nominal sovereignty) against the Ottoman Empire in the First World War ten years earlier (ibid., 138).

The abolition of the caliphate had sent shockwaves through the Indian Sunni Muslim community, provoking the formation of the Khilafat movement under the leadership of Maulana and Shaukat Ali. Gandhi famously endorsed its demand for the restoration of the caliph. Less well known is the fact that Shaukat Ali, determined to ensure that the British did not fill the position of the caliph with a pliant figure of their choosing and convinced that Osman Ali Khan would make a better choice, suggested a marital alliance between the two eldest sons of the Nizam and the princesses Durrushehvar and Niloufer, the daughter and niece respectively of Abdülmecid. Disregarding rival offers from the royal houses of Egypt, Iraq and Persia, the beleaguered Abdülmecid accepted the Hyderabad proposal in gratitude for the Nizam's long-standing generosity. The double royal wedding of November 1931 was reported by the *Washington Post* as a merger of "the mightiest houses of Islam," and hailed by the Muslim press in India as portending the restoration of the caliphate (ibid., 138–46).

By all accounts the marriages were unhappy affairs, their protagonists ill-suited to one another. And yet the Ottoman princesses adapted quickly to life in Hyderabad, outstripping their unimpressive husbands in popularity on account of their jettisoning of purdah and other aspects of court culture, their philanthropy and their glamorous social lives, becoming early fashion icons in a dawning age of celebrity. By sheer coincidence, at the time of this writing I happened to visit a photo exhibition on princess Niloufer in Hyderabad on the occasion of her centenary birth anniversary. I watched as members of old Hyderabadi families, Muslim and Hindu, pored over the exhibits, exclaiming in delight as they recognized parents, uncles, aunts and grandparents in sepia-tinted photographs. Attended by the Turkish consul general, the exhibition was inaugurated by K. Kavitha – member of parliament and daughter of the chief minister of the state of Telangana – who, eager to celebrate the cultural heritage of India's newest state carved out of the erstwhile Andhra Pradesh in 2014 (Muppidi 2014), promised to throw money at the neglected Niloufer Hospital, originally founded by the princess. Clearly Ottoman Turkey remained a living memory in the upper-class drawing rooms of Hyderabad.

Not long after the royal weddings, Hyderabad would undergo political changes that were no less cataclysmic than those that Turkey had been through. Since 1800, the Nizams had exercised a highly qualified form of sovereignty over their dominions, having ceded control over external affairs to the British. Yet their considerable internal sovereignty, exercised under the watchful eye of successive British Residents, ensured that Hyderabad remained relatively insulated from nationalist politics, with the Congress establishing a presence in this most feudal of princely states only at the very end of the 1930s. The Communist Party, spearheading agrarian insurgency in Telangana, had been banned but was then cynically unbanned in the late 1940s when it entered into an improbable and short-lived tactical alliance with the Nizam in an attempt to check the growing influence of the Congress. In 1947, the 565 nominally independent princely states in the Indian subcontinent were given the option of acceding to either India or Pakistan, or remaining independent – this last being an option in theory, but actively discouraged in practice. When the Nizam asserted his independence, not least by seeking the intervention of the United Nations in the resolution of the Hyderabad Question, the Government of India responded swiftly with a military operation that unfolded over five days in September 1948, forcibly integrating Hyderabad into the Indian state (Sherman 2007). Euphemistically dubbed "Police Action," it would result in some of the most extensive violence since Partition (Muralidharan 2014).

No one can quite tell me why Madhusudan gave his horses the names that he did. Sometimes the names he chose were derived from the foal's parentage. Sometimes they reflected his interests and preoccupations, or were suggested to him by friends and relatives. Some names were jokes. I would like to think that in naming his horses Kemal Pasha, Atatürk and Durrushehvar, Madhusudan was saying something about the choices that faced both Turkey and Hyderabad in the times that he lived through, capturing both a nostalgia for the old world that was passing and the shock and excitement of the new one being birthed.

TOWARDS BANDUNG

Inaugurating the 1947 Asian Relations Conference in New Delhi, itself an important milestone on the road to Bandung, Jawaharlal Nehru said to the assembled delegates:

> India has always had contacts and intercourse with her neighbour countries ... with the coming of British rule in India these contacts were broken off and India was almost completely isolated from the rest of Asia. ... This Conference itself is significant as an expression of that deeper urge of the mind and spirit of Asia which has persisted in spite of the isolationism which grew up during the years of European domination. (cited from Abraham 2008, 199)

While granting that Nehru's rhetorical mourning of India's supposed loss of contact with the rest of Asia as a result of colonialism was intended to spur a renewal of such contact, it was not strictly accurate. As the foregoing account should make clear, imperialism intensified a desire among modernizing elites to look to other parts of Asia for ideas, strategies and techniques with which to engage with modernity on more favourable terms. If anything, imperialism provided both the material infrastructures as well as the political grievances that made pan-Asianism both possible and necessary. Nor was pan-Asianism simply a language in which representatives of states or proto-states expressed their friendship and alliance with one another at anti-imperialist meetings. As I have tried to show, pan-Asianism had deep social roots that shaped the identities of the elite classes and castes that were preparing to wrest power from the British in India. As such, it was never simply an anti-imperialist discourse but also accommodated within itself a range of conservative and reactionary agendas.

When I started writing this chapter, I was excited by the possibility that lurking beneath the everydayness of family pet names that evoked an unmistakeable pan-Asianism were stories of the international as it was perceived, experienced and transformed in a place that scholars of international relations might consider a provincial backwater. As I began to locate these naming decisions in their full social complexity, a darker picture began to reveal itself. The internationalism that these names seemed to represent began to look like a double-edged sword wielded by conservative modernizing elites against both an imperialist West and the restive lower orders at home. Sub-altern studies long ago alerted us to the conservative "passive" revolutionary character of bourgeois anti-colonial nationalisms (Chatterjee 1999), but it has been slower to reveal analogous dynamics at work in their internationalist imaginaries. If autobiographical genealogical projects are typically driven by some combination of love, pride and desire for affinity, I have to confess to an increasing squeamishness, even dis-identification, as I delved further into my family archive.

And yet, there is nothing uniquely venal about the characters in my story. For all their distance from the centres of official state power, they seem repre-sentative of the elites who populated those centres rather than different from them. At Bandung, Nehru is reported to have said, "We do not agree with the communist teachings, we do not agree with the anti-communist teachings, because they are both based on wrong principles" (Ahmad 1994, 297). Aijaz Ahmad parses this sentence to reveal the many balancing acts that Nehru was attempting to perform. At the international level, he was courting Soviet aid while reassuring the West and the right wing of his Congress party that he did not intend to become a Soviet client. But it is his domestic agenda that makes the avowedly socialist Nehru sound like a member of my family: uncannily enough, from the perspective of this chapter, Ahmad reads his utterance as a signal to the electorate of the newly created state of Andhra Pradesh (formed in 1953 by merging Hyderabad with the Telugu-speaking regions of Madras state), where the Congress was facing elections that the CPI was expected to win in the very year of the Bandung Conference. In Ahmad's reading (ibid., 298–9), Nehru's "we" effectively conflates the interests of the Congress, the government and the nation itself, in an ideology whose inescapable implication is that voting for the CPI is an anti-national activity, while also reassuring the communists that he would not go so far as to join the US camp. As it turned out, the Congress won the 1955 Andhra elections. Ahmad cites EMS Namboodiripad, who became the communist chief min-ister of neighbouring Kerala when the CPI won elections there in 1957, as suggesting that the stature that Nehru had gained at Bandung played a part in the Congress's anti-communist Andhra victory. Bandung, then, was also double-edged: simultaneously a forward thrust against the imperialist pow-ers and a rearguard action against domestic opponents. Whatever the truth of that assertion, the meaning of Bandung on these smaller stages remains to be fully written.

ACKNOWLEDGEMENT

Thanks are due to Quỳnh N. Phạm and Robbie Shilliam for their comments on earlier drafts of this chapter. For their time, patience, logistical support, stories, arguments, criticism, laughter, tears, gossip, rumour mongering and nourishment, I must thank Deepika Rao, Gayatri Rao, Jithender Babu, Mohini Reddy, Nitya Rao, Pradeep Reddy, Pratap Reddy, Ravinder Reddy, Rukmini Reddy, Santosh Reddy and the original storyteller Kamala NVR Reddi.

Chapter 8

False Memories, Real Political Imaginaries

Jovanka Broz in Bandung

Aida A. Hozić

My cautionary tale about Bandung begins in a small Bosnian town called Konjic. It then meanders through art and nuclear shelters, false memories and biographies of Non-Aligned women to question the prospects of solidarity when/if built upon histories of exclusion.

Konjic is a sleepy, provincial town in a breathtaking setting: the stunningly beautiful river Neretva runs through the town surrounded by green hills and snow-capped mountain peaks of Prenj. Resting on a boundary between continental Bosnia and Mediterranean Herzegovina, the town has always had some strategic importance. During the Ottoman Empire, Konjic was the seat of legal power for the surrounding area; in Austro-Hungarian times, it became an important stop on a railroad line between Budapest and the Mediterranean coast; in the Second World War it was the site of heavy fighting between the Nazis, Tito's partisans and Serbian Chetniks. More recently, it became known that it had surprising relevance during the Cold War: in the early 1990s, at the onset of the war in Bosnia and Herzegovina, it was revealed that a large nuclear shelter had been carved into its mountainous side.

The shelter, known as Bunker ARK D-0 (Atomic War Command D-0), was built in absolute secrecy over the period of twenty-five years – from 1953 until 1979. Its estimated cost was 4.6 billion dollars, with the funding mostly provided by US military loans. The bunker spreads over 6,000 square metres and has more than a hundred bedrooms, two large conference centres, a small hospital and a surgery. Equipped with air conditioning and satellite links, it was supposed to house President Tito and 350 of his closest collaborators in case of nuclear warfare. The bunker was hidden from view by several plain-looking Bosnian houses and remained totally unknown until 1992. At that time, faced with the dissolution of the country, the Yugoslav Army was planning to destroy the bunker but a few defecting Bosnian soldiers miraculously saved it for posterity. Its interiors have remained intact to this day – down to the last roll of toilet paper prepared for the survival of the Yugoslav elite beyond nuclear Armageddon.

Since 2009, thanks to European Union funding, the bunker has been opened to the public as an art space. By the summer of 2015, three biannual exhibitions – Project Biennial of Contemporary Art – had been organized in its space, with many works produced in situ. Artists from Italy, Turkey, Serbia, Albania, Bosnia and Herzegovina, Croatia, Iraq, Germany, the United States etc., have found inspiration in the contradictions of the Cold War shelter built in a Non-Aligned country with US money, intended for the survival of a handful of the state's leaders amidst the disappearance of its peoples.

In the inaugural edition of the biennial – "The First Time Machine" – Bosnian artist Maja Bajević placed a wig on a vanity table in the room intended for President Tito's wife, Jovanka Broz. By the time the bunker was finished, in 1979, Jovanka – the only woman on the list of its possible inhabitants – was no longer allowed to see her husband. All of her possessions, including personal jewellery and photographs, had been taken away from her; the wig of her famous bun was the only adornment she was allowed to keep. Maja Bajević's installation of Jovanka Broz's hair-bun in the secret bunker was, therefore, both a vivid reminder of her disappearance from public life and a gesture in favour of her continued afterlife in a decommissioned nuclear shelter.

Jovanka Broz, Tito's third wife, once had an enormous presence not just in Yugoslav public affairs but also on the world stage. As a very young woman, during the Second World War, Jovanka joined the anti-fascist partisan movement; at the war's end she was the highest ranked woman – a major – in the Yugoslav Army. She married Tito in 1951 or 1952, after working as his personal secretary for several years. During the 1950s and 1960s, as Tito's stature grew internationally thanks to his prominent role in the Non-Aligned Movement (NAM), Jovanka – "a symbol of elegance" – helped him host countless world leaders in Yugoslavia and accompanied him on his travels abroad. When she died, an obituary in the English press noted that "she was photographed dancing with the women of Ghana, and astride – or perhaps side-saddle – on a camel in Egypt, as well as in evening dress graciously receiving tributes, her hair swept up in the bun that became her signature, or in an open-top car, smiling at her husband's side" (Keleny 2013).

Despite her global appeal, "Comrade Jovanka" was never much liked or appreciated in Tito's inner circles or, frankly, in Yugoslavia itself. Her marriage to Tito – thirty-two years her senior – was shrouded in secrecy; it was rumoured she had been planted into his cabinet as an NKVD spy or as a tool of the Yugoslav secret services. Her carefully chosen wardrobe – her fur coats, her jewellery, her brocade dresses – was viewed as ostentatious in a poor if rapidly modernizing communist country. Some complained about her "peasant background" and the ease with which she stepped into the pleasures of the bourgeoisie. Others thought she was too loud, had too many opinions, meddled too much in political or security issues and had a dangerous influence on her husband's views and decisions. "Forced to live at heights she could not conquer, and for which she was not equipped," as Tito's close collaborator and then famous dissident Milovan Djilas (1980, 149) remarked, "Jovanka rapidly succumbed to the dazzle of power and fame." But she was lonely. She had no children and no friends. Apart from Tito, she was only close to her two sisters; her public life of glamour and high-level diplomacy was paired with seclusion, intrigues and paranoia in her private domain.

In 1977, the "First Lady of the Non-Aligned Movement" did not travel with Tito to the Soviet Union, North Korea and China ("Former 'First Lady'" 2013). Her absence was widely noted and speculated about in the world press. Even *People* magazine – not known for its coverage of international politics – wondered about Jovanka's disappearance and called it "one of the more titillating scandals of the Communist world" ("Marshal Tito's Wife" 1977). Later, it would become known that the "case of comrade Jovanka" was apparently initiated by Tito himself, in 1974, when he formed a special commission to look into her allegedly suspicious behaviour (Didanović 2007). According to Jovanka's memoirs, she was simply trying to protect her ageing husband from various spies in his environment (Jokanović 2013); while according to the party leadership close to Tito, she was suspected of plotting a coup to remove him from power. In 1975, Tito was moved out of the villa they had shared together into another residence. For the rest of his life, he would be taken care of by a small coterie of party leaders and secret service officers.

Between 1974 and 1988, the case of Jovanka Broz and her marriage to Tito were discussed in fifty-nine special meetings at the highest levels of power in the former Yugoslavia. Her last appearance, at Tito's funeral, on May 4, 1980 was made possible thanks to the intervention of her Non-Aligned friend, the Indian prime minister Indira Gandhi. Indira Gandhi, whose father Jawaharlal Nehru had been one of Tito's closest allies in the formation of the NAM, threatened not to attend the funeral unless Jovanka was present (ibid.). The threat gave Jovanka a temporary reprieve. After Tito's death, she was placed under house arrest. She lived through several different political regimes under squalid conditions – without documents or health care, in a house with a leaky roof and no heating, assisted only by her sister. Eventually, she was unofficially pardoned for her unknown crimes. She received a passport and an identity card in 2009. Upon her wish, she was given a state funeral and buried next to Tito in 2013. Thousands of people came to say their farewells; a popular Italian partisan song – "Bella Ciao" – played in the background as her body was laid to rest ("Uz vojne počasti" 2013).

Non-Alignment was the pillar of the Yugoslav foreign policy. The host of the first Non-Aligned summit in Belgrade in 1961, Yugoslavia played a pivotal role in the movement's evolution. The city was all dolled up for the meeting – forty new streets were constructed, infrastructure was updated, the first neon signs appeared in the city centre ("Vremeplov" 2011). A new city park – The Park of Friendship – was created. Visiting leaders were expected to plant new trees "to give visible expression" to their newly found solidarity (Dinkel 2014, 214). The only European country in the movement, Yugoslavia saw itself lending an aura of its whiteness to the processes of decolonization, racial solidarity of the coloured peoples and the real or feigned resistance to the bloc politics of the Cold War period. In return, it acquired access to markets all around the world and the stature of a "great power" totally dispro-portionate to its size or location (Rubinstein 1970).

And precisely because it was a European country, Yugoslavia was not invited to the Asian-African Conference in Bandung in 1955. Nonetheless, as Robert Vitalis (2013) carefully documents, journalists and historians frequently place Tito in Bandung. Photographs of Tito, Nehru and Nasser from their meeting on Tito's island of Brioni in 1956 are often labelled as "Bandung, 1955" as are the photographs of Tito, Nehru, Nasser, Nkrumah and Sukarno from New York in 1960. Given the importance of Bandung in the mythologized history of the NAM, and the role of Tito and Yugoslavia in the movement's creation – it is probably not surprising that Yugoslavia imagined itself in Bandung. It is, perhaps, more surprising that Jovanka Broz, in her memoirs, also imagined herself at the Bandung Conference. Not only that, she imagined herself as the ideational creator of the NAM. The idea of Non-Alignment, she said, was hers:

> It came about when we were in Indonesia, at the conference in Bandung. There were two blocs at the time, East and West. The situation was tense; everyone was fearing that some spark would start another world war. Tito and Nehru talked about it all the time. They were constantly complaining about the situa-tion in world affairs.
>
> And so, in Bandung, while sitting next to Nehru, I told Tito: "Why do you keep whining about these two blocs? Why don't you do something about it? Let us create something else, a third thing, a tampon between these two powers. Why wouldn't we do it when we are already inhabiting such circumstances?"
>
> Nehru heard what I said and welcomed it. He said I was right.
>
> Future developments followed that direction. The Non-Aligned Movement was thus formed. (Jokanović 2013, 49)[1]

Apart from the young Indira Gandhi, who attended the Asian-African Conference with her father, there were no women in Bandung. Jawaharlal Nehru did not speak Serbo-Croatian making it unlikely that he would have understood what Jovanka said to Tito. Tito and Jovanka visited Indonesia only once, in 1958, when they celebrated New Year's Eve with President Sukarno and his wife in Bali. They stayed in Bandung briefly, on their way to Bali. The visit was largely ceremonial – Tito received an honorary degree from The Padjadjaran University of Bandung – and it included a visit to the building where the Asian-African Conference was held. One of the photographs from the visit shows Sukarno, Tito, Jovanka and Sukarno's wife Hartini sitting in the conference chairs. Sukarno and Tito are eating bananas in the photo.

The conversation between Nehru and Tito that Jovanka remembers could not have taken place during this visit. In short, there is little doubt that Jovanka's account of her role in Bandung, and in the creation of the NAM, is an emblematic case of a false memory. That, however, does not make it irrelevant to our understanding of Bandung. Quite the contrary.

Psychologists view false memories – recollections of events that did not actually occur – as a subset of autobiographical memories, intimately entwined with identity, sense of self and self-understanding. While they are often related to trauma or abuse, they can also be symptoms of aspirations, consistent with the way that one wishes to see himself or herself. Although objectively unfounded, they are constitutive – they generate their own realities, produce tangible consequences and inform other memories. Once set in motion, they can become cornerstones of individual or political narratives, hard to disentangle from events that have actually taken place.

The NAM was an anchor for Jovanka Broz much as it was for her country. Tito's biographers note that she often spoke on behalf of Yugoslav women's organizations – and reached out to their counterparts on her travels, even though she was not officially their representative. Touring the world, she actively participated in conversations between Tito and representatives of foreign governments. After she was deposed, one of the generals close to Tito allegedly said: "For as long as she was hiring and firing waiters and chefs, she could be tolerated. But once she started meddling in affairs of the state – that was unacceptable" (Goldstein and Goldstein 2015).[2]

A mere First Lady deposed to a persona non grata, Jovanka viewed herself not just as a witness of history but as its protagonist. "My memories do not suit anyone," she wrote further in her discussion of the NAM. "No other woman from this part of the world had such access, such an opportunity to meet so many people, to speak to them and get to know them, to observe them in closed meetings. But my testimonies are useless, if I am not free from this pain" (ibid., 85–86). She remembered most fondly Indira Gandhi and Sirimavo Bandaranaike – the two most prominent female leaders in the NAM. "They both valued my contributions to the Non-Aligned movement and I am grateful to them for that recognition" (Jokanović 2013, 86).[3]

In 1992, already at war, Yugoslavia's membership in the NAM was suspended. As the country fell apart, the membership was never reinstated. Some of Yugoslavia's successor states – Bosnia and Herzegovina, Croatia, Montenegro and Serbia – now have an observer status in the organization. At the fiftieth anniversary of the first summit in 1961, Belgrade was honoured to host another conference of Non-Aligned leaders. The city was again all dolled up for the event. Yet in the course of the last few decades of aggression, genocide, sanctions and transitions, some of the landmarks of Non-Alignment have lost their meaning. The Park of Friendship, for instance, where Fidel Castro, Muamar Gaddafi, Queen Elizabeth, Jimmy Carter, Leopold Senghor, Haile Selassie and hundreds of other world leaders once planted trees of peace now lies neglected.

Jovanka Broz was supposedly invited to one of the state dinners during the conference but did not attend. The invitation had never been delivered.

At her funeral, Ivica Dačić, Serbian minister of interior and once a protégé of Serbia's infamous leader Slobodan Milošević, said: "By forgetting Jovanka, we have forgotten ourselves" ("Uz vojne počasti" 2013).[4]

ACKNOWLEDGEMENT

I would like to thank Quỳnh Phạm, Jelena Subotić, Srdjan Vučetić and Valerie Bunce for their thoughtful comments on this essay. The responsibility for its content remains mine.

NOTES

1. Translated from Serbian by the author.
2. Translated from Croatian by the author.
3. Translated from Serbian by the author.
4. Translated from Serbian by the author.

Chapter 9

Casting Off the "Heavenly Rule Book"[1]

Bandung's Poetic Revolutionary Solidarities

Anna M. Agathangelou

INTRODUCTION

The more the people understand, the more vigilant they become, the more they realize in fact that everything depends on them and that their salvation lies in their solidarity. (Fanon 1967; Agathangelou 2011, 581)

If you have come to help me you are wasting your time. But if you have come because your liberation is bound with mine, then let us work together.[2]

The opening texts offer provocative notions of anti-colonial and anti-national internationalisms and solidarity to redress lynching, colonialism and theft of land. Contemporary (re)configurations of critical internationalist revolutionary movements, such as the Arab revolutions, indigenous insurgencies, anti-racist, feminist, queer and Black Lives Matter movements, are pushing us to creatively envision an anti-colonial liberation guided by an ecological analysis of the relationship of colonial violence, anti-black violence, and violence against stateless, displaced peoples, and their ecologies. A participant in Black Lives Matter says, "We need to be internationalists." Another adds, "But we have to have a program for self-determination that helps us to build power against the capitalist forces and the state," referring to the cultivation of economic self-sufficiency, boycotts and labour strikes (Zee 2014). Harnessing critical re-engagement and memory for a feminist anti-colonial-nationalist and anti-racist movement today means acknowledging that diverse tactics are necessary for a meaningful confrontation of the toxic complex of white supremacy, gender violence, environmental degradation and capitalism.

In this chapter, I argue that the 1955 Bandung Conference culminated in a revolutionary constitutional moment with worldwide reverberations, redefining the international community and its dominant ideas of unipolarity or bipolarity governance, politics and sensibilities (Jasanoff 2003). It was the vital site of new idioms and experimentation, what I call a poetics of solidarity, using verbs, tropes, and strophes to challenge and transform the consciousness of peoples. Coming together at Bandung, leaders formerly subjugated by Western imperial powers proposed a dream of South-South connections with alternative forms of modernity, industrialization and social expressions. They evoked images of solidarity between peoples and states – ideas and projects of a new world and a new humanism. The vocabulary that emerged challenged European imaginaries of anarchy and exotic disordered places. At the conference, leaders "wrestled with each other," "made friends with each other" (Nehru 2001) and articulated a way of thinking and a mode of intervention that fully engaged in the global fate of the world and its contingent ecologies (Fanon 1967). Their coming together was an impetus to experiment with ending colonial shackles and "other shackles of [their] own making" (Nehru 2001). Indeed, Bandung co-constituted an experiment with transnational anti-colonial and decolonial thought and an order whose emerging relationships across multiple worlds embodied what the power of the colonized peoples could and can do.

My interventions are threefold. First, I explain poetic solidarity as a feminist mode of poetic praxis in the form of word, verse, and soliloquy that breaks down the gendered interiority of the European experiment about the international, simultaneously reaching for ways to radically transform racism's and capitalism's notions of the international. Second, I reassess speeches by three notable leaders: Nehru, Sukarno and Zhou Enlai. While they entered from different vantage points, together their efforts created what I call a poetics of solidarity – a verse that transforms the consciousness of the target audience by using rhythms, language, and saturated bodies of frustrated desires for their eruptive possibilities and concerns of that very audience. Third, I conclude with some thoughts on the meaning of Bandung as a historical event and as a set of imaginations and expressed grammars. As an imaginative and generative event, it inspires grammars, radical, creative and innovative possibilities for decolonization and decolonial thought in international relations today.

Informed by sexual revolutionary poetics of solidarity orientation, my reading attends not only to the conceptual logic of the texts I analyse, but also to their literary dimensions and visceral charges. I observe the tonalities of their words and the distinctive contours of their images to point to how the medium of the conference and the writing material express solidarity. Writing this piece reflects my deeper need to imagine and conjure a poetics of solidarity, a dream of transformation, the word's construction of an alternate international whose locus is the tabula rasa, that is, the disinvestment from and the "changing of the whole social [colonial] structure from the bottom up" (Fanon 1967, 27).

THE BANDUNG RUPTURE AND POETIC SOLIDARITY

The Bandung Conference and many of the congresses in its aftermath have experimented with poetic solidarities. More recently feminists engage with poetry, arguing it is a site "for the birthing of alternative histories and the forging of solidarities – particularly in moments of world shattering violence" (Spira 2011). Jahan Ramazani (2009), for instance, challenges the notion that poetry is less capable of circulating transnationally than other forms of cultural work, such as film, television and digital media. Many incorrectly consider poetry "stubbornly national" (Spira 2011; see also Borstelmann 2006). Many feminists, including Tamara Spira, Kyle D. Killian, and myself, agree with Ramazani. For us, poetry expresses "earlier iterations of struggle" reverberating into the present to invent a dialogue with the "refreshed climate of protests in our midst" (Spira 2011). These kinds of poetics, as Édouard Glissant (1997, 159) argues, and I argue elsewhere (Agathangelou and Killian 2006), not only refer to styles of writing, but also to modes of knowing, being and acting in the world: "The world's poetic force ... kept alive within us, fastens itself by feeling, delicate shivers, onto the rambling presence of poetry in the depths of our being." Being in the world is pivotal to understanding how the world's poetic force creates and expresses itself: "The expression of this force and its way of being is what we call Relation: what the world makes and expresses of itself" (Glissant 1997, 183–4).

Those who participated at Bandung challenged the mode of organizing and the circumscribing of the world in imperialist and nationalist terms. The solidarity dance of the poetics expressed there and elsewhere[3] created a global aesthetic imaginary and movement; multiple worlds converged in the shaping of an international order whose crime of colonization and extermination of peoples and ecologies did not presuppose remembrance or mercy. When delegates spoke, they embodied the space of the colonial archive, queering it with alter visions and imaginaries even though their speeches and archival documents were marginalized, erased or even exterminated from the international and intimate archive of a bipolar international society that promised peace, freedom and democracy.

Bandung shaped our understanding of world politics, especially the anti-colonial and decolonial knowledge for international relations as a field, as a method, as ethos, and as a Relation. Mustapha Kamal Pasha (2009) argues that the conference manifested in what he calls the Bandung impulse. This is still alive today as a radical orientation and imagination of knowledge in international relations and world politics. It is important to recognize how the era produced spaces for "a post-Westphalian ethics in a world of strangers" challenging the "post-secular sensibility" inherent in "modernity's global march" (ibid.). Relying on multiple sources, including Gandhi's critique of modern civilization, he challenges the "cosmopolitan impulse nested in secularism" by pointing to how the Bandung impulse ruptured, and still ruptures, imperial reason and practices that occlude alternatives calling for equality and recognition of difference and non-hierarchical cultural agency (ibid.).

Manifested in the form of imaginaries, visions, affective matrices and lives that co-produce meaning for many peoples whose subjecthood is bracketed outside normative Western structures, the Bandung impulse reveals an investment in anti-colonial and decolonial affects (i.e. Fanon's [1963] nausea, trembling, ejaculation, passion, warmth) challenging the enduring archives of empire and stimulating many peoples to action and to radical dis-orientation. The Bandung event was and is a revolutionary paradigm, confronting the secular premises of the political and the attempts to forget the crimes allowing Western projects such as the sovereign and the state to erect themselves and sustain their *salus*. Importantly, Bandung's planetary vision does not confine people within narrow nationalist borders to be protected at all costs.

INTIMATE POETICS OF SOLIDARITY

We have been like the "Monkey King Upsetting Heaven" in the old play. We have thrown away the Heavenly Rule book. Remember this. Never take a Heavenly Rule Book too seriously. One must go by one's own revolutionary rules. (cited in Strong and Keyssar 1985, 505)

Drawing on the epic novel *Journey to the West*, written in the sixteenth century by Wu Cheng'en, in a time of mortals, gods, and Buddhas, in the passage cited above, Mao Zedong reminds us how important it is to throw out the Heavenly Rule book. The given worlds, he says, are not necessarily desirable, and other worlds ought to be engineered and with the "few poems [of each one of us] ... and no other personal weapons."[4] And if the Bandung Conference indicates a set of social-technical imaginaries and otherwise fluctuating worlds, then applying Mao's comment to the conference reveals its poetics and the multivalent systems of meaning making at play, opening up the complexities through which African and Asian solidarities are imagined and practised.

The Bandung Conference was a "galvanizing event in the revolt against the West" (Devetak, Dunne and Nurhayati 2016, 6). Its poetics generated a radical imaginary and possibility for an anti-colonial solidarity, along with the vision of a peaceful coexistence for the whole world. While there were twenty-nine countries present and the air was rife with tensions, the texts, speeches and conversations embodied an epistemology of a radical transnational social production, a source of life. Those present can be considered to have expressed the major poetics of the colonized world; they are the poets and "citizens of imaginative webs formed by cross-national reading and writing" (Ramazani 2009, 48) of an anti-colonial and peacefully coexisting international order.

In the opening speech of the conference, Indonesian president Sukarno alerts his listeners to the significance of the "first intercontinental conference of coloured peoples in the history of mankind" (*Africa-Asia Speaks* 1955). He is "filled with emotion," including "sadness recall[ing] the tribulations through which many of our peoples have so recently passed, tribulations which have exacted a heavy toll in life, in material things, and in the things of the spirit." Using powerful and tactile language, he reminds his audience of the sacrifices in sweat, labour, and blood which made the West possible: "This hall is filled not only by the leaders of nations of Asia and Africa; it also contains within its walls the undying, the indomitable, the invincible spirit of those who went before us" (ibid.).

Sukarno echoes the rhythms of the lives of those upon which the Western world was built. Drawing on militant anti-colonial and labour strife, he extends the attention of his audience beyond those present to include the dead. He speaks to social abandonment, to the anxiety and fear generated by the colonizer who violated life and cosmos. Social abandonment tugs at the roots of our sense of belonging, and Sukarno's speech raises key questions of what constitutes Indonesia and the international or who might have a direct stake in combatting the amnesia of colonialism. Sukarno also speaks of and from an affective disposition that allows him and his audience to remember to extend their attention span, lifting them to experience time and space differently from the entrenched ways of the colonial, reaching into those familiar senses of a misconceived modernity whose promises of freedom and prosperity were just rhetorical codes. For Sukarno, the conference clearly marks a pivotal moment in the struggle against colonialism, enabling Asians and Africans to experiment with unprecedented solidarity:

> Sisters and Brothers, how terribly dynamic is our time! ... This line runs from the Straits of Gibraltar, through the Mediterranean, the Suez Canal, the Red Sea, the Indian Ocean, the South China Sea and the Sea of Japan. For most of that enormous distance, the peoples were unfree, their futures mortgaged to an alien system. Along that lifeline, that main artery of imperialism, there was pumped the life-blood of colonialism. (ibid.)

In his evocative invocation of "sisters and brothers," on the one hand, Sukarno expands an allegiance to the two largest continents in the world, while on the other, he expresses a collective avowal of a revolutionary project, in the demand for the social expansion and envisioning of a new poetic-political solidarity.

Sukarno works with the transformative affectivities already existing in the people of these two continents and harnesses solidarity energies through his deployment of language. Consider the following:

> Our envoys then were rifles, and cannon, and bombs, and grenades, and bamboo-spears. We were blockaded, physically and intellectually. ... It was at that sad but glorious moment in our national history that our good neighbor India convened a Conference of Asian and African nations in New Delhi, to protest against the injustice committed against Indonesia and to give support to our struggle. The intellectual blockade was broken! ... "Have no doubt of the omnipotence of a free people." (ibid.)

Sukarno challenges the masculine European modernity's approach that turns everything into technologies and things to co-produce certain subjects' lives and social orders. The reader/audience is reminded of the incapacitation of the colonized, pointing to how the affective and temporal logics of this blockade ought to be unleashed and transformed; it will take assembly and poetic solidarity to loosen up the blockade and ultimately to destroy the colonial order.

By and large, then as now, the bipolar order's rules, norms and institutions excluded the majority of the world under the assumption that the colonized peoples would not be able to contribute much to the thinking and its formation, including its imaginaries.[5] In contrast, the conference offered a multilateral forum to awaken those new feelings and desires for liberation and freedom (even when and what form was unknown) and "learn to be aware with a new awareness" as well as "envisag[e] the possibility of creating new races from the latent heat in [their] dark brown bodies" (Anand 1940, 152–3). Probing the poetics of these visceral figures, and the systems of meaning making at play, opens up the amalgamations through which revolutionary consciousness is imagined. In projecting such a revolutionary vision, these leaders articulated a human collective whose very ways of sensing and being could be a site of an alternative conception, embodiment of the world and transformation.

Indicatively, after poetically expressing the sobs of those colonized and brutally left out of the process, Sukarno speaks of the changes, indeed, the storm over Asia and Africa that generates the possibility for a sonic/social contract of solidarity:

> Yes, there has indeed been a *Sturm uber Asien* – and over Africa too. ... The last few years have seen enormous changes. The passive peoples have gone, the toward tranquility has made place for struggle and activity ... Hurricanes

of national awakening and re-awakening have swept over the land, shaking it, changing it, changing it for the better. ... The affairs of all the world are our affairs. (*Africa-Asia Speaks* 1955)

Sukarno's metonymic focus on the ecology is twofold. He gestures to the process of making the world through the toil and sweat in noxious plantations and fields and also to the South's shaking up and redirecting their energies and power towards a new kind of revolution and world. The storm acts as a central trope structuring the temporal grammar, from Asia and Africa's emergence from colonization to awakening the land, changing it and ecologizing its revolutionary potential, metaphorically replacing the impalpable struggle of the South with a palpable one.

Jawaharlal Nehru (2001), as the architect of non-alignment (not neutrality), offers his poetics of solidarity through his declarations of intent, linking his vision of peaceful coexistence to international politics: "Asia is dynamic, Asia is alive and full of life. Asia will make mistakes, has made mistakes, but it does not matter. If life is there, every mistake is tolerated and we advance. ... But we shall cooperate only as friends, as equals." Nehru's repetition of Asia ... Asia ... Asia ... alerts the ear to life, mistakes, change and advancement. Within the same speech, questions of a visceral poetics of solidarity bring him to questions of time. Will the decolonized subject become the object or subject of historical development? Nehru asks: "Our influence must be exercised in the right direction, in an independent direction, with ideals and objectives behind it, if we represent the ideals of Asia, if we represent the dynamism of Asia. Because if we do not represent that, what are we then?" (ibid.).

He addresses the question of racialism by talking about the ways in which the world is based on it.

> I think that there is nothing more terrible, nothing more horrible than the infinite tragedy of Africa in the past few hundred years. When I think of it everything else becomes insignificant before that infinite tragedy of Africa ever since the days when millions of them were carried away into America or elsewhere; the way they were taken away, fifty per cent dying in the process, we have to bear that burden, all of us, I think the world has to bear it. ... And it is up to Asia to help Africa to the best of her ability, because we are sister continents ... I hope we will be worthy of the people's faith and our destiny. (ibid.)

Nehru's poetics brings these two continents together in a sexual, intimate, intellectual space to make, imagine, live and generate not just the possibility but ultimately also the creation of a new world. In this, he engages the world and reaches a new transformative experience of time. His verse points to the significance of a solidarity that attends to Africa both as a "metaphor for reclaiming a stolen humanity" (Spira 2011) and as a historical entity that allows the linking of specific nodes of struggle within a larger architecture of movement building – bringing the Americas in as well.

Nehru, like Sukarno, expresses the transformative potential of sentiments that already exist in their communities of whom – and with whom – they speak. What I call here the sexual poetics of solidarity as an analytic continues to animate and catalyse community relationships in more recent movements, including Arab protests and revolutions, the Black Lives Matter movement, feminist and queer movements, and indigenous insurgencies, making structural linkages across geographies, ecologies and humans towards a unity of a Global South decolonial struggle.

While Nehru recognizes that the Asian or African inhabits a densely saturated, suspended immanent temporality (i.e. "are we copies of Europeans or Americans or Russians?"), he theorizes this as a condition for a solidarity expressing a world otherwise. In this, he is informed by the "five principles" of peaceful coexistence in international relations as agreed in 1904 between China and India over Tibetan territorial rights, that is, mutual respect for a state's territorial integrity, mutual non-aggression, mutual non-interference, equality and mutual benefit, and peaceful coexistence. Nehru (2001) calls for world peace, cooperation and peaceful coexistence, as opposed to the "false values and false standards" of the two "colossuses, the US and the Soviet Union." "The difficulty," he says, "is that while governments want to refrain from war, something suddenly happens and there is war and utter ruin" (ibid.). To prevent total "annihilation," all states should be treated as equal partners, sharing in the decision-making and management of world affairs, not held hostage to the whims of superpowers and their blocs (Nesadurai 2008): "The question we must put to ourselves now is, are the actions we take here going to serve the cause of peace or the cause of passion and mutual recrimination?" (Nehru 2001).

Similarly, the Chinese delegation and Chinese Prime Minister Zhou Enlai moved rhetorically beyond the sexualized (i.e. masculinized and feminized) divisions of the Cold War to state, "Our voices have been suppressed, our aspirations shattered, and our destiny placed in the hands of others. Thus, we have no choice but to rise against colonialism."[6] At the conference, in fact, Zhou cultivated an alternative platform for international relations and a world otherwise.

Personally and collectively, Chinese delegates challenged the rigid and dangerous bipolar division of the world and pushed for the emergence of a multipolar international system. When the Lebanese delegation argued the conference should support the UN's "Universal Declaration of Human Rights," controversy broke out, as Taiwan was part of the UN and China was not. Many expected the Chinese delegation would renounce the proposal, but the prime minister swiftly said the conference was not the place to put

Chinese communist ideology or China's position against the West and the Soviet Union on trial. In the following, he asks participants to use the conference to "seek common ground," not "emphasize their differences" ("Interview with Chou En-lai" 1955):

> We are against outside interference. ... We are prepared now to establish normal relations with all the Asian and African countries, with all the countries in the world. We have no bamboo curtain, but some people are spreading a smoke-screen between us. Let us the Asian and African countries, be united and do our utmost to make the Asian-African conference a success. (Zhou 1955)

The tension between communism and expansionism came up in a call by John Kotelawala, prime minister of Sri Lanka, for delegates to denounce colonialism,[7] thereby challenging Chinese foreign policy and its stance on imperialism. Instead of shying away, China played a leading role in the committee deciding what colonialism meant. The Chinese delegation used this opportunity to establish nationality agreements with the Philippines, Thailand and Indonesia, ending any claims to those lands and silencing those who argued China was an imperialist nation (Kahin 1956, 14). Upon concluding their deliberations, this draft committee signed a statement condemning "colonialism in all its manifestations." (ibid.)

Zhou emerged as a great persuader of conference participants, especially as he was willing to not only compromise but also to experiment with the new affects emerging at the conference. Recognizing that the sensorial nodes of African and Asian bodies had been monopolized or destroyed by the projects of empire, he reminds his audience: "The first atomic bomb exploded on Asian soil and ... the first man to die from the experimental explosion of the hydrogen bomb was an Asian" (Zhou 1955).

The new awareness articulated by Zhou unsettled the tautological architecture of fictional notions of world, community and bodies, opening them up to a vision of what it means to be no longer colonized and endangered. Metaphorically and materially, Zhou threw away the Heavenly Rule book of the West because of its inability to guide the world beyond the Western ontological problematic of political sovereignty in its multiple masculinized iterations. He shaped pivotal alliances, and at the conclusion of the conference, delegates seconded his call to institutionalize the *Panchsheel* – five principles – and articulate a unified Afro-Asia platform.[8]

AS A WAY OF CONCLUSION: AGONISTIC EMBRACES?

Africans and Asians used the Bandung Conference as a major moment, a platform from which to articulate their visions for the planet. Speakers and participants critiqued and problematized the co-produced universal (and secular) humanism of the West and its contingent orders. In its place, they proposed and pushed for an all-inclusive humanism that could dismantle racist and imperial tendencies by valuing all people for their inherent humanity. The conference marked the beginning of a new era in global political economy, one lasting into the 1970s; during this period, projects of nationalization and various experiments with states, economies and cultural productions attempted to forge an independent Third World path to economic development and human freedom. While national liberation movements generally oriented themselves towards either the United States or the USSR, the spirit of Bandung informed many Third World peoples who did not automatically choose the first or the second world. Indeed, non-alignment was an important strategy that emerged out of this moment.

The meaning of Bandung also "went deep into the psyches of the colored oppressed of the world" (Rollins 1985, 64). Pan-Africanists like Shirley Du Bois saw how China, for instance, inaugurated racial liberation as expressed at events as far removed as the Suez crisis, Ghanaian independence and desegregation at Little Rock Central High, all of which permanently reconfigured race as a central feature in world politics. It was Beijing and "not white Moscow that was standing firm against US imperialism" (Frazier 1956, 7–8; Horne 2000, 224–5) and supporting pan-Africanism through its multiple socialist projects. Ultimately, "no American can feel the struggle of China more keenly than does the American Negro" (Horne 2000, 236). Du Bois was clear: Mao's socialism could transcend the differences between communism and nationalism, crafting a movement of what the sensorial nodes of the enslaved and the colonized body and the power of the people could do.

While Du Bois and other pan-Africanists and anti-colonials argued for a nationalist/socialist economic development, others with very different ideological positions believed differently. For example, Richard Wright (1956, 204) says Bandung represented a new postcolonial situation that signalled the end of imperialism and "would result in the need for radical reconstruction of the social and economic systems of the Western world." A year after Bandung, the Congress of Black Writers and Artists met in France. Speaking at this congress, Franz Fanon drew a sharp line between the perpetuators and objects of imperialism by challenging gradations and fictions in thinking about the colonized. Waging a critique against imperialism and (masculinized) racism, he says that because "military and economic oppression most frequently precedes, makes possible and legitimates racism … a colonial country is a racist country" (Fanon 1956, 125, 127). He speaks of those emerging from the colonizing and enslavement conditions as working together in a "fluctuating movement which they are just giving a shape to, and which, as soon as it has started, will be the signal for everything to be called into question." Fanon speaks of the existence of a "zone of occult instability" (1967, 227) where our impalpable corporeal registers, our racialized and gendered awareness, can turn themselves into sites of calling into question the fictional privilege of whiteness and of race.

With today's global shifts (e.g. the rise of BRICS [Brazil, Russia, India, China and South Africa], intense militarization worldwide to erect neo-liberal markets vs. movements challenging neo-liberalization, ecological degradation, toxic contamination and neo-colonial violence), the Bandung intensity has returned, along with several of its key questions: What constitutes the global today? What kind of a world do we want? Should some ideas, such as self-determination and decolonization, be reanimated towards a new poetic solidarity for a world otherwise?

Bandung's leaders pushed for autochthonous forms of writing and making the world. Through radical verses, language and strophes, a poetics of solidarity (Agathangelou 2012), they expressed revolutionary orientations that continue to animate anti-colonial and internationalist creativity, informing and shaping our contemporary revolutionary internationalisms. In their very bodies and ways of being, new movements express such poetics of solidarity pushing us not only to advance towards multipolarity and away from bipolarity but also to defy prevailing divisions of labour and fetishizations of collectivity. Multipolarity as a notion and practice questions the nature of states, their economies, their social/cultural practices, actions and effects. However, to this point it has failed to question the ways knowledge and order are co-produced, including what powers (i.e. the corporate world) make this possible. Indigenous movements, black lives movements, and occupy movements are calling for political, economic and ecological decentralization of the world's resources, better management and fair distribution of these resources. These movements demand self-determination and participation in the invention of worlds and lives that are not terror ridden and exclusive.

Instead of multipolarity, we could talk about multilateralism and seek governance institutions that allow for cooperation and partnerships benefitting larger numbers:

> If the building of a bridge does not enrich the awareness of those who work on it, then that bridge ought not to be built and the citizens can go on swimming across the river or going by boat. The bridge should not be "parachuted down" from above; it should not be imposed by a *deus ex machina* upon the social scene; on the contrary it should come from the muscles and the brains of the citizens. (Fanon 1967, 200–1)

Direct substantive democracy, self-determination and poetics of solidarity stretch our imaginaries of the political to include the pursuit of peace and development in ways that do not destroy us and our life sources. Such interrelated values should be central to any conversations of re-imagining and inventing the state, state-societal and ecological relations. It is equally important to challenge the capital/property model of development, as it has been destructive for humans, non-humans and ecology. Finally, African-Asian direct democracy, self-determination and poetic solidarity ought to take similar directions.

These various disruptions and contingencies represent the points from which we must start our analysis of the social, economic, political, ecological and intimate productions of the world. As I write elsewhere (Agathangelou 2012), we learnt from the Arab revolutions in 2011 that our poetic solidarity ought to begin with saying goodbye to all givens. Whatever we work in or with will not allow us to create that fugitive social field without those other folks who, along with us, are trying to get to that something otherwise. As Fanon (1967, 204) reminds us: "The living expression of the nation is the moving consciousness of the whole of the people; it is the coherent, enlightened action of men and women. The collective building up of a destiny is the assumption of responsibility on the historical scale." It is indeed with such solidarity that "we" don wings and introduce "invention into existence" (ibid., 229).

ACKNOWLEDGEMENT

Thanks to my mother who always sang songs of solidarity that expressed fugitive feelings. Kyle D. Killian, Elizabeth Thompson, Robbie Shilliam and Quỳnh N. Phạm, thank you for your excellent editing suggestions.

NOTES

1. Strong and Keyssar (1985, 505).
2. This motto was on a poster by Aboriginal Activists, Group Queensland, ca. 1970.
3. Including the following: All Indian Women's Commission; All-Asian Women's Conference, Lahore, 1931; Egyptian Feminist Union, "Al-Mu'tamar al-Nisa al-Arabi," Cairo, 1944.
4. Mao said his only weapons were a few poems.
5. Ministry of Information 1955a, 2.
6. Zhou Enlai, Premier, Head of the Delegation of the People's Republic of China, Speech 19 April 1955, Wilson Center, Digital Archive, available at http://digitalar-chive.wilsoncenter.org/document/121623.
7. Kotelawala condemns "all types of colonialism, including international doctrines resorting to the methods of force, infiltration, and subversion."
8. The final resolutions included nine major principles consistent with the UN Charter.

Part II

LINEAGES OF BANDUNG

Chapter 10

Remembering Bandung

When the Streams Crested, Tidal Waves Formed, and an Estuary Appeared

Siba N. Grovogui

How does one remember and what is the relationship between memory and cognition? The answer to this question is not straightforward. Yet, remembrance and cognition are ultimately connected by perception. In this sense, remembrance is a function of cognition, or of knowing, a process by which perception, judgement and even reasoning are committed to mental processes of recollection. So little has been said about the 1955 Bandung Conference in the general literature of international relations that one can only remember it. For instance, unless I am mistaken, Bandung does not appear in the literature on norm formation as one of the most important generative moments of norms in the twentieth century.[1] Historically, norm formation in our discipline has combined three factors that seem retrospectively to reflect back on the pre-eminence of Europe and the West: (1) a classical notion of social psychology that presumes uneven development within and among social entities (Friedkin 2001) from which international relations scholars have inferred unequal influences among regions of the world; (2) a set of comparative approaches to norms or standards of behaviour that are based on false dichotomies between the West and the rest and that also dubiously infer causal links between observed behaviours and comparable Western practices; and (3) a materialist notion of power that mistakes mechanisms of dominance for hegemony and therefore confuse deference due to the effect or fear of coercion for moral influence (see, for instance, Martinsson 2011). As a result, the literature on norm formation and diffusion[2] generally elides the reasons for conformity to posit consent in norm adoption – and therefore to falsely attribute the fact of norms with acceptance by followers of norms to a general agreement.

Much can be said about the rise and propagation (or diffusion) of norms that can be verified in fact. The following is not, therefore, an indictment of theories of norms, whether they be of the agent model type or else. Rather, it concerns the imaginaries of agency, rationality, power, causality and performance that abide already presumed hierarchies of reason, values and interests among the different elements of the international system, and its orders of subjects, institutions and values. I am in particular in disagreement with the manners in which facts are mobilized to infer evidence of Western authorship of nearly all the norms of international behaviour after the Second World War. The following recollection of Bandung is intended to suggest that this inference is mistaken. Still, the purpose of remembrance in this context is not merely to demonstrate the baselessness of much of the assertions of the centrality of the West in producing certain international norms. It is also to reconstruct, by way of insistence, alternative generative moments of norms since committed to memory that, although lost to disciplinary truisms, might have defined international practices among vast majorities around the world.

METAPHORS AND FRAGMENTS

Of all the metaphors that have been applied to the Bandung Conference to explain its historical significance, I have always preferred that of an estuary. To be sure, Bandung itself is neither an estuary nor located on one. On the other hand, nothing short of the meetings of distinct political streams, of a historical confluence of ideas and of tidal waves of subjects and their wills occurred at Bandung. Indeed, the leaders who met in Bandung from April 18 to 24, 1955, hailed from convergent political streams in modern parlance: liberals, communists, social democrats, and the like. For instance, it would not surprise anyone that Nehru's Congress Party's approach to the questions of democracy and nation-building looked very different from that of the Chinese Communist Party that sent Zhou Enlai to the event. Yet, they were united by the singular desire to create an international environment and corresponding modes of organization that allowed all of them to express themselves. Second, the condition of enactment of this desire was the result of historical confluences whose gravitational force defied the diverse political orientations of the attendees. This force was the realization, or consciousness, and judgement that Western imperialism had been falsely predicated upon modern, humanist underpinnings. Consistently rejecting varying degrees of the ideational and cultural predicates of Western imperialism and empire, Bandung also took aim at the attendant mechanisms and institutions of power, value and interests. This consensus or confluence on the nature of the imperial (or colonial) order allowed participants to envisage new modes of governances and related institutions of subjectivity as foundation for justice, global solidarity and coexistence.

From this perspective, Bandung was a junction, a coming together of many rivers of approximately equal width and depth that formed a tidal wave. This tidal wave was rushing towards an open ocean of freedom – a mare liberum of sort that stood against reigning international practices steeped in empire and imperialism. This image of the tidal wave suggests that the road to freedom and a just international order has not been easy and the end not yet in sight. This is not to discount the great debates that followed Bandung in international fora, such as the United Nations, around such topics as the Law of the Sea; the New International Economic Order (NIEO); the Transfer of Technology; the Demilitarization of Earth, Sea and Space, and the like. Then again, such is the nature of the estuary before us today that its apparent calmness betrays the turbulence before it as well as what lies beneath it: the historical tidal waves connecting Bandung to decolonization and near-revolts at the United Nations, UNESCO, and elsewhere may no longer be perceptible. Still, these tides were the result of universal gravitational forces that continue to reverberate today through different settings with unpredictable outcomes. The post-Bandung era has been tumultuous, to say the least. But each subsequent moment has been marked by contests that still bear echoes of Bandung in both reflections and politics. For instance, in their final celebration of the demise of Soviet communism as an alternative sociopolitical model, Western hegemons have systematically attempted to dismantle the commons to parochial ends. One such event is the defanging of the UN Economic and Social Council (ECOSOC), which was a prelude to the diminishing role of the UN Conference on Trade and Development (UNCTAD), as a context for discussing matters of international trade and related issues of investments, transfers of technology and the ends of science and life. The politics of the so-called Washington consensus did not merely dispense with ECOSOC and UNCTAD, it substituted them with Western-controlled institutions, including the World Trade Organization (WTO), that give both currency and legitimacy to past unequal terms of trade under new guises, such as Trade-Related Aspects of Intellectual Property Rights (TRIPS) and Trade-Related Investment Measures (TRIMs).

To say that the themes and reflections of Bandung reverberate even today is not to suggest that the response to the reinvention of the imperial order in new guise should, or would, take the form of a unified forum like Bandung. It is to say that the postcolonial world – including the West – is now looking at the sea from this estuary that is the post-Bandung era. The ecology of world politics was forever altered in Bandung. Just as fresh water and salt water mix where the river connects with the sea, new reflections have been brought to bear on old universal truths by new subjects who can no longer be discounted. As it often happens in estuaries, postcolonial entities – and not merely states – have emerged as new subjects to inject new species of sovereignty, rights and ethics into global politics that will permanently stand in opposition to any attempt to reinvent old imperial orders. In sum, Bandung reverberates today because the reasons for that meeting keep appearing in different forms to the same effects: attempts to claim political hegemony for some and the disenfranchisement of others through global or universal political, economic, cultural, scientific and technological instruments.

My central contention is that, unbeknown to us today, the sound of Bandung continues to reverberate around us through a range of bodies that continue to replicate analyses and reflections leading up to it. These reverberations can be heard emanating from any postcolonial entity whose political analysis and actions are predicated upon the certainty of the decay of imperialism and its modes of sovereignty and subjectivity. So can Bandung's echoes be heard in any attempt to fashion anti-imperialist or just and equal world order. Bandung confirmed the changing fundamentals of the world politics which preceded it, but it gave its own imprimatur to a set of practices that continually return in multiple settings where postcolonial entities confronted the fundamentals of empire and imperialism: whether it be during wars of national liberation; nationalization of national resources; or claiming equal access to the resources of life and humanity. Certainly, the "eruption" of Bandung caused seismic changes in the world that permanently altered the international system and international *relations* themselves. Bandung forever delegitimized the language, institutions and techniques of empire and imperialism and, in the process, attempted to chart a new course for global politics. The latter task remains incomplete and, yes, yet to be fulfilled. It remains the case, however, that any effort in this latter sense takes place today in the estuary that was Bandung. There was sailing to the open oceans from the different rivers that lead to Bandung – Asia, Africa, communist, liberal, social democrat, Buddhist, Muslim – that does not lead to this metaphorical estuary: again, where fresh and salty water meet as happiness and disappointment; trials and failures; and successes and reversals. This time, however, the subjects are as self-aware as they are aware of the stakes.

WHEN THE WATERS CRESTED

Bandung was the culmination of historical formations originating in anti-colonialism. After all, anti-colonialists from Africa, Asia, the Middle East and elsewhere had been acquainted either in person or through their respective position on the emergent imperial proposals intended to appease them. This space may not be the appropriate venue to spell out the extent of metropolitan networks among colonized populations. I shall only mention one example. When he moved to Paris around 1917, for instance, then Nguyễn

Ái Quốc ("Nguyễn the Patriot") became involved with other activists from around the world against colonial rule. His petition in this sense to the Versailles Peace Conference (where the League of Nations was formed) was widely supported by others in Asia, Africa and beyond. When the conference refused to recognize his petition, the now Hồ Chí Minh founded the anti-colonial Le Paria (the Pariah) for anti-colonialists throughout the French empire to express and disseminate their views. One could find similar cases in England, the Netherlands, Portugal and Spain too numerous to list here.

Anti-colonial solidarity, sometimes modelled on or fostered by socialist or communist internationalism in the metropoles, was therefore a reality before Bandung. It also created intimacies and comraderies that were manifest in the ease with which the Bandung conveners reached consensus on the language and text of the final statement. This prior intimacy among anti-colonialists is one that is often lost in scholarship. It was never lost on anti-colonialists that by necessity they needed one another across the imperial realms to fulfil their objectives. As early as in the 1920s, for instance, Sun Yat-Sen had appealed to the Chinese diaspora to aid in supporting the Chinese revolution. One of those who answered his call was Eugene Bernard Achan, a leftist writer of English with mixed Chinese-Spanish-Black ancestry from Trinidad, who later became known simply as Eugene Chen. While advising Sun, Chen founded and edited the bilingual *Peking Gazette* (Peking 1915–1917) and then later the *Shanghai Gazette* (1918–) (Wagner 2012). Later, following Sun's death, he would be foreign minister, a position from which he negotiated the return of foreign concessions to Chinese control.

I mention Chen's case to illustrate connections between West Indian movements of (Pan)African emancipation and the struggle of China to recover its dignity from under the unequal treaties that had been imposed upon it. This is to say that although many Chinese had not heard of nineteenth- and early-twentieth-century West Indians such as Edward Wylmot Blyden, Henry Sylvester Williams and Marcus Garvey, the literary expressions of the English-speaking Chinese of early twentieth century and most importantly, the views on empire and decolonization of the founding figure of revolutionary China, were influenced by pan-African anti-colonial views. This is *not* to say that China's conditions were not unique and the problems faced by China could be resolved by solutions taken from Trinidad. It is, however, to suggest that each imperial dominion faced imperial techniques that, taken together, could provide colonized populations everywhere with a fuller view of imperialism generally and, specifically, the modes of government and legal and cultural edifices erected around each imperial regime.

Again, the streams heading to our estuary may have come from different hilltops and traversed many ridges and valleys, but they each added to the chemistry and ecology of the eventual opening to the sea. It is therefore to be expected that Zhou Enlai's representations at Bandung reflected the indignities of the unequal treaties that had been imposed upon China. Yet, just as the unequal treaties proceeded from treaties of capitulation and protectorates imposed throughout the world, other countries could just as easily relate to, for example, India's painful experiences of the British East India Company and its role in the famine of 1770, and beyond.

Still, Bandung was not merely about the past. Quite the contrary. Barely a year before the meeting, it became apparent that the rules governing traffic and engagements over the opening estuary were about to be perverted. Those rules, enunciated on Newfoundland Island in the middle of the blue sea, were compiled in the so-called Atlantic Charter. The meeting between Churchill and Roosevelt was an immediate response to the geopolitical situation in Europe by mid-1941 but its goals soon extended to the future of the world itself: to enunciate (eight) common principles on postwar international relations. These were to not seek territorial expansion; to seek the liberalization of international trade; to establish freedom of the seas, and international labour, economic and welfare standards; and most importantly to support the restoration of self-governments for all countries as well as the right of all peoples to choose their own form of government. The commitment of both the United States and the United Kingdom to these principles was tested in Iran in 1953, with the conflict between the elected government of Iran and United States and American oil companies established in the country under conditions judged by the Iranian government as less than ideal.

To be sure the Atlantic Charter was not a binding treaty but it set the context for the 1942 Declaration by the United Nations, the precursor to the UN Charter. It was presented to the world then as now as laying out "Roosevelt's Wilsonian-vision for the postwar world; one that would be characterized by freer exchanges of trade, self-determination, disarmament, and collective security."[3] What the Iranian Crisis demonstrated was the opposite of the enunciated norms of the Atlantic and the UN charters. In fact, the overthrow of Prime Minister Mossadegh was the result of a conspiracy based on secret accords between Anglo-American oil corporations, the US and UK governments and secret agencies (the CIA among them) to subvert a legitimate government whose only sin was to do exactly what the UN Charter had allowed: determine its own future under the system of government freely (democratically) chosen by its people.

This is to say that by the time of the Bandung Conference, the principles of diplomacy and national self-determination as well as the right to self-determination and peaceful coexistence were under assault by former imperial and colonial powers. It is easy, in this context, to understand the emphasis placed on economic and cultural cooperation at Bandung as well as the space given to human rights and self-determination, on the one hand, and, on the other, the problems of dependent peoples. The latter were represented by Cambodia, the Gold Coast (Ghana), Laos, Libya, Sudan and the two Việt Nams (the republic and the state), among them. Most centrally, Bandung placed a premium on world peace by insisting on the resolution of the situation in Palestine (based on the right of Palestinians to self-determination); urging the Netherlands to peacefully resolve its disputes with Indonesia; supporting Yemen in its drive to unity; and "declaring that colonialism in all its manifestations is an evil which should speedily be brought to an end" (*Asia-Africa Speaks* 1955).

This was not mere theatre. Nor was the need to insist that diplomacy be given primacy in order to eradicate "mistrust and fear" for the restoration of "confidence and goodwill towards each other." Nor was it, in light of the UN Charter, to reprise the basic principles of

- "Respect for fundamental human rights and for the purposes and principles of the Charter of the United Nations;
- Respect for the sovereignty and territorial integrity of all nations;
- Recognition of the equality of all races and of the equality of all nations large and small;
- Abstention from intervention or interference in the internal affairs of another country;
- Respect for the right of each nation to defend itself singly or collectively, in conformity with the Charter of the United Nations;
- Abstention from the use of arrangements of collective defence to serve the particular interests of any of the big powers;
- Abstention by any country from exerting pressures on other countries;
- Refraining from acts or threats of aggression or the use of force against the territorial integrity or political independence of any country;
- Settlement of all international disputes by peaceful means, such as negotiation, conciliation, arbitration or judicial settlement as well as other peaceful means of the parties' own choice, in conformity with the Charter of the United Nations." (ibid.)

The Bandung Conference instead added to these principles a prognosis. That is, it perfectly anticipated the French and British reaction to the nationalization of the Suez Canal by Egypt (leading to the Suez Crisis of 1956); the refusal of France to grant Việt Nam and Algeria their right to self-determination; Portugal's refusal to undertake any steps towards granting independence to its colonies (principally Angola, Guinea-Bissau, and Mozambique); and the US wars (open and secret) on Việt Nam, Laos and Cambodia. Bandung was not mistaken either that the Americans and the Soviets would use their instruments and treaties of collective defence under NATO and the Warsaw Pact to exert undue pressure on other countries. The participants detected in both NATO and the Warsaw Pact a perversion of Article 51 of the UN Charter,[4] such that the two superpowers and their allies would use their instruments of war to threaten the territorial integrity of the new nations and thus to effectively undermine the principle of peaceful resolution of conflicts through diplomacy, negotiation, conciliation, arbitration or judicial settlements.

TIDES, STORMS AND SHAKY GROUNDS

To be sure, Bandung attendees were not just about riding the rising tides of history against imperialism and the institutions of empire and colonialism as well as their hierarchies of subjects, values and interests. Beyond the excitement over the idea of a successful gathering of formerly colonial entities, Bandung conferees were also mindful that their positions threatened existing norms and the prior terms of public and private lives within the international order. They thus anticipated countervailing forces and movements among former colonial powers against any alterations of international norms and institutions that would undermine their hegemonic positions. But the threat was not exclusively external. The grounds upon which the leaders of the postcolonies stood were themselves unstable, owing to perceptible fissures. There were not only lines of division within the group (as illustrated by the presence of two Việt Nams), the postcolonies had also inherited states that were divided along the lines of geographies (regions), ethnicities, languages, cultures and the like.

The final communique of Bandung did not explicitly make references to these problems. But it did point to cultural cooperation, mutual learning and the existence in Asia and Africa of great religions and civilizations as the foundations for political and institutional experimentation in the interest of nations and their populations. The communique also acknowledged the facts that "the cultures of Asia and Africa are based on spiritual and universal foundations." The emphasis here is on both spirituality (a nod to essential non-cognitive and psychic faculties) and universality: that Asian and African cultures are open to abstractions towards the imagining of universal categories and institutions. The development and promotion of cultural cooperation in this sense not only meant the need to recognize the internal resources that once produced the "great religions and civilisations" of Asia and Africa, but also the desire to recognize that Asia and Africa had been – and could yet be again – home to institutions and social and political arrangements that enriched peoples' lives. Again, among them was "the age-old tradition of tolerance and universality," which conference attendees thought would add new dimensions to the "promotion of world peace and understanding."

Bandung justly understood the role of education in recovering great traditions from oblivion as well as the need to place this recovery in the context of national cultures that favoured the basic right of populations as well as the development of domestic "personalities." In the language of anti-colonialism in the early to mid-twentieth century, "personality" was the idiomatic equivalent of subjective autonomy and self-affirmation. The conference made this meaning clearer by denouncing the fact that French colonial authorities violated the basic right of the populations of Tunisia, Algeria and Morocco "to study their own language and culture" just as apartheid did in South Africa. To remedy this situation, Bandung was insistent on the need of "countries in Asia and Africa ... to develop their educational, scientific and technical institutions." Finally, once each country had done so, they could turn their attention to "the acquisition of knowledge of each other's country" through mutual cultural exchanges, and exchanges of information about society and the means to its development: social organization, science, technologies and related institutions.

This concept of exchange of ideas on social and political organization was already in effect by the time of the Bandung Conference. For instance, Jawaharlal Nehru, one of the key proponents of Bandung, belonged to one of the most successful political organizations of the twentieth century. That party, the Indian National Congress (INC 1885), also had a pedigree within both India and the British Empire. The Congress had many namesakes but the most important one was the African National Congress (ANC 1912). Between the two, they generated Mahatma Gandhi and Nelson Mandela, two towering figures of the twentieth century. But that is not all: the INC, and to some extent the ANC, had the merit of creating political organizations based avowedly on an ethos of spirituality, tolerance and togetherness – not necessarily unity within political and ideological uniformity. The reasons and the trajectories are important as to why the model of the Congress Party captured the imagination of more anti-colonial entities than any other political model.

Briefly, the INC was founded by Indian activists with the support of British members of the Theosophical Society, who believed that a knowledge of God may be achieved through spiritual ecstasy, direct intuition, or special individual relations. One need not indulge in theosophy to note a special kinship at the dimension of mystical insight with some South Asian religions, including Hinduism. This connection is important for two reasons. First, because of the importance it placed on spirituality in the final communique of Bandung. And second, it explains why fractured societies around the world thought that the idea of Congress was best suited for them in contemplating political pluralism and competition. Again, it is not my intent to give a summary of the history of the INC, but it might be worth noting that it underwent multiple transformations – starting from being a mere advocacy organization for elites (just as the ANC had been) to becoming a mass (anti-colonial) movement before independence (again just as the ANC became particularly after the events of Sharpeville); and to become a manager of the affairs of state (like the ANC). My point is not to defend the manner in which either the INC or the ANC managed the affairs of state. I merely wish to stress the fact that at the time of formation, the INC, ANC, and countless namesakes in Asia and Africa aspired to – and did in fact – provide institutional answers to the real dangers of social fractures – particularly social, racial and ethnic divisions – and political disunity. Both the INC and the ANC had the distinction during the Cold War of achieving successful coexistence (INC) and cohabitation (ANC) between political parties and factions of seemingly incompatible ideological orientations, from liberals to communists and beyond. This herculean feat ran against superpower orthodoxies (of both the United States and the Soviet Union). Specifically for India, this coexistence allowed it to survive the Cold War as the only non-permanent Security Council Third World state to not undergo a military or authoritarian takeover, notwithstanding the state of emergency.

It is also worth noting that the transformation of the INC into a mass political movement occurred subsequently to Mahatma Gandhi's return from South Africa. Afterwards, the INC opened the way to successful political experimentation that, at the time of Bandung, gave credence to the idea that all postcolonies had within themselves the resources to imagine new institutions that cohered with historical or universal aspirations while allowing for their respective singularities – or personalities, to use the then reigning language. Consistently, the ANC experimented with non-racialism, an idea crystalized in the following by Nelson Mandela during the Rivonia trial: "I have fought against white domination, and I have fought against black domination. I have cherished the ideal of a democratic and free society in which all persons live together in harmony and with equal opportunities. It is an ideal which I hope to live for and to achieve. But if needs be, it is an ideal for which I am prepared to die."

The post-Bandung era witnessed a multitude of political movements and experimentations from Asia and Africa that affected the international order. These were in the areas of moral spaces, international cooperation, and interregional solidarity, to name just a few. By now, it goes without saying that Bandung was largely responsible for the advent of the so-called Third World. Although it eventually came to connote developing countries – and to some underdevelopment – the Third World was in actuality a moral space for setting up agendas and debates that otherwise lay outside of the concerns of the superpowers and their Cold War allies. It was also conceived to blunt superpower interference in conjunction with their hegemonic designs. Beyond the above two goals, the Third World also enabled cooperation and solidarity among postcolonial entities. The effectiveness of Third World cooperation could be seen during the transition from mandate to statehood in Namibia, with the institution of the UN Council on Namibia. It was also evidenced in the pressures on the United States to end its war on Việt Nam; the enactment of the International Seabed Authority as part of the Law of the Sea; the worldwide mobilization against apartheid; successive General Agreement on Trade and Tariffs (GATT); the demilitarization debates; the legitimacy of postcolonial nationalization of extractive and natural-resource industries; support for the right of Palestinians to national self-determination leading to the observer status to Palestine today at the General Assembly; and more.

To the non-initiates, the above might appear merely as a list of claims and contestations. Yet, these events provided structure and content to the sorts of public freedom that emerged from decolonization, including self-determination and national sovereignty. They defined through contestations and counterpoints the boundaries of the (international) public domain, the spaces of possibility (or of realization) of (collective and individual) autonomy. In other words, the public freedoms envisaged by Bandung enabled the structuring of the spaces for enacting public policies and the legal, moral and ethical codes of private lives and individual and personal liberties. To be sure, in many postcolonies, the transition from the enactment of public freedom to the extension of private freedoms to the citizenries has proven to be more troublesome than anticipated. It remains that the acquisition of public freedoms, or the ones that defined the terms of public life and its sovereign spaces of enactment, was an indispensable transition.

The institutional contexts of Third World solidarity are many but the most important one will remain the Non-Aligned Movement (NAM), a movement whose universal character was sanctified by the adherence of Cyprus (emancipating itself from British control) and Yugoslavia (casting off the shadow of Soviet communism). From this context, there emerged institutions of solidarity, including but not limited to the Organization of Solidarity with the People of Asia, Africa and Latin America (OSPAAAL). The founding of OSPAAAL was equal in its significance and commitment to decolonization as Bandung. This time, however, the focus was the expressed desire to defeat colonialism and imperialism. To Cuba, one of the most active proponents of this doctrine of defeat of imperialism, the adherence to this principle meant occasional opposition to Soviet policies as well, particularly in Africa. In any case, the doctrine of anti-colonial and anti-imperialist solidarity, which was captured cryptically as tri-continentalism, was the primary motivation for Cuban interventions in Africa as well as its support for revolutionary liberation movements. The determination to rid the world of colonialism and imperialism dragged Cuba into successive (civil) wars in Africa. It also stood behind Cuba's assistance to Angola in defeating South Africa's military incursion at Cuito Cuanavale in south-central Angola.

FACING TIDAL WAVES

The goal of the Bandung conferees to emancipate themselves from colonialism and to chart new courses towards modern universalizing projects quickly
unleashed exceptionally quick and consequential political repercussions from
former colonial and imperial powers. Working through the extant superpower
configuration, the new would-be masters of the world reacted to Bandung as
if they had been hit by a volcanic eruption that threatened their very existence. Compounding the ramifications and consequences of challenges to
the international order were tremors from within most postcolonies in the
forms of ethnic, political and cultural fissures. Indeed, Bandung attendees had
underestimated the instability of the grounds upon which they stood.

In regard to the domestic terrain, India was a case in point. The trouble
facing the country began at the inception of its postcolonial constitution and
it had a personal quality. Dr Bhimrao Ramji Ambedkar, one of the chief
architects of its constitutional order, was himself a Dalit, or untouchable. He
was not only a precursor of today's Dalit movement, he had also objected
to Nehru's approach to the question of Kashmir. Like India, all but a few
postcolonies faced internal divides that would take time to resolve, if at all.
Whether they were the result of colonial designs or the weight of traditions,
governments everywhere faced ethnic, racial, caste, religious and linguistic
divides. In retrospect, politicians, activists, and other humanists and secular-
ists within the new states had underestimated the complications attendant to
the dismantling of social and belief systems, and their resulting hierarchies, in
which so many were invested. Thus, while the Dalit movement was forming
against the caste system, Hindu nationalists were setting themselves up for a
revival and indeed ascendancy of Hinduism within the body politic. As we
see today with the Bharatiya Janata Party (BJP), this Hindu parochialism was
not merely a quest for hegemony (which would depend on some combination of consent and coercion). It is not beyond the realm of signification that
events at Ayodhya, Gujarat and elsewhere in recent decades had ominous
subtexts of historical confessional redress (from Mughal-era grievances)
against Muslims. Of course, this is not diminishing the gender and caste
dimensions of post-independence.

The other reversal was the transformation of national unity political parties
into single-party systems and, indeed, authoritarianism. This was the case
throughout Africa where, with the exception of a few, "founding fathers"
of national independence espoused near-tyrannical methods of government
under the "party-state" that had once competed in multiparty democratic
elections. The turn towards authoritarianism was the consequence of state
failure to deliver on anti-colonial promises. This failure to deliver had strictly
domestic dimensions as well as international ones. In Rwanda, for instance,

the failure of the Tutsi government to significantly democratize at the time of independence (1959) led to the so-called revolution that brought about a Hutu-majority government. The failure by Juvénal Habyarimana himself to instil democracy and democratic institutions set in motion events leading to genocide. Under distinct but not so dissimilar conditions, Gamal Abdel Nasser reverted to authoritarianism after the defeat of his army in the war that positioned his country against Israel in 1967. In these and in examples elsewhere, defeat and failure often led to the fear of losing power and therefore repression.

The international environment also affected the turn of domestic politics in many of the postcolonies. For their independence of spirit, Patrice Lumumba (of the Congo), Sylvanus Olympio (Togo), and Kwame Nkrumah (Ghana) were first to succumb to military coups under national intrigues that had significant international dimensions in 1960, 1963 and 1966 respectively. The host of the Bandung summit himself, Sukarno, was overthrown a year after Nkrumah in a coup in which the CIA had been implicated just as it was in the overthrow of Lumumba. By then, of course, the superpowers had refined the art of regime change: beginning with Iran, the list of regimes overthrown with the assistance of foreign services grew. The list extended to Latin America, most notably Jacobo Árbenz (Guatemala 1954) and Salvador Allende (Chile 1973). Even when regime change had not been preferred, post-independence African regimes were subject to pressures and intrusions in their domestic spheres of decision-making. Thus, Guinea incurred the wrath of France for opting for independence in 1958, leading to French complicity in the 22 November 1970 Portuguese invasion of the country. Likewise, West Germany and its Western allies suspended foreign aid to Tanzania for "daring" to establish diplomatic relations with the German Democratic Republic (GDR). In instances like Guinea, French obsession against the regime and actual foreign intrusion (such as the Portuguese invasion) profoundly distorted domestic politics. In Guinea, particularly after 1970, the country lived under a permanent state of emergency with its toll of political prisoners.

The 1980s' structural adjustment policies dictated by the International Monetary Fund and the World Bank Group ushered in the erosion of national capacity to meet domestic demands. They also fomented political instability leading in French West Africa and Madagascar to what many call the second wave of independence: the 1990s' national conferences for constitutional and democratic reform. The democratic achievements of these conferences were later overturned by the neo-liberalism adopted under the Ronald Reagan and Margaret Thatcher revolutions and, later, the so-called Washington consensus. What has been termed "the retreat of the state" and the social abandonment of social needs by the state can be linked directly to the resource wars in Liberia, Sierra Leone, the Democratic Republic of Congo and elsewhere where any enterprising "thug," armed with AK-47s and supported by a willing militia, can lay claim to land for the purpose of extracting gold, diamonds and other exotic stones and minerals.

RESONANCES, ECHOES AND REVERBERATIONS

It would be a misunderstanding of the physics of postcolonial international relations as well as historical illiteracy to imagine that the Bandung Conference is without resonances and reverberations today. To be sure, Bandung may be ascribed to an overwhelming desire for an alternative postwar order and a manifestation of such a desire at a particular location, a particular moment and during a particular historical epoch. Yet, it was a phenomenon destined to reverberate beyond the moment of its eruption. The initiate still hears echoes of bounding and moral experimentation in the estuary that is today's landscape of global politics. The first reverberation of Bandung is manifestly of a psychic order, a disposition to express autonomy and subsequently give expression to the sovereign will of the multitudes seeking change to the imperial fact and to do so without the authorization of would-be "emperors." This was the necessary condition for many of the (international) public freedoms that the postcolonies required to unambiguously determine their own interests; to autonomously give effect to their own values through their own or collectively designed institutions; and to independently define the standards by which they and others would be judged.

In the first instance, one might view the Iran Crisis, the seizure of Suez, and similar waves nationalizing natural resources such as oil as the condition for international morality today that grants postcolonies the sovereign right to dispose of their natural resources, the right to territorial integrity, and to own (as an effect of property) and to trade (by consent) with partners of their choosing. In the second instance, Bandung set in motion a desire to revisit and revise or transform international practices and institutions. In this regard, it is easy to forget the extent to which the much-maligned "Afro-Asian Confraternity," in association with allies in the Americas and the Mediterranean, altered the face of the United Nations, and therefore the world. India did not just intervene in Bangladesh to prevent genocide as Việt Nam did in Cambodia to prevent the unfolding murderous experiment of the Khmer Rouge. (Tanzania did the same when it intervened in Uganda to depose Idi Amin.) India, Pakistan, Mexico, Brazil, Turkey and Yugoslavia played crucial roles in the settlements of the crises in Congo, Rhodesia, Namibia and South Africa. During the Congo crisis, for instance, Ghana, Guinea and Egypt who (unsuccessfully) opposed the machinations of the United States and Belgium against Patrice Lumumba received crucial support from India, Indonesia and others at the UN. India joined Nigeria to bend the will of the United Kingdom through the Commonwealth determination that there will not be any support for Rhodesia until there was majority rule. During the struggle against apartheid, Nigerian president Murtala Mohammed asked and obtained from his country's civil servants voluntary contributions to the liberation movements in the form of withholdings on incomes. This is not to omit the sacrifice of Tanzania on behalf of all liberation movements in Africa or the efforts of the so-called anti-apartheid Frontline States of South Africa.

These interventions were not roles that the former colonial powers anticipated. This is because the related acts and actions occurred from without the UN-prescribed conflict resolution mechanisms and institutions. In fact, the post-Bandung "Afro-Asia Confraternity," later assembled in association with others within the NAM, often defied international institutions when they deemed them out of phase with the historical mood. This is what makes the decision to create the UN Commission for Namibia so remarkable. To achieve this end, the non-aligned – led by Indonesia, Chile, Colombia, Pakistan, Turkey and Yugoslavia – had to denounce a 1966 ruling on the matter of South West Africa by the International Court of Justice for its antiquated colonial underpinnings; defy the UN Charter prescribed pre-eminence of the Security Council on the question of Namibia; and thus had to create a special body to act in the trust of Namibia's people thereby bypassing the UN Trusteeship Council. In effect, the NAM, whose core was the "Afro-Asia Confraternity," was setting its own rule, albeit within the constitutional parameters of the world body.

The (mistaken) conventional wisdom today is to assume that Bandung accomplished nothing and that the "West" has been the key generator of international norms. The key evidence for most is the failure of the attempted NIEO. Perhaps! The collapse of the Soviet Union also muddled international historiography to the detriment of clarity. In this latter regard, I just wish to note that the aims of the post-Bandung coalitions at the UN and elsewhere were neither anti-Western (they were anti-imperialist) nor anti-capitalist. The West may take credit for the present institutions and practices of investment, production, distribution and consumption of capitalism (which were and are still in dispute) but not capitalism itself or its desirability. For better or for worse, capitalism is a universal good and has been so since its inception. Thankfully, Bandung conferees and the postcolonial coalitions had come to realize that the rights and norms that they envisioned were not inscribed in the Atlantic Charter or affirmed by postwar international or transnational institutions. Nor did the emergent postcolonial rights, norms and institutions figure in the imaginaries or scenarios of interdependence envisaged by the founders of the Bretton Woods institutions and the UN system.

Like the sources of the rivers and streams converging on the estuary, the politics of Bandung might seem distant to us today. Like watersheds too, it might be difficult to comprehend that such a distant and small gathering might have profoundly and inextricably transformed the terms of global politics and, in the process, refashioned the dispositions or impulses of all actors – whether they be national and international or state and non-state actors. But it did. The sounds of Bandung – indeed, its discourses, protestations, affirmations and their syntaxes, melodies and lyrics – do not belong to the past. They still echo in our collective ears and reverberate in our collective consciousness. Bandung altered the collective historical sense of things, of what is right and what is disallowed. Bandung conferees not only produced a general sentiment against certain (prior) international practices – including imperial injunctions applicable to sovereignty, international law, treaties etc., but they also set in motion new practices, including but not limited to solidarity, intervention, trade and the commons – as illustrated, for instance, in the Law of the Sea. In short, Bandung persists today and its sounds linger on in contemporary practices of international relations.

To say that the themes and reflections of Bandung reverberate today is not to suggest that the Bandung coalition may be reconstituted today or that attendees' response to the neo-liberal reinvention of global hierarchies would or should look like it did in Bandung. It is to take stock of the fact that Bandung was the cresting of waters from distant and distinct places that converged towards the same place. Thanks to Bandung, the world, although not entirely postcolonial, has nonetheless entered a moment of history that may usher in the postcolonial. We are now looking at the open sea from our metaphorical estuary whose ecology brings the coarseness of lingering imperial impulses against the exhilarating desire of the multitudes for freedom, equality and justice. I say coarseness of the imperial projects because dimensions of those projects as well as their ideologies may be separated from their institutions, hierarchies, and order of (mal)governance and (in)justice and oriented towards different ends, all consistent with the acknowledgement of the conjoined collective fate of our estuary, which must ultimately lead to the open seas (of globalization) with its abundant riches (of cultures, ideologies, technological instruments, and spirits and sentiments), its varied environments and micro-ecologies (of desires, inclinations, passions), and countless possibilities (of forms of life and futures).

The genius of Bandung was to have recognized that the promises of modernity, universalism, and their underlying emancipatory and cosmopolitan projects must be upheld with the proviso that they must be adjusted to reflect two other realities: one, the postcolonial/post-imperial temperament (temperature?) of the moment as determined by subjects – old and new; and, two, a recognition of the limits and excesses that risked undermining those promises. This last stipulation was an acknowledgement of the still relevant import of religion, spirituality and morality to contemporary material and symbolic cultures and their forms of power and authority; their modes of governance and base legitimacies; and their mechanisms of production, distribution (or adjudication) and consumption as justice.

The greatest contribution still of Bandung was to forever connect the rivers, to find the language and forge the will to adapt to the concurrence of sea water with fresh water, to juggle the coarseness of history with the potable (or palatable) of hope and imagination in order to create a liveable estuary, reflected in today's ecology of world politics. It was an aspiration of Bandung to initiate new reflections on or reconsiderations of "old" universal truths and to do so with the contributions of the formerly free and the new free. This struggle and its aims are not behind us. They are of actuality today more than ever. As we witness today, there are new attempts by the West to delegitimize collective governance, for instance at UNESCO; undermine the principle of self-determination (as with the Palestinians); forge neo-imperial coalitions (e.g. during the two wars on Iraq and the overthrow of Gaddafi); or institute new modes of encumbrance in politics, moral, and scientific and technological production for the purpose of new hierarchies in the international order. This tendency is also obvious for instance in the contemporary rivalry between China and India in advancing the interests of domestic capital and state power abroad onto other postcolonies. Regrettably, mal-governance, authoritarianism, and corruption have also taken root in the postcolonies against the aspirations and interests of vast pluralities of postcolonial entities. In this context, rather than heap scorn on Bandung, the attitude ought to be to reconvene a new Bandung, to actualize the debates and discourses that it initiated, and to broaden participation in the interest of democracy, self-governance, inclusion, equality and justice on all scales: communal, societal, national, state and international levels. The very survival of the estuary formed in Bandung in 1955 depends on it. So does our collective future.

Salaam.

NOTES

1. It is not my claim that norms theorists universally eschew references to the role of the postcolonies. Some do. Mine is that even when they do, individual authors do not show a great deal of understanding or appreciation for postcolonial interventions and innovations. In fact, norms theorists are more likely to view postcolonial innovations as merely corroborating the mandate of intergovernmental organizations such as the UN. See, for instance, Finnemore (1996).

2. For a general reading on the state of the literature on norms and political change, see Sikkink and Finnemore (1998).

3. US State Department, Office of the Historian, "The Atlantic Conference & Charter, 1941" (Milestones: 1937–45), https://history.state.gov/milestones/1937–45/atlantic-conf.

4. "Nothing in the present Charter shall impair the inherent right of individual or collective self-defence if an armed attack occurs against a Member of the United Nations, until the Security Council has taken measures necessary to maintain international peace and security. Measures taken by Members in the exercise of this right of self-defence shall be immediately reported to the Security Council and shall not in any way affect the authority and responsibility of the Security Council under the present Charter to take at any time such action as it deems necessary in order to maintain or restore international peace and security."

Chapter 11

The Racial Dynamic in International Relations

Some Thoughts on the Pan-African Antecedents of Bandung

Randolph B. Persaud

INTRODUCTION

Bandung is often, and rightfully, seen as the launching of the Third World into modern global politics. It is also rightfully acknowledged as the definitive symbol of Third World solidarity. Bandung, in other words, was a new beginning; it was about the future. Yet, in important ways, that meeting of twenty-nine nations in Indonesia in 1955 was as much about the past as it was about the future, and this, despite the direct links to the Non-Aligned Movement (NAM), the New International Economic Order (NIEO), G77 and other institutional demands for greater global equality. The Afro-Asian Conference, in fact, marked the culmination point of a long process of historical development, much of it anchored in the social forces of race and racism. In my own view, Bandung was a platform for the affirmation of self-worth by what Vijay Prashad (2007) has thoughtfully called "the darker nations."

A more comprehensive understanding of the meaning of Bandung requires us to examine what I shall call the *racial dynamic* in the structuration and restructuration of world orders. By racial dynamic I mean the ways in which race and racism, as both ideology and practice, have been active in the making of history (see Anievas, Manchanda, and Shilliam 2015). Accordingly, the racial dynamic is a kind of cultural law of motion that has within it the (seemingly contradictory) capacities for both relations of oppression and projects of emancipation. Keep in mind, however, that relations of oppression and projects of emancipation are not reciprocally exclusive.

There are general connections between the racial dynamic and the construction and diffusion of norms. Norm construction is a product of struggles among historically evolved social forces in the body politic of world order. The state itself must be seen as a configuration of different sets of social forces. The racial dynamic is one of the most enduring and "productive" social forces in the emergence of the modern inter-state system and the global capitalist economy. The long processes of state formation and capitalist modes of accumulation on a global systemic scale were in part dependent on the formulation of narratives of difference and philosophies of supremacy between the European and their various Others. Sven Beckert uses the concept of "war capitalism" to characterize this process. War capitalism was a configuration of imperial expansion, slavery, land expropriation and colonial domination. This violent form of capitalism from the early seventeenth century through the mid-to-late eighteenth century laid the foundation for modern industrial capitalism (Beckert 2014, 52). Thus "slavery, colonial domination, militarized trade, and land expropriation provided the fertile soil from which a new kind of capitalism would sprout" (Beckert 2014, 60).

This chapter pays particular attention to the ways in which the struggles by Africans and the African diaspora (especially in the United States and the Caribbean) not only anticipated Bandung, but had also actually begun the process of norm construction and norm diffusion on the fundamental principles of human rights and political/cultural equality (Acharya 2014; Anievas, Manchanda, and Shilliam 2015).

AN INSIDE VIEW OF THE RACIAL DYNAMIC

Let us take a look at the centrality of the racial dynamic embedded in Bandung. We begin with the thinking of US Secretary of State John Foster Dulles, who took increasing interest in the Afro-Asian Conference as the plans for it developed. Dulles initially thought the event would never happen and in fact predicted that "2 to 1," the conference "is likely to collapse because of inherent weakness."[1] Dulles's dismissiveness was not to last too long. In fact exactly one week later he authorized a message exposing major anxieties about Bandung. The Circular Telegram which he authorized actually betrayed a major struggle in his own mind on the meaning of Bandung. In a 25 January 1955 Circular Telegram signed by Dulles, the issue was now about "risks inherent in the Conference." The "inherent risk" apparently was "that fraternity of peoples must not be divided by arbitrary geographical or racial distractions."[2] By February 1955 Dulles was at pains to distance American interests from the "subjugation" of the Third World by colonial powers, almost all of them allies of the United States. More than that, he saw a situation where the Third World might look to China as a leader against colonial domination.[3]

If, in January and February of 1955, Dulles was beginning to see Bandung as a threat to American (as distinct from European) interests, by the first week of April he had moved to higher levels of abstraction, much of it resembling the thinking of Samuel Huntington, who a few decades later characterized international affairs as an impending "clash of civilizations." Strategy, culture and race were now directly linked. Dulles met with the British ambassador Sir Roger Makins and observed that the problem with Bandung and of Asia went beyond what the press was reporting. For him, it was not a matter of this or that incident. He told Makins that Bandung would lead to "anti-Western and anti-White" tendencies which was very dangerous and which would threaten the "whole concept of human brotherhood, of equality among men, the fundamental concept of the United Nations."[4] The secretary's outpouring to Makins was both candid about the grounds of the terrible foreboding he saw before the Western world and indicative of his own limits in understanding the emancipatory potential of the Asian-African Movement, so defined. For Secretary Dulles:

> It is true, of course, that in the past the record of the Western Powers in Asia had not been without regrettable faults. There was nothing to be gained ... by the Asian and African powers falling into the same faults, particularly the fault of racialism in the opposite direction.[5]

And again:

> The West, of course, has been dynamic and aggressive and frequently shown a sense of racial superiority – but it also contributed to human welfare in the realm of technical and material progress, and it has carried with it the Christian outlook on the nature of man.[6]

This very brief examination of Secretary Dulles's views on Bandung underlines an important fact, namely that the racial dynamic exists at the very highest levels of policymaking. Note also that in this case race is not simply "background matter," but it is at the centre of what is transpiring. With this in mind, we can now go backward and briefly examine the ways in which the racial dynamic had been at work well before 1955, and how Bandung must be understood in a much broader historical sweep.

THE LEAD-UP TO BANDUNG

Although Bandung has been widely known as the Afro-Asian Movement or the conference itself as the Asian-African Conference, there is no doubt that the Asian part was more dominant. Part of this is due to the enormous pressure put on the most influential leader in sub-Saharan Africa, Kwame Nkrumah, not to attend. In the end, the only African nations that attended were Egypt,

Liberia, Libya, Ethiopia, Sudan and the "Gold Coast." Nkrumah's absence, plus the outsized presence of India's Jawaharlal Nehru and China's Chou Enlai (Zhou Enlai), diminished the impact of at least sub-Saharan Africa on the proceedings. Of course, Gamel Abdel Nasser also made a huge impact. Yet, the African influence on Bandung must have been enormous.

I argue that the international activism done through the Pan-Africanist Movement and other organizations such as Marcus Garvey's Universal Negro Improvement Association (UNIA) had already set a path for global solidarity among the colonized nations and oppressed peoples. More broadly, the argument is that the emancipatory aspects of the *racial dynamic* had already been in play in an organized and structured form for over fifty years prior to the Bandung Conference itself. Bandung, therefore, must be understood as the outcome and simultaneously a major moment in a cumulative history of struggles and resistances, a good deal of it through agitation for African rights as universal rights.

While Nehru, Nasser and Chou En-lai (and others) were the "heroes" and voices of the nationalist movement after the Second World War, W. E. B. DuBois, George Padmore, Richard Wright and Sylvester Williams (among others) were the early intellectual voices joined to international activism in a long and determined challenge to global white supremacy and colonial domination. The activist-scholar configuration of the early twentieth century was a preparatory moment in the upcoming nationalist struggles, which had already begun in many places including India.

It is important to remember the context of the early twentieth century in terms of race. This was the time when racial science surfaced in its worst forms, a time that coincided with the rise of international relations as a discipline, or at least as an area of study (Vitalis 2015). The ideology of white supremacy at the turn of the century was not only to be found in supposedly scientific disquisitions in biology but also in practices of domestic and international politics. In the United States, Theodore Roosevelt, a cranial theorist, became president. He embarked on a kind of racial imperialism with wars in Puerto Rico, Cuba and the Philippines (Beisner 1968, 165).[7] In Europe, not long before that, Africa had been divided up and distributed. It was also at the turn of the century that King Leopold was at the height of executing one of the most brutal projects of colonization in history. At the intellectual level, *The Journal of Race Development* (1910) was founded in order to promote – well, the development of other "races."

In the United States, Marcus Garvey built the largest progressive black nationalist movement in the UNIA. Despite legitimate criticisms of Garvey's economic self-interest, the Jamaican was able to advocate for the rights of blacks in America, the Caribbean, and on the African continent. Arriving in New York in 1916, by the early 1920s Garvey's UNIA had formed seven hundred branches in the United States and more than a thousand branches in forty countries. Among Garvey's most important contributions, and one that would seep into Bandung, was the notion of transnational solidarity of the oppressed, all of it based on the singular concept of the sovereignty of the people and their lands. Garvey also attended numerous international events aimed at promoting independence for African states and peoples. Significantly, he attended the 1919 Paris Peace Conference where the UNIA advocated the following principles:

1. That the principle of self-determination be applied to Africa and all European controlled colonies in which people of African descent predominate.
2. That all economic barriers that hamper the industrial development of Africa be removed.
3. That Negroes enjoy the right to travel and reside in any part of the world even as Europeans now enjoy these rights.
4. That Negroes be permitted the same educational facilities now given to Europeans.
5. That Europeans who interfere with or violate African tribal customs be deported and denied entry to the continent.
6. That segregatory and proscriptive ordinances against negroes [sic] in any part of the world be repealed and that they be given complete political, industrial and social equality in countries where Negroes and people of any race live side by side.
7. That the reservations land acts aimed against the natives of South Africa be revoked and the land restored to its prescriptive owners.
8. That Negroes be given proportional representation in any scheme of world government (Hill 1983: I, 288, quoted in Persaud 2001).

An examination of the *Final Communique* of the Asian-African Conference, as well as the ten principles of Bandung that were propounded, shows some remarkable similarities. Much like Garvey's document (and previous documents/declarations issued through the Pan-African Movement broadly defined), Bandung focused a great deal on economics factors, cultural and specifically racial equality, and national sovereignty, meaning in this case independence. The Bandung Conference obviously also placed considerable weight on international peace, disarmament and an end to nuclear weapons, while Garvey's Paris document focused a good deal on the internal violence against blacks in the United States. (At that time, lynching was near its height.)

W. E. B. DuBois, a contemporary of Garvey, attended the First Pan-African Conference in London in as early as 1900. It was here that he gave both intellectual and political expression to his deep understanding of the problems of global racialism. This is where DuBois stated that "the problem of the twentieth century is the problem of the color line, the question as to how far differences of race which show themselves chiefly in color of the skin and the texture of the hair will hereafter be made the basis of denying to over half the world the right of sharing to utmost ability the opportunities and privileges of modern civilization." DuBois also attended the First Universal Races Congress at the University of London in 1911 and the first formal Pan-African Congress held in Paris in 1919. Although he has been criticized for not doing too much at the former conference, DuBois did in fact meet some scholars, especially anthropologists, who were making important headways in their work on race. Frantz Boaz was one of those. Anievas, Manchanda, and Shilliam (2015, 8) argue that "it was Frantz Boaz, ... who in the early twentieth century pioneered the critique of the typological rendering of race common to anthropological studies."

These congresses and the others to follow were major platforms for the global advocacy of racial equality, national self-determination and cultural authenticity. All of these elements of liberation made their way into the Bandung documents, and as such, Bandung was a much grander event advocating the fundamental principles that had been taken up in the United States and further afield through the Pan-African Movement. It goes without saying that struggles all over the colonial world also fed into the spirit of Bandung.

THEORIZING NORM CREATION AND DIFFUSION

Debra Thompson (2015, 52) has forcefully argued that "changing global ideas about the nature of race set the conditions of possibility for state action and inaction towards race relations, creating a transnational cultural code that provides actors with a range of acceptable options to draw from when making decisions." Thompson's argument about the diffusion of ideas about race is consistent with Amitav Acharya's more general argument about the ways in which normative agency spreads. A closer examination here makes the connection between the earlier work of pan-African transnationalism and the consolidation and formal expression of key values at the Bandung Conference in 1955.

Acharya advances five aspects of norm construction and norm diffusion, all of which are apposite to our concerns here. First, he states that "norm making seldom involves a single source" (Acharya 2014, 405). While the concept of "source" is not fully fleshed out, it is immediately important to note that the normative claims of equality, human rights and other similar values did not simply emerge from the theoretical treatises of international relations scholars. Second, for Acharya, it is important "to look at ... regional and interregional sites of dialogue" since, indeed norms need not necessarily emerge from the global level (ibid.). The point underlined by Acharya is that "some supposedly global norms can have regional origins, influences, and manifestations" (ibid.). The third aspect of norm creation and diffusion, or what he also calls norm subsidiarity, concerns the non-linear and contested nature of norm creation and diffusion. Norms advanced from one source may be resisted by other parties. As he puts it, "Once articulated, norms do not remain static, and resistance and contestations do not end but persist" (ibid., 406). Fourth, weaker states lying at the margins of the international system can also create norms, since it is not only the powerful states that are capable of norm creation. Although this particular point is formulated around state actors, the idea might be easily adapted to non-state actors for our purposes. Fifth and finally, norms can take multiple forms through widening, deepening and thickening. Moreover, Acharya argues that the construction of a norm and its circulation are both important because its agents affect diffusion.

Acharya uses this norm circulation model to analyse the construction of human rights and non-intervention norms by non-Western countries. In our case, we can apply it to the ways in which human rights defined as norms of racial equality did indeed circulate "out" from weaker (in terms of material capabilities) actors – in this case non-state actors.

The intellectual and political activism of the Pan-Africanist Movement was unique because it was at once national, regional and transnational. Exactly the same applies to the Bandung Conference. What we can determine here vis-à-vis Acharya's model is that the Pan-Africanist Movement fed into Bandung, and that both "movements" are the products of multiple sources – one of Acharya's elements in democratizing our understanding of norm construction. In a 2005 interview, the noted scholar Samir Amin underlined the multiple sources and different political inspirations of those who went to Bandung (Herrera 2005, 546). The second aspect on possible regional origins of norms, which ties in with the fourth element on the capacity of weaker agents to engage in norm construction, is self-evident in the case of black internationalism and advocacy for basic human rights.

The third aspect which focuses on norm creation and resistance is at the epicentre of both the Pan-African Movement and Bandung. The creation-resistance dialectic operated at several levels not least because of the multiplicity of sources at work in the creation of norms. At one level, attempts by both black activists (in Pan-Africanism) and statesmen at Bandung were met with resistance from powerful actors in the international system. It is well known that the US government made it very difficult for black activists to travel to the Paris Peace Conference. Marcus Garvey himself was consistently harassed and eventually deported from the United States. The pressure on Nkrumah noted above is already widely known. What is also widely known is that the Western states made multiple efforts at penetrating the Bandung Conference through "surrogate" states in attendance.[8]

At a broader level, the dialectic of norm affirmation and norm resistance can perhaps be best understood in terms of what Partha Chatterjee (2012, 337) has called the *colonial exception*. The concept of the colonial exception refers to (among other things) the refusal by the imperial powers to apply their own supposedly universal norms to states that they consider lesser. This certainly was true at Bandung, especially with respect to the questions of Palestine and Algeria (among others) that demanded national sovereignty based on universal principles of equality. In the case of the Pan-Africanist Movement, the applicability is still there even though the referent objects are not states. In the case of the United States, blacks were asking for the rights and privileges in the constitution of the United States to be applied to them. Chatterjee notes that there are multiple ways in which the colonial exception might be invoked, meaning that different grounds might be used to justify the exception. Bandung was a massive rebellion against the apparatus of the colonial exception. More than anything, it was a rebellion against the oppressive foundations of the racial dynamic and simultaneously a call to transnational anti-imperial and anti-racialist solidarity.

Acharya's fifth point concerns norm circulation, noting that it takes multiple forms. The observation on widening, deepening and thickening is of importance because it indicates that norm construction that advances democratic values and practices does not necessarily have to be developed from scratch. Norms can be productively stretched, a process that the Bandung Conference certainly engaged in on behalf of well over half of humanity.

Acharya is correct when he argues that norm construction and diffusion can and often does emanate from the "margins," and that once created, norms do not fade away but persist. This is most apposite to the impact of pan-Africanism on the Bandung Conference, practically all of it embedded in the racial dynamic. The racialization of state formation and the emergence of capitalism in its various forms did not take place in a vacuum. Rather, the multiple strategies of coercion and subordination employed by European states, planters, merchants, slave owners, as well as joint-stock companies ran up against continuous resistances, also in multiple forms. In the Caribbean alone, we may, for example, note the gallant efforts at Demerara (British Guiana) in 1823, the Morant Bay Slave Rebellion in 1865, and of course, the cataclysmic rupturing with violent capitalism and French imperialism in the Haitian Revolution. In every case, narratives of freedom and equality were propounded. What the results were, and what form they took was dependent upon the balance of social forces, all of it racialized, that is to say, the *racial dynamic*. The Pan-Africanist Movement continued to articulate norms and values of universal freedom and equality (among others), these latter widely distributed from the late nineteenth century right through the take-off of decolonization. Many of the general principles put forth at Bandung clearly had roots in the African and pan-African struggles, at least dating back to the Haitian Revolution. The Asian-African Conference was first an Africa-Asia Movement.

CONCLUSION

This chapter has argued that there were multiple sources of democratic norm creation and norm diffusion aimed at democratizing world order. The Bandung Conference was a major moment in this regard but it was itself a continuation of intellectual and political activism that began well before 1955. While that claim is indisputable, I was keen to look at some of the transnational sources of the spirit of Bandung. It should be clear that although African (especially sub-Saharan) states did not play a pivotal role in Indonesia, the influence of black activism was very much at hand. The point is not so much to insist on the importance of African/Afro-American contributions but rather to assess the significance of Bandung as the product of some proximate historical forces, instead of focusing on the meaning post-1955. Meaning is not only or always about consequences.

Acharya's "model" of norm creation and norm diffusion was especially useful in making sense of who makes norms, for whose benefit, and with what consequences. I was able to show that the central norms associated with human rights, respect for national sovereignty, and racial equality (as a special form of human rights) have emanated from multiple sources, and in this case from actors who are usually seen as consumers rather than creators of norms. The Bandung Conference of 1955 was a massive moment in the advancement of a more democratic world order. It has contributed much to Third World solidarity, resting as it did, in part, on a solid foundation laid though several decades, if not centuries, of prior activism.

ACKNOWLEDGEMENT

I would like to thank Robbie Shilliam and Quỳnh N. Phạm for excellent feedback on this chapter.

NOTES

1. Minutes of a Meeting, Secretary Dulles's Office, Washington, DC, 18 January 1955. State Department Central Files 670.901/1-215.

2. Circular Telegram from the Department of State to Certain Diplomatic Missions, Washington, DC, 25 January 1955.

3. Circular Telegram from the Department of State to Certain Diplomatic Missions, Washington, DC, 25 February 1955.

4. Memorandum of a Conversation between the British Ambassador (Makins) and the Secretary of State, Department of State, Washington, DC, 7 April 1955. Department of State Central Files 670.901/4-755.

5. Op. cit.

6. Op. cit.

7. The United States also had strong anti-imperialist currents. In one famous case Andrew Carnegie offered to buy the independence of the Philippines for twenty millions dollars.

8. Secretary of State Dulles was also confidentially briefed on the conference by the Lebanese Ambassador (Dr Charles Habib Malik) to the United States. Dulles wanted to know if the Asian and African countries would form an "exclusive club" outside the UN and was assured that was unlikely. Dulles was keen on knowing if "the colored races" would form a grouping against the West, to which Ambassador Malik said "there was no clear decision." Malik also said that the conference did more "harm than good" but that "it could have been worse." Memorandum of a Conversation between the Lebanese Ambassador (Malik) and the Secretary of State, Department of State, Washington, DC, 5 May 1955. Department of State Central Files 670.901/5-555.

Chapter 12

Spectres of the Third World

Bandung as a Lieu de Mémoire

Giorgio Shani

INTRODUCTION

The conventional trope through which Bandung is approached is through the prism of Bull and Watson's "revolt against the West" where the newly emerging postcolonial states of Asia and Africa articulated their opposition to the colonial and Cold War world order by laying the foundations of the Non-Aligned Movement (NAM). Over time, this civilized revolt, according to English School authors, subsided once the new members were socialized into the norms of (European) international society and enjoyed the benefits of participating in an international political economy based on capitalist lines (Bull and Watson 1984). The "most striking feature of international society," Bull and Watson (1984: 433) remarked over thirty years ago, "is the extent to which the states of Asia and Africa have embraced such basic elements of European international society as the sovereign state, the rules of international law, the procedures and conventions of diplomacy and International Relations."

This narrative reflects the "double movement" (Inayatullah and Blaney 2004: 10–11) which lies at the heart of the colonial encounter: the "other" is simultaneously assimilated to the "self" through the projection of the values of the Westphalian international society, articulated in a language of rights, territory and authority, onto the colonized; or its difference is translated as inferiority (as articulated through conventional narratives of development) and pathologized as danger (as articulated through failed states). As such, there are unmistakeable continuities between the mid-twentieth century's "expansion of international society" and the "civilizing mission" of a century before, in that the new missionaries at Bandung – (ex) colonial subjects donned in "native" dress yet more at home speaking their colonial masters' language – sought to actively impose a *cultural conversion of non-Western*

143

states to a Western civilizational standard" (Hobson 2012: 27 – emphasis in the original).

However, Bandung can also be read as a "decolonial moment," delinking the newly emergent Third World from the master narratives of the Cold War. Indeed, for Mignolo (2011: 273), "decoloniality" has its origins in Bandung for it spawned the NAM. The main goal of the conference was "to find a common ground and vision for the future that was neither capitalism nor communism. That way was 'decolonization.'" Decolonization, however, was not to be understood as a historical event whereby former colonial territories in Asia and Africa were given their freedom, but as a "rupture" of linear, historical time. What the Afro-Asian Conference symbolized was not a decolonization that would lead to the inevitable "expansion of international society" whereby "newcomers" were socialized "into the established norms and practices of the international" but the "promise of *perpetual decolonization*" (Pasha 2013: 146, 148 – italics in the original). International relations, as Pasha has convincingly argued, "has failed to recognize decolonization as a rupture" (ibid.). A rupture opens up a "way of thinking that delinks from the chronologies of the new epistemes or new paradigms" (Mignolo 2011: 274). Despite the adoption of the formal trappings of state sovereignty bequeathed by colonial rulers, Bandung came to represent the "condition of active contestation" (Pasha 2013) to norms of an international society which had its roots in colonialism. Bandung, therefore, constituted a powerful challenge to the epistemology of Cold War international relations and the "new" paradigms of capitalism and communism with their teleological, fixed visions of the future.

BANDUNG AS A *LIEU DE MÉMOIRE*

For Pasha, Bandung continues to haunt as *memory* rather than as history. Bandung as an "event" in terms of linear historical time is of limited significance tied to a specific period of world history which has long since disappeared. At first glance, the world of today bears little resemblance to the post–Second World War era defined by two events which shaped the history of the twentieth century: formal political decolonization, first in Asia and then Africa, coinciding with an ideological confrontation between the "free world," led by the former colonial powers, and the socialist bloc led by the Soviet Union. Seemingly forced into the categories of East and West by escalating rhetoric which promised mutually assured destruction (MAD), the twenty-nine delegates at the conference held at Bandung, Indonesia, asserted the collective agency of the majority of humanity which they represented by choosing to proclaim themselves non-aligned. Although the NAM no longer appears the same force as it was given the geopolitical transformations wrought by the sudden collapse of the Soviet Union and the retreat from state socialism in a postwar world defined by the globalization of neo-liberal capitalism, Pasha (2013) argues that the memory of Bandung produces normative ideals that reappear in new global sites. During the Cold War, the United Nations, through the UN Conference on Trade and Development (UNCTAD) and subsequently through the General Assembly, became a new "global site" animated by the spirit of Bandung. At Bandung, the Third World, a term which reproduced rather than challenged the Eurocentrism of the postcolonial order, found a voice. Through the UN system, it found a platform.

Fragments of the memory of Bandung still continue to animate the contemporary international political order through the emergence of the Brazil, Russia, India, China and South Africa (BRICS), and of the People's Republic of China and India in particular. Both appear to have abandoned their fellow brethren in the "darker nations" (Prashad 2007) and to have embraced a neo-liberalism that concentrates wealth in the hands of an increasingly assertive middle class at the expense of the marginalized sections of society as the only alternative to poverty and impotence. Nevertheless, their attempts to translate rapid economic growth into geopolitical power by contesting Western hegemony both in the Asia-Pacific and international fora such as the G-20 illustrate that the spirit of Bandung remains very much alive even though its "memory" has faded. Bandung, therefore, is not ready to be confined to history but, as Pasha argues, continues to haunt as memory.

A clarification here of the distinction between history and memory is needed. Whereas memory can be likened to "life" in permanent evolution and susceptible to "being long dormant and periodically revived," history is a representation of the past. Memory is "blind to all but the groups it binds," while history "belongs to everyone and no-one" (Nora 1989: 8). The history recorded in textbooks and recited by students aspires to lay exclusive claim to a "truth" based on a universal standpoint. It seeks to articulate a coherent narrative which binds members of a group, or different groups, together. In the patchwork quilt of the nation or a "world," this universal "History" provides a common thread. Different histories may exist but they are always subsumed beneath the master narrative of the collectivity. Power relations are rendered invisible as the individual histories of subaltern and oppressed peoples are woven into the master narrative without compromising its message. Peoples "without history" (Wolf 1982) can only exist if they are brought into "History."

Unlike History, which has "always been in the hands of the public authorities, of scholars and specialized peer groups," memory resembles the "revenge of the underdog or injured party, the outcast, *the history of those denied the right to History*" (Nora 2002: 6 – italics mine). Although History was always "founded on memory," as a discipline it aspires to a "scientific status" that had "traditionally been built up in opposition to memory" which was "thought to be idiosyncratic and misleading, nothing more that private testimony" (Nora 1989: 9). History, in Pierre Nora's words, was the sphere of the collective; memory that of the individual. Consequently, "History was one; memory, by definition, plural." The idea, however, that "memory can be collective, emancipatory and sacred turns the meaning of the term inside out" (Nora 2002: 6). *Collective* memory – which is more than the aggregate of individual memories – contests the hegemony of History.

Bandung as *memory* disrupts the linear narrative of the "expansion of international society" into which Bandung as *History* has been inserted. The memory of Bandung seeks not only to contest established narratives of the Cold War as a globalized clash between two different ideological systems with their origins in European political and economic thought or as a "Long Peace" marked by peace and stability (in Europe) but also to refocus our gaze on the *longue durée* of relations between North and South, the colonized and the decolonized. Viewed in this light, the Cold War appears as a continuation of a distinctly European "civil war," a "cold" one, to be sure, in contrast to the genocidal violence which Europe inflicted on itself a decade before Bandung. However, in comparison to the violence Europe unleashed on the rest of the world, the Second World War appears as an apocalyptic interlude; a mere six years in contrast to the six centuries of exploitation, genocide and slavery formally instituted through colonialism. It was this shared "memory" of colonial oppression which gave rise to the Third World and NAM as articulated at Bandung (and formally instituted later at Belgrade). Anti-colonial sentiment, in a world in which the majority of the "darker nations" (Prashad 2007) had not yet gained independence, was the glue which bound the delegates at Bandung, divided by geography, culture, language, religion and ideology. In the words of the host, Indonesia's President Sukarno, the delegates were "united by a common detestation of colonialism in whatever form it appears ... by a common detestation of racialism [and] by a common determination to preserve and stabilize peace in the world" (Prashad 2007: 35).

While History binds itself to temporal continuities and relations, memory takes root in "the concrete, spaces, gestures, images and objects." This chapter builds on the spectral presence of Bandung in international relations by arguing that it represents what Pierre Nora (1989) termed a *lieu de mémoire*. Although *lieu de mémoire* defies translation, it has come to mean the places, institutions and cultural phenomenon which have shaped the way the past is remembered in the present. Nora distinguishes between three different *lieux*: material, symbolic and functional. The three different conceptions of *lieu* coexist and reinforce one another making a separation between the material and the symbolic impossible. All three meanings are present in Bandung. Bandung is a *material* site, a conference attended by delegates from twenty-nine different states from Asia and Africa. Bandung became a *symbolic* site for anti-colonial nationalist movements and later for the NAM. Finally, Bandung became a *functional* site in terms of being constitutive of a community of postcolonial nation-states that used the UN system to attempt a "regime" change in the heart of the global capitalist economy through UNCTAD and the New International Economic Order (NIEO).

Although Bandung is no longer a functional site, the postcolonial community of nation-states was sundered apart by the sudden collapse of the communist bloc and the resurgence of a neo-colonial neo-liberalism on a global scale, Bandung retains its symbolic aura. The "memory of Bandung" continues to haunt the practice of the BRICS like a spectre. The BRICS represent a very different *lieu*, with its origins in a neo-colonial world order which Bandung once sought to contest. The term the BRICS was first coined in a Goldman Sachs policy paper (Global Economics Paper 66) where it was argued that, as a bloc, Brazil, India, the People's Republic of China, Russia and later South Africa could outstrip the GDP of the United States and the European Union. The BRICS were chided for not playing a more prominent role in policing the economic order. The emergence of the BRICS appears, at first sight, to further the narrative of global development along neo-liberal lines. Certainly, the BRICS have done little to alter the prevailing patterns of marginalization and inequality within the world economy. Despite increased investment in the Global South and particularly Africa, most overseas investment by BRICS continues to be in developed countries. Forty-two percent of BRICS's outward FDI stock is in developed countries, with 34 percent in the EU. Africa accounts for only 4 percent of BRICS's FDI outflows (most from South Africa whose economy is dwarfed by the Asian giants) (http://unctad.org/en/PublicationsLibrary/webdiaeia2013d6_en.pdf). The BRICS in practice are complicit in the perpetuation of an economic system based on "accumulation by dispossession" (Harvey 2007) which *excludes* most of the Global South from a share of the fruits of economic growth. Furthermore, high economic growth rates cannot hide the fact that most of the world's 1 billion (or 800 million according to latest UNDP and World Bank statistics) absolute poor live in the BRICS (most within India, which played a key role in facilitating Bandung through the 1947 Asian Relations Conference).

However, the "spectre" of Bandung continues to "haunt" the BRICS, interrupting the linear, historical narrative of neo-liberal "development." Faint echoes of the demand for a NIEO were audible at the 5th BRICS summit meeting in Durban in the proposal for the creation of a new development bank and the pooling of foreign currency reserves to act as bulwark again currency crises and financial speculators. These proposals constitute a powerful challenge to the hegemony of the IMF/World Bank which is perceived to be an instrument, through conditionality, of maintaining Western control over developing economies. The proposals, however, leave intact the underlying structure of the world capitalist economy and represent at best a "provincial-ization" (Charkrabarty 2000) of the Western concept of "development" with its genealogy in Enlightenment notions of "progress" and "civilization." The seeds of this provincialization were sown at Bandung where the postcolonial and anti-colonial nationalist leaders committed themselves to development as a political goal.

THE DARKER NATIONS ARISE! BANDUNG REMEMBERED

Bandung, for the first generation of postcolonial subjects, was synonymous with an assertion of the sovereignty of postcolonial peoples and a statement of anti-colonial *unity*; a sentiment based, as both Richard Wright and later Vijay Prashad make explicit, on *race*. Postcolonial subjects of different "reli-gions," ideologies and ethnicities, from West Africa to East Asia, could take pride in this transnational declaration of independence. The "darker nations" had arisen. The populations of the Third World were nobody's "puppets" but *sovereign* peoples.

Less than a decade after Partition, the prime ministers of India and Pakistan put aside their territorial claims over Kashmir, and temporarily attempted to "forget" the horrors their peoples had inflicted upon each other, in order to convene the Bandung Conference with regional neighbours, Ceylon and Burma, at the instigation of the host, President Sukarno of Indonesia. Half the world sent delegates. The conveners were joined by the six independent states of Africa (Ethiopia, Egypt, Gold Coast, Libya, Liberia and Sudan); eight from the Middle East (Iran, Iraq, Jordan, Lebanon, Saudi Arabia, Syria, Turkey, Yemen) and a further ten from the rest of Asia (Afghanistan, the People's Republic of China, Cambodia, Japan, Laos, Philippines, Nepal, Thailand and both Việt Nams). Bandung, in other words, attempted to rectify the *failure* of nationalism; a nationalism which had, in South Asia, divided neighbours on the basis of religion and legitimized acts of violence, torture and rape against "others" who had been previously seen as part of the community. By contrast, Bandung sought to *unite* strangers who had never even heard of one another. If, following the Indonesian specialist Benedict Anderson (1983), the nation can be seen as an "imagined community," then what feat of imagination inspired the organizers of Bandung to dream up a community inclusive of almost two-thirds of humanity! The Afro-Asian Conference was an assertion of postcolonial agency on a global scale. It was Wright's impression that "with the exception of Nehru, Chou En-lai and U Nu, no delegations or heads of delegations came to Bandung but with the narrowest of parochial hopes and schemes." Yet, once they arrived, "something happened that no Asian or

African, no Easterner or Westerner, could have dreamed of" (Wright 1956: 129). The "parochial" interests were transformed into a *global* vision.

This was reflected in the *Final Communiqué* which committed the participating countries to extending economic, cultural and political cooperation in an attempt to transform the international order. The principal mechanism to foster the desired cooperation was to be the United Nations System itself. Reference was made to the Charter of the United Nations in the statement of support of "the principle of self-determination of peoples and nations" and to the Universal Declaration of Human Rights in its opposition to "racialism as a means of cultural suppression." The conference agreed (a) "that colonialism in all its manifestations is an evil which should speedily be brought to an end"; (b) that the "subjection of peoples to alien subjugation, domination and exploitation constitutes a denial of fundamental human rights, is contrary to the Charter of the United Nations and is an impediment to the promotion of world peace and co-operation"; (c) it declared "its support of the cause of freedom and independence for all such peoples"; and (d) called "upon the powers concerned to grant freedom and independence to such peoples" (*Asia-Africa Speaks* 1955: 6).

However, it also accepted borders designed by colonial powers as *national* borders and agreed to play by the rules of a game they had a limited role in designing. The Afro-Asian delegates at Bandung affirmed their commitment to the "purposes and principles of the Charter of the United Nations," their "respect for the sovereignty and territorial integrity of all nations," and for "the right of each nation to defend itself singly or collectively, in conformity with the Charter of the United Nations." Furthermore, they committed themselves to "the settlement of all international disputes by peaceful means, such as negotiation, conciliation, arbitration or judicial settlement as well as other peaceful means of the parties' own choice, in conformity with the Charter of the United Nations" (ibid.: 9). Viewed in this light, the "revolt against the West" was indeed "tamed"; instead of storming the Bastille, the Third Estate of mankind politely asked to be invited in and agreed to conduct themselves according to the rules of "civilized society." However, like unwelcome guests, they made their presence felt and used the UN Charter and Universal Declaration of Human Rights to remind their "hosts" of the commitments they had made a decade earlier. In particular, they reminded the former imperial powers and emerging superpowers to abstain "from intervention or interference in the internal affairs of another country" and, most importantly, of their commitment to recognize "the equality of all races" and of "all nations large and small" (ibid.: 9). Colonialism, in short, was declared to be incompatible with the UN Charter and those states that continued to cling to their imperial possessions would, as Britain and France were to find out in the Suez Crisis, be excluded from their own dinner party. Perhaps this was the greatest legacy of Bandung.

BANDUNG: A CRITICAL ASSESSMENT

Bandung, however, can also be remembered as a missed opportunity to rede-fine international relations along postcolonial lines rather than assert a collec-tive agency. By accepting the secular nation-state as *the* only sovereign form of political community, the delegates at Bandung committed themselves to a "nation-building" project which sought to construct secular, modern subjects out of ethnically and religiously diverse populations. The *nationalization* of the (post)colonial states and the pacification and homogenization of the populations under their control was accompanied by a messianic embrace of a new creed: secular development and modernization. In Nehru's and Nasser's views, political independence was inseparable from economic and social development which could only be achieved by harnessing the new powers of science and technology. Science, for Nehru ([1945] 2003: 511), offered a way to "break with the dead wood of the past" since it "opened up innumerable avenues for the growth of knowledge and added to the power of man to such an extent that for the first time it was possible to conceive that man could triumph over and shape his physical environment." In achieving mastery over nature with the application of modern scientific techniques to the economy, the Third World could cast off the colonial legacy of poverty and underde-velopment. By buying into Enlightenment narratives of progress, however, the participants at Bandung strapped their populations to Benjamin's Angel of History:

> His face is turned towards the past. Where *we* see the appearance of a chain of events, *he* sees one single catastrophe, which keeps pilling wreckage upon wreckage and hurls it before his feet. The angel would like to stay, awaken the dead and make whole what has been smashed. But a storm is blowing from Paradise, it has got caught in his wings with such violence that the angel can no longer close them. This storm irresistibly propels him into the future, to which his back is turned, while the pile of debris before him grows skywards. This storm is what we call progress. (Benjamin [1968] 2007: 257–8)

Unlike Benjamin's angel, the faces of the participants at Bandung, of Nehru, Sukarno and Nasser, were turned towards a future: a secular, socialist future of progress and prosperity for all, which never arrived. They were propelled *back* instead of forward by the colonial legacy, which aside from making economies in the periphery dependent upon demand in the core, also saddled the postcolonial states with ethnic, religious and racial divisions – the legacy of policies of divide and rule.

A critical assessment of Bandung would question the *desirability* of the secular vision of the future which the first-generation postcolonial elites bought into. For them, as for many first-generation postcolonial subjects like my father, a refugee from Partition violence in South Asia, religion was an atavistic primordial sentiment inextricably linked to violence. The retributive genocides which constituted Partition were viewed as *religious* violence, albeit religious violence exacerbated by colonial policies of *divide et impera.* Yet the "secularity" of the Nehruvian project was never brought into question, nor the complicity of "secular" elites in the organization of Partition violence.

The term "secular" is itself a *religious* term. Etymologically, "secular" is derived from the Latin term *saeculum* (literally "century") and connotes "profane" time in opposition to eternal or "sacred" time. In contrast to the "sacred," the "secular" refers to the "world" of the "lay" priests who lived among their congregation in opposition to those who sequestered themselves in monasteries. Consequently, "secularization" refers to the process of "making worldly." Secularism, therefore, can be seen to have its roots within "religion" and within a particular tradition: the Judeo-Christian. Central to my understanding of that tradition is the possibility of *transcendence* through an external form of authority whether it be God, the Messiah or the State. Time, in this tradition, is measured not as an eternal cycle of events as in some non-Western religious traditions (Hinduism, Jainism, Buddhism and Sikhism) but as *finite* culminating in "the day of judgement" (Shani 2014: 3). It is argued that the Judeo-Christian conception of secular time informs the modern understanding of development as "progress" as adopted by postcolonial elites at Bandung.

To use Benjamin's terms, Bandung represents a "weak messianic power" in contrast to the "empty, homogenous time" of linear historical development. The messianic has the power to "explode a specific epoch out of the homogenous course of history; thus exploding a specific life out of the epoch, or a specific work out of the life-work" (Benjamin [1968] 2007). However, it is a power which can *only* be understood from within a *specific* tradition. In opposition to the "universality" of History with its "empty, homogenous time" filled by a succession of events leading to the victory of the present, messianic time represents the "narrow gate, through which the Messiah could enter" (ibid.: 254).

Distinguishing between history and memory, therefore, allows us to understand the Judeo-Christian origins of the new international society into which the participants at Bandung found themselves inserted. By framing development in universalist terms as development and by accepting the nation-state as the *only* form of sovereign political community, it is argued that delegates at Bandung missed an opportunity to articulate a post-Western, *post-secular* world order (Shani 2008, 2014), one based on different conceptions of sovereignty and development embedded in *their own* religio-cultural traditions.

Giorgio Shani

CONCLUSION

The three worlds which Bandung helped to bring into being have long since submerged into one. There still appears to be no alternative to global capitalism but the inequalities which it has spawned can no longer be contained within the territorial container of the state. The Westphalian architecture imposed upon the colonized by the colonizers should have been jettisoned rather than embraced at Bandung. Similarly, with the benefit of hindsight, it might have been better for the newly decolonized states not to drink from the poisoned chalice of development in order to quench a thirst caused by centuries of colonial rule. However, the promise of Bandung, that of "perpetual decolonization" (Pasha 2013), remains and the invocation of the *place* continues to haunt the international system as *memory* even when the event itself has been erased from the *history* of International Relations.

Chapter 13

The Political Significance of Bandung for Development

Challenges, Contradictions and Struggles for Justice

Heloise Weber

INTRODUCTION

In Bandung's shadow, the "Third World" was no longer viewed as a pejorative term, but as a positive marker and virtue, a political alternative to colonialism and the hegemonic grasp of the two superpowers – the United States and the Soviet Union. (Pasha 2013: 148)

This chapter argues that Bandung ought to be a significant reference point for analyses of the politics of development in the post-1945 global social and political context. I make this case for two important and related reasons. First, as noted by the editors of this book, the development aspirations articulated at Bandung exemplify efforts to negotiate and deliberate a just settlement to the colonial global order. This was no small task and entailed conceptualizing development as a political project that emphasized, for instance, cultural rights as well as economic justice framed broadly in terms of aspirations for restorative justice. Second, as Mustapha Pasha argues in the conclusion to this book, Bandung constitutes an "alternative archive of knowledge": this alternative archive provides a distinctively different account of the dominant framing of the post-1945 development project. Through this alternative archive we can apprehend the extent to which colonialism and its legacies underwrote the post-1945 development project and the struggles for a "just settlement to the colonial order," both before and after Bandung. It is for these reasons that I argue that Bandung serves as a counterpoint to the dominant framing of the post-1945 development project.[1]

In most accounts of global development (post-1945) Bandung would not be the focus and point of departure for political analyses.[2] Instead, in these discourses we often begin with narratives of liberal internationalism, in one form or another; the United Nations would be posited as a key marker of progress emphasizing its human rights doctrines, while some analysts may also point to the significance of its specialized agencies, such as the World Bank Group. Similarly, in the dominant framework, statements identified as significant for development in the post-1945 era tend to begin with Truman's 1949 speech (with specific reference to his Point Four Program). At times, the UN Conference on Trade and Development (UNCTAD) receives some acknowledgement as one of the core UN agencies of development. To be sure, these organizations have been significant sites of struggles over development, and have been so precisely because they have operationalized a highly problematic colonial framing of development (with notable exceptions, such as the UNCTAD; e.g. Thomas 1985: 126–28). Indeed, from the dominant perspective the question of development has always been associated with states that were collectively identified as part of the Third World or, as they are referred to now, as "developing countries" or the Global South.[3]

An upshot of this is that the post-1945 development context is disconnected from its prior colonial history and its legacies – a history that enabled and sustained "development" experiences of the Western states not least through plantation labour and the social suffering of many in the Global South. Therefore, taking Bandung as our point of departure for analyses of the politics of development not only disrupts the ahistorical understanding of the dominant framing of development and "under-development" but importantly also allows us to restore colonialism and its legacies to our analytical framework, *against* which the "spirit of Bandung"[4] was enunciated. And it is a struggle that continues – even if in different fora – for restorative justice.

Building on the idea of taking Bandung as a vantage point for reconsidering the politics of development and its dominant framings, I develop my analysis in three connected parts. In part I, I reconstruct key elements of alternatives to the colonial project that were articulated at the Bandung Conference. There, emphasis was placed on support for decolonization through strongly formulated renunciations of colonialism and imperialism. Bandung also reflected early efforts to challenge the colonial division of labour, even if in somewhat (politically strategic) subtle ways. Through the "spirit of Bandung," a commitment to a form of "solidarist internationalism" was firmly established, or what Prashad (2007: 12) has referred to as "internationalist nationalism," as a counterpoint to the liberal international order. The question of development was hence an important meta-narrative at Bandung, which inspired the subsequent call for an New International Economic Order (NIEO).[5]

In part II, I consider the extent to which the struggle for development by what came to be known as the Third World was politically undermined by the core capitalist states. As a political strategy, this played out both at the level of policy and also in terms of a politics of epistemic erasure in the sense that the challenge of Bandung and the NIEO remains in the shadow of dominant accounts of international development. The undermining of struggles for justice by the Third World occurred in spite of it being framed comprehensively as *the* space for concerns of development!

In the final part, I briefly return to the significance of Bandung for critical political analysis of development. Here I identify some important contradictions that Bandung confronted, including imposed colonial constrictions as also experienced (if under different circumstances) prior to Bandung, as for instance in the Haitian struggle for self-determination. I also identify the way in which the post-1945 development project encouraged colonial logics in addition to colonial legacies that the postcolonial states inherited. Thus, the significance of Bandung for politics of development must be appreciated through the lens of the struggles for a just settlement to the colonial order in its specific historical context. I conclude that the "spirit of Bandung" resonates today not only as a memory of political struggle but also in concrete struggles for development otherwise.

DEVELOPMENT AS A META-NARRATIVE AT BANDUNG: A PROJECT OF RESTORATIVE JUSTICE?

It is important to note at the outset that "development" was conceived at Bandung holistically, and not in economically reductive terms. It was conceived in relational terms (in contrast to GDP which was formalized as the key measure of national development in the post-1945 context) and the delegates were acutely aware that they were establishing themselves as a new "formal" political force in world politics and were cognizant of the challenges they faced.

For example, the *Final Communiqué* agreed: (Section D; point no. 1): "In declaring that colonialism in all its manifestations is an evil which should be speedily brought to an end." On cultural cooperation they agreed on the following (Section B; point 1):

> Asia and Africa have been the cradle of great religions and civilizations, which have enriched other cultures, and civilizations while themselves being enriched in the process. Thus the cultures of Asia and Africa are based on spiritual and universal foundations. Unfortunately contacts among Asian and African countries were interrupted during the past centuries. The peoples of Asia and Africa are now animated by a keen and sincere desire to renew their old cultural contacts and develop new ones in the context of the modern world. All participating Governments at the Conference reiterated their determination to work for closer cultural cooperation. (*Asia-Africa Speaks* 1955)

These statements perhaps best convey the essence of the "spirit of Bandung." What we can apprehend are sensibilities *otherwise* to the colonial project with aspirations to cultivate deep relationships by drawing on the resources of what Shilliam refers to as un-colonized spaces of the "hinterlands" (2015: 30). The cultivation of deep relations with other colonized peoples was thus identified as significant not merely for politically strategic reasons, but because of an awareness of its intrinsic value for recovering human dignity and strength through solidarity.

The *Final Communiqué* also made explicit reference to the need to redress the (economic) legacies of the colonial development architecture. For example, though it included a formal endorsement of the UN agencies, it was agreed that there ought to be a "Special United Nations Fund for Economic Development," something which did not eventuate but nonetheless testifies to the intent of comprehensively working to address the harmful effects and legacies of colonial rule. The recommendations also specifically addressed concerns relating to the colonial (international) division of labour that the newly independent (and soon to be independent) states had inherited. Cognizant of the fact that a consequence of colonialism was that many of the postcolonial states had inherited economies that relied on plantations and the production of agricultural commodities, the delegates were in agreement about the following (Section A; point 5).

> The Asian-African Conference recommended that collective action be taken by participating countries for stabilizing the international prices of and demand for primary commodities through bilateral and multilateral arrangements and that as far as practicable and desirable they should adopt a unified approach on the subject of the United Nations Permanent Advisory Commission on International Commodity Trade and other international Commodity Trade and other international forums.

However, the "spirit of Bandung" was much more than what was explicitly articulated in the fine print of the *Communiqué*. Many commentators agree that Bandung enunciated an anti-colonial project through efforts aimed at cultivating deep relationships (cf. Shilliam 2015) with other colonized peoples not just in Asia and Africa but also in Latin America. We see this for example in the various political initiatives that followed Bandung such as the formation of the Afro-Asian Peoples Solidarity Organization (AAPSO) after the 1957 conference in Cairo as well as the Tricontinental Conference in Havana in January at which the OSPAAAL was launched (cf. Farid 2016: 14). It should thus come as no surprise that the Bandung Conference is conceived as a key moment and movement of the political project of Third Worldism. As Vijay Prashad (2007: xv) has argued, "The Third World was not a place.

It was a project." Prashad (2012: 1) later elaborates on this point stating that the "Bandung dynamic inaugurated the Third World Project," which was "for peace, for bread, and for justice" (ibid.: 3).

The "spirit of Bandung" encompassed a deep sense of solidarity with aspirations for restorative justice that was to be pursued through concrete proposals to realize development goals. The development concerns and concrete strategies cultivated at Bandung (and subsequent solidarist forums) gathered momentum and were re-articulated in terms of a more comprehensive project for restorative justice in the 1970s during the call by the coalition of postcolonial states for the NIEO at the UN.

FROM BANDUNG TO THE NIEO: THE STRUGGLES FOR JUSTICE THROUGH INTERNATIONAL SOLIDARITY

The NIEO is politically significant because it explicitly articulated for structural transformations of the colonial division of labour (cf. Thomas 1985: 130–31). In keeping with the "spirit of Bandung" and the collective power of solidarist internationalism, the call for an NIEO was forceful and demanded nothing short of restorative justice: Point 1 of the NIEO included the following:

> The greatest and most significant achievement during the last decades has been the independence from colonial and alien domination of a large number of peoples and nations which has enabled them to become members of the community of free peoples. ... However, the remaining vestiges of alien and colonial domination, foreign occupation, racial discrimination, apartheid and neo-colonialism in all its forms continue to be among the greatest obstacles to the full emancipation and progress of the developing countries and all the peoples involved. ... *The developing countries, which constitute 70 per cent of the world's population, account for only 30 per cent of the world's income. It has proved impossible to achieve an even and balanced development of the international community under the existing international economic order. The gap between the developed and the developing countries continues to widen in a system which was established at a time when most of the developing countries did not even exist as independent States and which perpetuates inequality.* (my emphasis)

These demands were already expressed at Bandung but they take on added force in the context of the 1970s. This is reflected in Point 4 of the declaration and included the following principles:

> Full permanent sovereignty of every State over its natural resources and all economic activities. In order to safeguard these resources, each State is entitled to exercise effective control over them and their exploitation with means suitable

to its own situation, *including the right to nationalization or transfer of owner-ship to its nationals, this right being an expression of the full permanent sov-ereignty of the State.* No State may be subjected to economic, political or any other type of coercion to prevent the free and full exercise of this inalienable right (my emphasis);

The right of all States, territories and peoples under foreign occupation, alien and colonial domination or *apartheid to restitution and full compensation for the exploitation arid depletion of, and damages to, the natural resources and all other resources of those States, territories and peoples* (emphasis added);

Just and equitable relationship between the prices of raw materials, pri-mary commodities, manufactured and semi-manufactured goods exported by developing countries and the prices of raw materials, primary commodities, manufactures, capital goods and equipment imported by them with the aim of bringing about sustained improvement in their unsatisfactory terms of trade and the expansion of the world economy.

The addition of the language of restitution and full compensation for colo-nial exploitation captures the essence of the political project of Third World-ism. The resolution for the NIEO was translated into the Charter of Economic Rights and Duties of States (CERDS) in 1974. However, core capitalist states vetoed the CERDS at the United Nations. It is precisely during the struggles for a NIEO that neo-liberal politics of development was pushed through core institutions of liberal internationalism, thereby undermining the struggles and political project of Third Worldism.

SOLIDARIST INTERNATIONALISM VERSUS LIBERAL INTERNATIONALISM: CRITICAL OBSERVATIONS

It should not come as a surprise that the *political* project of "solidarist interna-tionalism" was directly (and from its inception) challenged by the very project of "Atlantic Liberalism" itself (Prashad 2012: 15–85). Solidarist internation-alism was cutting at the heart of liberal internationalism while the latter itself was being reorganized to align with neo-liberal politics already reflecting an ideological shift away from welfare capitalism. (For instance, the embedded liberal compromise that enabled the welfare state was already slowly being undermined in the West by the sanctioning of offshore financial markets and later the re-regulation of finance to enable financial and credit markets. Under the embedded liberal compromise this was something that was regulated against). As Caroline Thomas (1985: 139) noted in what was perhaps one of the earliest studies on the NIEO: "To all intents and purposes, the Westerns Industrialised states were ignoring the Charter's [the Charter of Economic Duties and Rights of States] existence, let along its dictates. In no way were they tailoring their international economic activities to meet its guidelines."

However, Thomas also demonstrates how initially, through the UNCTAD, Third World concerns about unequal terms of international trade achieved some success with the establishment of the generalized system of preference (GSP) in 1970, which reflected the growing influence of Third World concerns at the level of international institutions. For instance, from the 1960s onwards collective power against structural inequalities gathered momentum and culminated with the institution of the Organization of the Petroleum Exporting Countries (OPEC). It is noteworthy that it was the Algerian international lawyer and diplomat Mohammed Bedjaoui who led the call for the NIEO. Algeria had become a member of OPEC in 1969.

The CERDS (reflecting aspirations articulated in the NIEO) called for, among other things, "primary commodity producers to form associations" (ibid.: 135), as well as indexation, "which advocated that the price received by developing countries for their primary products should be linked to the price of their imports" (ibid.: 136). As Thomas notes, the Third World continuously strived for full implementation of the charter but it continued to receive pushbacks from the capitalist core. Efforts including an attempt to address the impact and implications of the charter through a clarification of international economic law were made, but this too was opposed by the core capitalist states (ibid.: 142–43). For instance, the position of the United States was that it would only be interested in any discussion of economic cooperation if the "liberalization of trade and the improvement of the climate for foreign investment in developing countries" would be accepted (ibid.: 145).[6]

The denial of fundamental entitlements to the majority of the peoples in the world was also justified through epistemic silencing by the mainstream of the discipline of International Relations (IR) and the field of International Political Economy (IPE). For example, there continues to be a denial of the substantive implications of colonialism for IR, IPE and development, reflected not least in the widely shared commitment to narratives about interdependence between states originating in the 1970s! It is only through a denial of the actual concrete histories of colonialism and its legacies that discourses can continue to be framed in terms of a "poverty stricken south" (Cohen 2007: 201), as if this were an originating condition, together with a deafening silence about the struggles aimed at redressing historically constituted unequal relations prior to, during and after Bandung that culminated in the call for an NIEO in the 1970s. This colonial framing of development through a commitment to formalism is held up as a scientific method in contrast to critical historical approaches categorized as "judgemental" (cf. Cohen 2007: see esp. 199–200; for a critique see Weber 2015).

Against the above background, it should also be noted that, sadly, the recycling of petro-dollars (a consequence of the success of OPEC) partially explains the debt crisis of the Third World which opportunistically enabled the World Bank and the IMF to institute neo-liberal conditionalities (through

Structural Adjustment Programmes – SAPs) in exchange for further credit, or debt relief. These developments coincided with the institutionalization of the World Trade Organisation (WTO) through which basic life-sustaining needs (public goods) have been progressively commodified, such as water, health care and education. This globally constituted neo-liberal development project is for the most part shared by former postcolonial states, with the attendant inequalities organized and experienced globally. Sixty years after the Bandung Conference we are experiencing relations of affluence through inequalities, including conditions of abject poverty in the Global South as well as livelihood insecurities in the Global North.

In the face of such outcomes, should we countenance Bandung as an elite project (cf. Chakrabarty 2005)?[7] Considering this possibility would, however, lead us on to note that there was nevertheless a commitment to provide for the welfare of their peoples whether inspired through questions of justice or motivated by strategic reasons and/or indeed as responding to social struggles for basic entitlements and beyond. For example, it is no coincidence that Sri Lanka, which played a very active and highly visible role at the conference, was a key exponent of approaches to redistributive policies. But it is also the case that colonial logics of domination and rule were frequently reproduced by the postcolonial state.[8] The case of Indonesia, as documented in this book by Budi Hernawan, could be cited as another example of postcolonial states reproducing colonial logics. But there are also cases of solidarist efforts to undermine and circumvent colonial logics and legacies (cf. Shilliam 2015a). To what extent then has the postcolonial state been constrained and limited by colonial strictures?

THE BANDUNG SPIRIT IN CONTEXT: CHALLENGES, CONTRADICTIONS AND STRUGGLES FOR JUSTICE

At one level, constraints faced by the postcolonial states were multiple: in the immediate post-1945 context the state became the aggregated unit through which development and progress would be measured (McMichael 2016: 48). Not only did the key measures of development become focused on state-centred indicators of economic growth, but importantly state-centrism became the dominant method of analysis of social and political order (if not relations). In this framework, the human experience of development (as well as its ecological implications) could arguably be rendered instrumental and subordinate to the broader aspiration of realizing the security and progress *of the state*. In a context of a politics of comparison understood in accordance with "stages of development" logic of discrete units of development (based on economic growth) substantive historical relations have been denied in favour of formal relations between states, while also devaluing the lived experiences of "development."[9] To some extent, the political project of Third Worldism attempted to circumvent problems aligned with this logic by subscribing to a political practice of solidarist internationalism. Yet, in the commitment to "catch-up" measured against the standard of civilization (inherited at decolonization), to quote McMichael (2016: 50), "Development was not just a goal; but a method of rule" – the displacement and dispossession of some served to justify the development of the state. But this post-1945 context is not unique.

For example, Shilliam (2008) provides an excellent account of the constraints and obstacles that Haitians encountered as they resisted colonial expropriation as part of the ongoing struggle for freedom and emancipation. In the context of the struggles to maintain Haitian independence in a racially organized world order that continued to support enslavement, Shilliam (2008: 800) notes the following:

> His options drastically curtailed, Boyer led Haiti back to France. In order to open up the channels of investment and trade, he accepted in 1825 an ordinance issued by Charles X requiring payment of an indemnity of 150 million francs for loss of the colony. Fourteen French warships rested off Port-au-Prince to ensure that Boyer sign the document, which also demanded French trade receive a one-half reduction of duties paid by other trading states. But even with the indemnity agreed, and with black nationalism now formally construed as a politics of theft, much of the international community extended only partial recognition. Neither the British Parliament nor the U.S. Congress wished to further antagonize their planters.

As Shilliam (ibid.) goes on to state: "To pay the indemnity within five years, as agreed, Boyer had no choice but to resurrect the militarized plantation system. Thus familiar steps were taken to halt the increase in small farms and the sale of national lands, outlaw cooperative ownership and, with the 1826 rural code, tie workers back to the plantations." As Grovogui (2011) has also argued, against these odds it was those formerly enslaved in Haiti who in their struggle for emancipation drew up the first constitution that aspired to bring justice and rights for all in substantive terms, and especially for those orphaned, dispossessed and conceived as illegitimate. In another case, Anghie (1993) offers an excellent account of the social and ecological implications and effects of colonialism in Nauru, and the struggles by Nauru to secure acknowledgement and reparations for stolen lives and livelihoods. Important parallels can thus be drawn between Haitian struggles for decolonization and Bandung (and its aftermath); as the case of Haiti demonstrates struggles against colonialism persisted in the face of utmost cruelty and domination, including colonial demands set as the condition of freedom and independence (backed up by brute force). Efforts to realize in concrete terms the essence of the "spirit of Bandung" including the struggles for the NIEO have encountered similar challenges albeit in significantly different contexts (cf. Bissio 2016; Farid 2016).

ON THE SPIRIT OF BANDUNG AND
ITS CONTINUED RESONANCE

By taking Bandung as the significant referent of development in the post-
1945 context we disclose an "alternative archive of knowledge" of the
politics of development. It allows us to move through time (not in a linear
way) to apprehend colonialism and its legacies. Restoring Bandung as a key
site, movement and moment in the struggles of development allows us to
disrupt dominant narratives of development that absent social and political
struggles.[10] Learning from Bandung means learning to appreciate the "spirit
of Bandung," and finding ways to navigate outside of colonial logics. A key
question in this context is whether such a project is feasible within the contradictory framework of the postcolonial state, which been associated with
reproducing colonial logics, partly as a consequence of inheriting colonial
strictures at the point of decolonization (including the idea of "catch-up"
as an ordering principle of development).[11] It would seem that the case for
alternatives is increasingly convincing. There continue to be some important
efforts by states in Latin America that have pushed back against neo-liberal
logics of development and attempted to articulate a politics of solidarity
through redistributive mechanisms. Most noteworthy here is the Bolivarian Alliance for the Peoples of our Americas – Peoples' Trade Agreement
(ALBA-TCP).[12] It is governed by "the principles of solidarity, cooperation,
complementarity, reciprocity and sustainability" (Muhr 2012a: 232). As
Muhr (2012a: 233) states:

> In contrast to existing (neoliberal) regionalisms, in the ALBA-TCP the social
> dimension, which comprises basic utilities (water, electricity, transport infra-
> structure) food, housing, health, sports, basic education and disaster preven-
> tion/emergency aid, has assumed a key integrationist role from the outset as
> important as energy (Venezuelan petroleum) and other areas of economic and
> industrial cooperation.

Interestingly, the governance of the ALBA-TCP has a space for progressive social movements such as La Via Campesina (i.e. the food sovereignty
movement) as well as Movimento Sem Terra (the "landless movement"), thus
including progressive movements from non-member countries in the Americas
and worldwide (ibid.: 234). The ALBA-TCP has at its core an incredible commitment to social welfare and redistribution (ibid.: esp. 235–36; Muhr 2012).
    As Siba Grovogui argues in this book, the "spirit of Bandung" still reso-
nates at multiple sites and through multiple relations. It can be apprehended
today in struggles for justice and acts of solidarity in the face of multiple forms
of domination and oppression, including those authored by the postcolonial
state(s). In a beautiful piece on the possibilities for "post-colonial repair,"

Niaah (2016: 160) demonstrates the presence of the "spirit of Bandung" in transnational solidarities between, for example, Rastafari sensibilities of justice and social welfare and those of female activists of the Peasant Union who were involved in struggles for rights to land, crops and their labour in an Indonesian context. As Niaah states of his field trip to Indonesia, it

> is the sensory echoes, perhaps the idea of the common expressions and spirit link-
> ing humanity and creation that bridges geo-political voids, offering genuine con-
> nection for thought and practice. This is part of the Bandung-spirit, now directing
> a universal advancement of concerted discourse on post-colonial repair. (ibid.)

The challenge continues to be not how to practice relations of development otherwise, but how to defend such relations in the context of intensified neo-liberal politics advanced in the name of development. Either way, by taking Bandung as our point of reference in the post-1945 context, we are able to apprehend a distinctively different "archive of knowledge" about the politics of (international) development from that of the colonial project.

ACKNOWLEDGEMENT

I would like to thank Quỳnh N. Phạm and Robbie Shilliam for their helpful comments on my chapter. My thanks also go to Quỳnh for inviting me to participate in a panel on Bandung at the ISA convention in 2014. This chapter has benefitted from the discussion that followed.

NOTES

1. As Rajagopal notes of the Bandung Conference, "it came to symbolize the new spirit of solidarity of the Third World. ... Despite several internal political tensions and contradictions, Bandung succeeded in two respects; first, it helped forge a common Third World consciousness that laid the basis for collective mobilizations by the Third World at the UN, through the Group of G-77 and the Non-Aligned Movement (NAM). Second, it underlined the two cardinal principles that would organize Third World Politics in the coming decades: Decolonization and economic development" (Rajagopal 2003: 74).

2. There are exceptions; see for example: McMichael (2016: 61–62, 112–13); Rist (1997: 81–88, 143, 149).

3. There is also the now common categorization of states in terms of their relative economic wealth (measured in aggregate terms); for example, low income, middle-income countries or high-income countries.

4. By the "Bandung Spirit" we aim to present the centrality of its "decolo-nial spirit" (Shilliam 2015: 1). As Shilliam goes on to note, while recognizing the

constraints within which the Bandung Spirit was enunciated, "Through this 'spirit of Bandung' the hinterlands of the (post)colonized proposed to break free from the global architecture laid by the colonizer" (p. 2); See also Pasha (2013) and Rajagopal (2003: 74). The "Bandung Spirit" as explicated by Prashad is similar (2007: 45–46): "From Belgrade to Tokyo, from Cairo to Dar es Salam, politicians and intellectuals began to speak of the 'Bandung Spirit'. What they meant was simple: that the colonized world had now emerged to claim its space in world affairs, not just an adjunct of the First and Second Worlds, but as a player in its own right. Furthermore, the Bandung Spirit was a refusal of both economic subordination and cultural suppression – two of the major policies of imperialism. The audacity of Bandung produced its own image."

5. The link between Bandung and the NIEO is recognized by several scholars, see for example, Rajagopal (2003: 74); Rist (2014: 82); Prashad (2012: 1).

6. For example, as Bissio shows the struggles against colonialism have always also encountered military force. He also notes the extent of a wave of "right wing" coups in Latin America since the 1960s (2016: 22), aimed at undermining struggles for social and economic justice. But he also shows that these struggles have persisted and to some extent are reflected in the election of redistribution-oriented political parties (p. 23). I expand on this below with reference to the ALBA-TCP.

7. It should be noted that Chakrabarty offers a carefully conceived discussion that does not *reduce* Bandung to an elite project; rather in his discussion he makes the point of the need to remember the "ambiguities and the richness of the moment of decolonisation" (2005: 4817) in the context of an examination of the perspectives of Wright and Ngugi which is contrasted with those of Senghor.

8. Amartya Sen (1983: esp. 101–03) has made much of this example in order to counter development orthodoxies, particularly those around associating GDP growth with welfare gains. However, one should be cautious on narrating such "success stories," as they only focus on aspects of postcolonial development struggles; in this particular example, not least as a consequence of colonial legacies, inter-communal violence, and repressive state tactics against political groups would have to be countenanced too. Again, this is part of the conundrum of the politics of decolonization.

9. For a critical discussion of the politics of comparison in development see Weber (2007).

10. For a sympathetic appreciation of Bandung as a "solidarist international" project that also acknowledges its contradictions, see Weber and Winnati (2016). That article draws on this chapter but expands a bit more on aspects of the argument.

11. In the context of a discussion of Bandung, Nigam also concludes on the following: "We might need, therefore, to think of Afro-Asian futures afresh, outside of the 'catch-up' syndrome" (2016: 50).

12. According to Muhr (2012: 232): "In 2011 the ALBA-TCP had eight full members: Antigua and Barbuda, Bolivia, Cuba, Dominica, Ecuador, Nicaragua, St Vincent and the Grenadines and Venezuela. A number of governments, including Haiti, Paraguay, Grenada and the Dominican Republic, have (had) observer status. Honduras, which joined the ALBA-TCP in 2008, was withdrawn from the agreement in January 2010, following the military–elite entrepreneurial *coup d'etat* against President Zelaya in 2009."

Chapter 14

Speaking Up, from Capacity to Right

African Self-determination Debates in Post-Bandung Perspective

Amy Niang

INTRODUCTION

Even while guarding against a memorializing or a romanticized reading of the Bandung moment, its importance as an aspirational morality for the decolonizing world was tremendous. In Africa in particular, Bandung provided an impetus for a reinvigorated politics of emancipation. As African militants, decolonization activists and other members of the African Democratic Rally (RDA) gathered in Bamako in 1957 for their third and largest congress, they drew constructively on the injunctions of Bandung still fresh in their minds. Bandung compelled them to face new questions. First, there was the tricky question: "How do we as political subjects locate ourselves within a radical geopolitical imaginary (a-decolonizing-world) and at the same time commit to an idea of community (Communauté) with the colonizer?" Second, "How do we stop obsessing about demonstrating to the colonizer our capacity to speak up, and start speaking about ourselves to ourselves?" This chapter draws on debates that were articulated around these two questions at the RDA Convention of 1957 and within the Assembly of the French Union (1946–1958) between African and French parliamentarians.

Bandung provided an opportunity, at once peculiar and exciting, to recover a capacity of thought and imagination, and a right to exercise a voice. This desire was grafted onto the possibility of an Asian-African approach to international relations – embedded in the desire of the formerly colonized to bring about a new political order in which to recalibrate the imperial footprint and to promote postcolonial ideals that transcended alienation and victimhood but also hubris and conceit as the unthought foundation of Western knowledge (Niang 2015). Bandung's most fundamental legacy was to be a point of reference for divergent but significant directions: non-alignment, regionalism and engagement, to which one could add the critical question of autonomy (Tan and Acharya 2008, ix). That the legacy of Bandung is contested should neither be a surprise nor a stumbling block for understanding its significance for Africa and Asia.

The hyperbolical qualifications then used to describe the significance of the event may now seem out of place. They however translated the intensity of the hope and the enthralling aspirations of actors faced with the indomitable challenges of a postwar world that left no doubt as to the compromised prospects of (their future) freedom, a world in which the formerly colonized were to continue to exist only as appendages of imperial interests. Appreciations – often sounding dramatic to the point of exhilaration – of the historic nature of Bandung are therefore to be engaged as originating in a particular time and context. If, for Richard Wright, Bandung was "a conglomeration of the world's underdogs, the dispossessed and the oppressed of the human race," for Leopold Senghor, one of the most prominent African leaders at the time, "lyrical appreciations abounded ... [hailing Bandung as] the most important event since the Renaissance."[1] To revisit Bandung is therefore to rethink founding political ideas often occluded in practices that have marginalized anti-racism and anti-imperialism in discussions over Third World communities.

In September 1957, seventy-five representatives of African political formations – the African Socialist Movement (MSA), the RDA, the Pan-African Socialist Party (PSP) among others – 254 delegates, 570 observers, twenty-five journalists and over 2000 non-mandated delegates overflowed the corridors of a conference centre in Bamako to convene the third congress of the RDA. On the French side, there were François Mitterrand (former minister of colonies), Edgar Faure (former head of the French government; member of the Rally of Republicans [RGR]), as well as a number of parliamentarians. The motto of the RDA Congress was essentially that *le temps du colonialisme est terminé!* [The time of colonialism is over!].[2] This was a federating idea variously reiterated by congress representatives. It was, in practice, not only a disavowal of imperial policies and the imperial political culture, but also a reversal of the moral burden, for the formerly colonized, to prove political and cultural maturity as sine qua non to being admitted into the "community of nations."

Were these ideas out of step with the context? How were these various deliberations relevant to, or speaking to Bandung? Obviously there is more continuity in the RDA struggle – the party being active up to 1970s. Albeit implied rather than strongly pushed forward, the argument suggested throughout this chapter is first that Bandung provided the questions, the perspectives and a degree of optimism that structured major debates among colonial subjects from the 1950s and the 1960s onwards. Secondly, Bandung helped enliven hitherto scattered, unfocused discussions about enduring imperial relations despite formal independence – a condition that was most relevant to French West Africa. Bandung thus provided an impetus for a more direct form of critique by bringing into focus *what needed to be overcome*. For the challenge was not just to attain independence but also to confront a divided world between those whose "established" sovereignty and therefore entrenched moral privilege arrogated the right to dictate the rules of engagement upon the formerly colonized whose past subjection stood as a normative liability.

This chapter is concerned with the way in which this new-found capacity was exercised by African politicians and intellectuals who embarked upon a direct dialogue with the former colonizer on the form and shape of a postcolonial future. I specifically revisit the third congress of the RDA in Bamako whereby this new source of empowerment was experienced as excruciating. I am therefore interested in the manner in which Bandung came in and out of focus in the postures, the visions and the positions of anti-colonial activists. The latter were able to pry open closures and legal walls as well as the ideological weight of subjects closed off from democratic deliberations for too long, especially concerning the status of citizenship and subjecthood. My comments relate in particular to the positions of African intellectuals and politicians in French West Africa. They attempt to capture not only a mood but also the fundaments of a broad-based aspiration largely inspired by the anti-colonial endeavour.

A DILEMMA: ASSOCIATION OR AUTONOMY

The RDA Congress was convened barely two years after Bandung, from 25 to 30 September 1957. The latter provided the former both a reference and a comparative background in addition to being a gripping inspiration for decolonization activists in the Third World. Bandung had defined the parameters for the emergence, literally, of over half the world's population onto the international scene. More crucially, it had provided a language for bridging the gap between subjection and decolonization.

Rather than a federation of parties, the RDA operated as a network and a framework for conceiving and mobilizing resistance against continued colonial bondage. A recurrent question was articulated around how to delink from a heavily committed stance given that the movement itself was born out of quasi-communist engagements. Ideological rifts were not only apparent, they were harshly divisive between an "old" guard – not by age but insertion into French colonial establishment (Houphouet Boigny, Leopold Senghor, Lamine Gueye etc.) – and a relatively radical branch. The latter would acknowledge a form of association with the metropole only after the question of independence was finalized. For this branch, to endorse association with France was a necessary evil. For instance, Alioune Cisse, member of Union Générale des Travailleurs d'Afrique Noire, advocated "a struggle for the total liquidation of the colonial system." David Soumah, union leader for the African Confederation of Believing Workers of French Equatorial Africa (CATC), on the other hand, advanced that "colonialism might have been disarmed in the political terrain, it would however catch up on the economic and social terrains." It therefore needed to be tackled upfront in its various aspects.

The RDA meeting in Bamako in 1957 was foundational insofar as it advocated a view of self-determination as a broader process of global historical progress rather than as a specifically African problem. A long-running thread in the various interventions that animated the Congress was an understanding of self-determination as that which enabled people to regain lost dignity, hence an insistence on the means, through access to resources, with which people could self-govern, rather than the formal requirements of territory, population and state institution as prerequisites for political autonomy.[3] In contrast to this view of self-governance, and in relation to the rift among different coalitions, the development question was approached with complacency by some, in other words, as a *technicality* that would naturally be extended to colonies in a federated system. The belief was therefore strong "that the 'technical' models constitute 'neutral' data, that can only be reproduced, would it be by controlling them" (Herrera 2005, 547).

For many delegates who supported the idea of a federation, political independence was to be conceived as a goal towards the greater purpose of gaining economic, social and cultural liberation. The Loi-Cadre (Reform Act) of 23 June 1956 was aimed at extending the powers of local territorial assemblies whose members were elected by direct suffrage into a single chamber; ultimately the aim was to enable overseas populations to govern their own affairs within executive councils. If troubled at all by the ideological implications of a politico-legal framework that reconstituted empire under a new form, a large number of African leaders barely recorded objections to the potentially limiting effect of a simple revision of Title 8 of the French Constitution as opposed to a full overhaul of the colonial apparatus. For Houphouet Boigny, then president of the RDA, the Loi-Cadre was just a sketch, an initial step in determining the nature of the relationship that was to be had between the metropole and the colonies, in other words a *"union librement consentie des populations d'Afrique au Peuple de France."*[4] However, for Gabriel d'Arboussier, prominent intellectual and a member of the Assembly of the French Union, the issue of federalism was too important to be imposed by the metropole and should be democratically debated among colonial territories.[5]

Standing in for Senghor, Mamadou Dia, the vice-president of the Senegalese Executive Council, insisted on the urgency of unification of MSA, RDA and other parties, with the aim of defining "jointly" a method and a "common doctrine" in order to achieve, without delay, a complete internal autonomy for the territories. Crucially with regard to the Algerian problem (*Le Probleme Algerien*), he suggested that they should take over from the French Left since the latter had completely disintegrated. Dia's firm stance against the Algerian war did not however translate into a further explicit condemnation against "the utilisation/use of black army."[6] Additionally there were eclectic tensions within the MSA, the African Socialist Movement and French liberals as "comrades" of the Internationale Socialiste who had divergent interpretations and expectations despite a common philosophical fund. It is, unfortunately, impossible to disentangle all the political subtexts that inform the various debates in the limited space of this piece.

However, the strongest objection to a somewhat conservative and timid interpretation of the Loi-Cadre came from representatives of Fédération des étudiants d'Afrique Noire en France (FEANF) (1951–1980), the powerful pan-African student federation. FEANF delegates not only established the link with Bandung most strongly, but they also defended associated principles of cultural nationalism and political self-determination most explicitly (Dieng 2009, 166–71, 364–70). If their literal – if not radical – stance on independence ruffled feathers among colonial authorities and their close African allies, it provided them with the means of an alternative interpretation of post-colonial solidarity that was not hinged on a reforming of empire as the only possible horizon (i.e. Communauté). On the one hand, the desire to speak for oneself could not be fulfilled as long as Africans continued to operate within the parameters of empire, no matter how progressive or egalitarian a project it was presented to be. On the other hand, they thought that Africans needed to look no further than Bandung for a framework in which to start apprehending the world as comprising full-fledged members. FEANF members made it a point to attend most, if not all Third World meetings from 1955 and to defend their version of cultural personality. In 1958, FEANF published a sixty-page pamphlet entitled *Le Sang de Bandoëng* (The Blood of Bandung) in which they outlined a view as to why Bandung should be seen as an impulse for a radical idea of *place* for the formerly colonized.[7] The condition for the fulfilment of the second aspiration of former colonial subjects that I noted in the introduction, namely to speak to each other, could potentially be realized in Bandung's ambition to build an alliance that was able to rethink the organization of global power from a non-Western perspective. The place in question was a new consciousness of the global order informed by a vision of humanity and solidarity, one which stood firmly in opposition to the ethical collapse of empire. In the pamphlet, the students denounced atrocities perpetrated by France specifically in Indochina and Algeria: "Will the French government finally come to understand that the dead of Africa cannot be forgotten any more than those of Oradour?"[8]

There were two difficulties to materializing a radical stance such as the FEANF's. First, the reluctance of many metropolitan intellectuals and politicians to understand, and further to recognize "them" – their African counterparts – as anything other than nondescript "African brothers," figurations of an uninterrupted imperial play. This was not just problematic, it was also an impediment to the emancipative project (Niang 2015). Third World countries were traditionally committed to multilateralism because they depended on it to deliver the promises of equality, freedom and well-being. In the francophone world, however, juridical equality hinged upon the prospect that the *indigene* became fully assimilated through education and incorporation into French ways (*assimilation par les moeurs*).[9] Their subjectivity was seen as *delayed*, even as/when they partook in the same intellectual citizenship undergirded by a shared competence in the language and practice of "francophone" colonial common sense. Second, recurrent references to an African personality[10] that run through the discourses of many delegates were, and could be a powerful force capable of federating divergent perspectives. Yet for some student delegates, there could be no African personality to speak of without full capacity to self-realize and without meaningful self-determination.

OUT-OF-EMPIRE: CONTEXT AND POSSIBILITIES

In the francophone world, questions of a common future out of the French Empire were confronted with ideas about redemption of the imperial project on the basis of values shared across the colonizer/colonized divide. Specifically, intellectuals and politicians faced the existential question of how to articulate freedom in the context of empire as they strove to reform empire, within its own parameters, as progressive, democratic and morally viable (Cooper 2014, 4). If this process was specifically negotiated within the context of French Africa, its significance has to be appreciated through the desire of the formerly colonized the world over to bring about a new political order in which to recalibrate imperial footprints and promote postcolonial ideals that not only transcended alienation and victimhood, but also hubris and conceit.

A concern common to the two communiqués of Bandung and Bamako was the issue of exclusion, and the idea that no exclusion should impede participation on the basis of divergent ideology, philosophy or political views.[11] Both strongly condemned the suppression of cultural expression and both advocated a new internationalism devoid of a racial logic or purely motivated by economic interests. However, the perspectives on decolonization that came out of these two meetings differed in the sense that while Bandung's internationalism was underpinned by a fundamental attachment to self-determination, Bamako's framework of rights was restricted by a commitment to a *colonial* union.

For many French participants in the deliberative institutions of the Communauté, the idea of the Franco-African Union was to reinvigorate the declining dynamism of colonial presence and influence. Among a majority of African participants there was a commitment to invigorate the imaginative potency of a body of thinking and a framework of rights that had been "compromised" in the course of the colonial endeavour. There was therefore no distinction to be made between intellectual and political engagement within and beyond the context of Communauté. Ideas and philosophies directly informed policies – hence, for instance, a naive belief that L'Internationale Socialiste was optimally egalitarian despite its commitment to universal, rather than particularistic therefore historicized, circumstances (see Cooper 2005, 54).

According to Frederick Cooper (2014, 8), "in 1946, France's African subjects acquired the right to have rights," therefore "the right to make claims." Colonial subjects appropriated the metropolitan terminology of human rights and citizenship and made these speak differently for themselves (Niang 2015). While colonial authorities castigated political movements outside of the imperial frame as "atavistic, demagogic or anti-modern" (Niang 2015), the fulfilment of the humanist and republican fundaments of liberté-égalité-fraternité could only be achieved through meaningful political empowerment. In other words the establishment, respectively, of an executive federalism (liberté), equal rights across the colonial divide (égalité)[12] and unity in common fate (fraternité) was required. For the purpose of the RDA Congress, therefore, African leaders changed the motto of the French Republic to better suit their circumstances: Liberté (exécutif fédéral)-Egalité (travail)-Fraternité (unité), and this motto was displayed on boards in the main conference room. Africans' belief in *fraternité* denoted something of an artful mix of imagination and naive optimism that made Houphouet Boigny say that *L'Afrique attend beaucoup de nous. Les esprits chagrins, les impatients nous reprochent notre mystique de la fraternité. … Ils n'y croient pas. C'est leur affaire.*[13] ("Africa holds tremendous expectations of us. The despondent … those that have become impatient, blame us however for our mystique of fraternity. It is their problem if they do not believe in it.") Senghor and Houphouet in fact believed that the Franco-African Community could be an assemblage in which all forms of subjection would be erased in favour of hybrid forms of subjectivity.

Although the very coloniality of the Communauté stood in contrast to Bandung's more radical idea of self-determination, it remains an important political, economic, ideological and epistemic project that has largely been written out of the history of international relations both as theory and practice. Its implications for our understanding of the making of communities, of attempts to institutionalize non-racialism and democracy at the global level, have largely been unheralded. For instance, a prerequisite to African support for a "yes" vote at Brazzaville (the famous Loi-Cadre) was a provision for the possibility of future secession, therefore the possibility for a member to leave the community if/when they wanted. This provision was an opportunity for Africans to shift focus from an obsession with demonstrating their worth to the metropole towards envisaging ways of engaging the latter on an equal footing. In fact, the PRA, a prominent party, was ready to campaign for a "no" were this condition not to be fulfilled. For d'Arboussier in particular, "the great Franco-African debates have found their solution. ... There is no more Franco-African problem. There remains an intra-African problem."[14] The Community was therefore as much about an alliance between France and its former colonies as it was about African colonies coming together in a federated unit across national-istic divisions. Arguably, the Communauté could be a means to a "francophone pan-Africanism." A sine qua non was that it had to be "neither sentimental nor theoretical, in other words a community in which members could properly administer their own affairs thanks to an appropriate internal autonomy."[15]

This all resonates with what Kwame Anthony Appiah (1992, xi) sees as the emergence of "an unsentimental form of African humanism that can under-gird [a] resistance to tyranny." Conceptions of political alliance were loose and flexible. On the one hand, political party interventions were framed on the basis of social movement (regardless of ideological allegiance): it was the beginning of the end of the Cold War, alongside other stories. On the other hand, the language of Bandung flowed – naively some might argue – from love and passion for an imagined world taking shape over the deadened hearts of declining politics, that is, Western imperial politics.[16] Then and now, the demand for a reformulation of the postcolonial critique of Western hegemony requires a reinterrogation of the premises of critique, not least continuities ingrained in the use of intellectual categories, but also a capacity to be attuned to the requirement for decolonization and moral rearmament variously articu-lated in mounting young voices the world over.

CONCLUSION

The radical singularity of Bandung, manifest in the quasi-mythical celebra-tion of the Bandung spirit,[17] reminds us that the richness of political thought coming out of the non-West is yet to be fully understood and integrated into IR. It also reminds us that values/ideas of solidarity, interdependence, and brotherhood are an important source of meaning in political discourse and practice. For many newly independent countries Bandung was the first event where they were able to "present" themselves rather than being merely "rep-resented" or spoken about. The limited effects of alternative formulation(s) of an international order in the postwar era have to be understood in a particular context, largely shaped, for Africans and Asians, by the anxieties of the political order of the time. Despite the moral and ethical resolutions intended to decentre Western power and epistemologies (Wa Thiongo 1991) the narrow choices imposed upon non-Western countries to align with either bloc meant that in the end, a hegemonic order prevailed.

For David Scott (2004), the requirement of postcoloniality – as new critical practice – entails a re-engagement with a notion of sovereignty post-Bandung. This injunction can be understood to mean two things. First, that we need to pay attention to the critical demands of our present, to engage the sources of continuities, historical and theoretical, of imperial rule in the present, while avoiding "teleologies, whether triumphalist or declinist" (Pitts 2010, 227). The Communauté, discussed above, can be seen to have operated, in this sense, a relatively smooth transition from imperialism to hegemony when it morphed into la Françafrique.[18] One can wonder whether this turn was simply a contradiction, or an indication of some deep structures of continuity that have remained unexamined.

The second injunction relates to both interdependence and self-determination. The intellectual and rhetorical lineages between Bamako and Bandung were overwhelmingly shared. For instance, they had in common an obsession with beginnings that is a concern about how to position Africa in a polarized world. How were those who until recently had not been part of the politically useful to determine a place and language for what it meant to experience emancipation? The telos of human emancipation lay in interdependence and the exercise of distinct – yet interconnected – subjectivities. Colonial subjectivity created precarious positions that spawned contradictory longings among the colonized, and an aspect of this condition was a strong desire for autonomy combined with a pursuit of ideals born out of imperial logics. Self-marginalization was not an option. It was neither practical nor consistent with a vision of an interdependent postcolonial world. The motifs of interdependence therefore had to be found in the articulation of the possibility of different permutations of the post-imperial subject.

ACKNOWLEDGEMENT

I am grateful to Quỳnh N. Phạm and Robbie Shilliam for their constructive and useful comments and for their patience throughout the whole process.

NOTES

1. "appréciations lyriques n'ont pas fait défaut … [Bandung étant] l'évenement le plus important depuis la Renaissance," quoted in Durdin (1956). See also Zorgbibe (2011). Richard Wright (1995) saw *The Colour Curtain* as defining the prevalent order.

2. See also various speeches at the Assembly of the French Union on the occasion of the celebration of the centenary of the abolition of slavery in April 1848, session of 31 December 1947, ANOM/BiB/50243/1947.

3. 1AFFPOL/2263, Rapports divers, Archives Nationales d'Outre-Mer, Aix-en-Provence.

4. Opening speech of the President of RDA, Congres de Bamako. Rapports divers. 1957 AFPOL 2263, Archives Nationales d'Outre-Mer, Aix-en-Provence [A Union fully agreed upon by African populations and the people of France].

5. Gabriel D'Arboussier, speech at the Assembly of the French Union, session of 29 December 1947, ANOM/BiB/50243/1947.

6. Mamadou Dia (1957). Discours-fleuve, Congres de Bamako. Rapports divers. 1957 AFPOL 2263, Archives Nationales d'Outre-Mer, Aix-en-Provence.

7. In Rapports divers. 1957 AFPOL 2263, Archives Nationales d'Outre-Mer, Aix-en-Provence. The pamphlet was subsequently edited by Diouf, Khar N'Dofene Diouf, E. Razafindralambo, Raymond Fardin and Jacques Vergès and published by Présence africaine.

8. Nazi massacre in the French village of Oradour-sur-Glane in 1944.

9. AFFPOL2186, Arcbives Nationales d'Outre-Mer.

10. [distinctions and varieties of what it was to be "African" or "French African"]; see debates at the Assembly of the Union, session of 29 December 1947, ANOM/BiB/50243/1947.

11. As Richard Wright noted in his foreword to Padmore's *Pan-Africanism or Communism* that "the Negro even when embracing Communism or Western democracy, is not supporting ideologies ... [but] seeking to use instruments for his own ends." quoted in Ndiva Kofele-Kale (1978, 258). This author is however critical of the *politique de la bascule* (a "policy of opportunism") practised by non-aligned countries in a bid to play out the East/West rivalry.

12. For example, the Labour question in West Africa.

13. Houphouet Boigny (1957) President's Report, Congres de Bamako.

14. *Le Monde* 26 August 1956; *L'Essor* 27 August 1958 in Cooper (2014, 312).

15. Extract from *La Lettre de France* N. 178, 26 February 1953 reporting the Congress of the Movement of the Independentist held in Bobo Dioulasso between 12 and 15 February 1953.

16. See for instance Louis Gordon on black existentialism and the use of "love" in black militant discourse.

17. The Bandung Spirit, according to Darwis Khudori, references the possibility that the world could be something other than a battlefield characterized by the tightening belligerent advances of the United States and the USSR.

18. La Françafrique is pejoratively likened to a family-like network of private interests run by Francophone political doyens, notably the late Houphouet Boigny and Omar Bongo, Abdou Diouf, and Blaise Compaoré, as well as junior political figures on the continent and in French political and media circles. It is characterized by its institutional, semi-institutional, and obscure practices, its annual get-togethers (the Franco-African summit), its elite protocols, its extended network of mediators and intermediaries. Its tentacles are said to extend into politics, business, and the military. See Niang (2016).

Chapter 15

Papua and Bandung

A Contest between Decolonial and Postcolonial Questions

Budi Hernawan

INTRODUCTION

It might not be too surprising to note that during the sixtieth anniversary of the Bandung Conference, we heard nothing about Papua.[1] The question of West Irian as a prominent decolonization issue at the 1955 Bandung Conference had been considered solved by the adoption of the UN General Assembly (UNGA) Resolution A/RES/2504(XXIV)[2] in 1969, which declared that the territory belonged to Indonesia's jurisdiction. Almost four decades later, however, the new Papuan generation questions the legality and legitimacy of the integration of Papua territory into Indonesia's sovereignty. The recent massive demonstration of Papuan students in Jakarta to mark the Papuan historical day of 1st December illustrates the resilience of the Papuan resistance. Organized by Aliansi Mahasiswa Papua (AMP/The Alliance of Papuan Students), the rally occupied the well-known roundabout of Hotel Indonesia, in the heart of Jakarta's business district, and turned it into a centre stage of Papua. The students publicly questioned the status quo of Indonesia's sovereignty over Papua. The act of reclaiming their identity resonates with what Mustapha Kamal Pasha (2013: 150–151) calls the "Bandung impulse" as it meets three characteristics that assert the struggle for recognition, unfinished history of decolonization and repressed history.

Just as the young generation of East Timorese challenged the legality of Indonesian occupation over East Timor in the 1980s, the current Papuan generation challenges the Indonesian authority over decolonizing Papua. The challenge does not derive simply from a spontaneous intention to resist. Rather, it is rooted in *memoria passionis*, the collective memory of the suffering of Papuans, that has consolidated Papua as a nation (Hernawan 2013: 76–80). The memory contains all narratives of human rights abuses,

including crimes against humanity, land grabbing and the suppression of
Papuan identity, that have been passed from one Papuan generation to the
next for more than four decades. The memory is the source of transformative
energy that is able to turn the status quo of the social and political structure
that governs Papua upside down.

Over the last four decades, Papuans have persistently demanded recognition not only from the Indonesian state but more importantly, from global
politics. During Suharto's authoritarian regime, the demand was violently
and effectively silenced. The history of military oppression, however, has
been documented and published by historians, activists and the Indonesian
National Commission on Human Rights (Komnas HAM) so it has become
public knowledge. The government response remains inadequate and one-
sided. The consecutive democratic governments post *Reformasi*, including
the populist Joko Widodo government, have not been able to meet the Papuan
demand of political recognition. The emphasis remains economic development driven by neo-liberal economic philosophy that fails to respond to the
Papuans' demand of recognition. As a result the legacy of the authoritarian
regime remains.

Since 2009 the Papua Peace Network and the Indonesian Institute of
Sciences (LIPI), a government think tank, have advocated a Jakarta-Papua
dialogue (Tebay 2009) as the way to solve the prolonged conflicts in Papua.
The government, however, shows disinterest. The fact does not stop
Papuans from appealing for dialogue. As a domestic remedy is not available, Papuan leaders have turned their attention to the Pacific, particularly
to the Melanesian Spearhead Group (MSG). It only took two years for them
to gain significant political support from the sub-regional diplomatic forum
in the Pacific. During the 20th MSG Summit in Honiara, Solomon Islands,
in 2015, the United Liberation Movement for West Papua (ULMWP), an
umbrella political organization which represents the Papuans, was granted
an observer status.[3] This decision has put the ULMWP and Indonesia at
the same diplomatic table. This major breakthrough laid a new ground for
Papuans to reclaim their agency by contesting the sovereignty of Indonesia
over Papua. This is the context that we must understand before we discuss
the contest between the decolonization of Papua and postcolonial Papua.
For the young Papuan generation, Papua has experienced colonization by
other means.

FROM DECOLONIZATION TO POSTCOLONIAL PAPUA

The current predicament cannot be understood without tracing back the historical roots of the decolonization process of Papua, which transformed the

political status of the area from a Dutch colony to a province of Indonesia in the late 1960s.

During the roundtable conference in The Hague, when the Netherlands transferred its sovereignty over the Dutch East Indies to the newly born state of Indonesia in 1949, the former colonial power retained West New Guinea (now Papua) which was to be transferred the following year. The promise never became a reality and this prompted Sukarno to take diplomatic efforts to complete the decolonization process of Indonesia. Borrowing Benedict Anderson's (1983) term "imagined community," Sukarno and Indonesia's other founding fathers imagined Indonesia as a construct from Sabang to Merauke and therefore the delay of the transfer of Papua was considered a serious attack on the integrity of Indonesia. The diplomatic efforts by Indonesia to convince the Dutch to give up Papua through the United Nations in the 1950s were never successful. On the contrary, the Dutch won more support from the West at the UN. These events encouraged Sukarno to leave the UN and build up Indonesia's military might with the support of the Soviet Union. This strategy worked well.

The strategy was proclaimed as TRIKORA (three people's commands) on 19 December 1961 and translated into the establishment of Komando Mandala (Mandala Military Command) led by Major General Suharto (Dinas Sedjarah Militer Kodam XVII/ Tjendrawasih 1971). The command was given the mandate to coordinate and prepare all Indonesian military forces to take over West New Guinea by force. Given Cold War politics, Sukarno's move to secure military support from the Soviet Union not only resulted in substantial financial credit but, more importantly, shifted US support from the Dutch to Indonesia for fear that the largest Southeast Asian country might turn communist. The US shift affected the position of all other allies who had previously supported the Dutch, particularly Australia and the United Kingdom. The military build-up was not a bluff. English historian John Saltford notes a remark of the US ambassador to Jakarta at that time that illustrates Sukarno's manoeuvre as follows:

> Sukarno understood the tactics of Realpolitik. He was a master of painting himself into a corner and waiting for someone to rescue him. In this situation, with the help of Russians, he created a real threat of war. It was not a bluff. (Saltford 2003: 7)

This political manoeuvre resulted in the 1962 New York Agreement, which served as the basis of the transfer of power from the Dutch to the UN and finally to Indonesia. The agreement was then translated into the so-called Act of Free Choice in which 1026 Papuan representatives were selected by the Indonesian army to participate in public consultation to decide whether they wanted to join Indonesia or to be separate. Despite UN supervision, the Indonesian army was fully in control over the consultation which resulted in a unanimous decision to join Indonesia. The following eyewitness account illustrates the atmosphere of control and coercion during the implementation of the Act of Free Choice in Southern Papua:

> For about a month we were interned. Not much happened inside the dorm. Every night, I had to practice loud reading with Mr Laurens, the commander of RPKAD [the Indonesian Army Special Forces]. "You can't be wrong" they told. ... We were coming from Asmat, Mappi, Marind Dek, Biau and the city of Merauke. The government and Opsus selected us. Some were teachers; some others were ordinary people. These were illiterate. ... I came forward and read the text to join Indonesia. I was so emotional because it was a total surrender. I could feel the burning fire inside me. I did not mean it. But such a feeling was not allowed to be expressed. It must be suppressed. Those who spoke out went to Kodim and many of them died because of electric shocks there.[4]

The testimony revealed a systematic pattern of silencing the voice of Papuans starting from the selection of recruits to internment to drilling and finally to the brainwashing of Papuan minds in order to conform to the instruction from the Indonesian army. The fact, however, did not deter the debate within the UN General Assembly (UNGA) from adopting the resolution A/RES/2504(XXIV) that accommodated the result of the Act of Free Choice regardless of its flawed process and oppositions from African countries. Saltford (2003: 175) illustrates the end of debate at the UNGA in a bitter tone:

> In the end the Dutch, British and eighty-two other states voted to adopt the original resolution taking note of the Act's result and acknowledging the fulfilment by the UN of its responsibilities under the Agreement. There were thirty abstentions, but no votes against. This resolution was then recorded as Document A/L. 576 in the official records of the UNGA. The UNGA moved on to Agenda Item 99 concerning the Korean question, and with that the UN ended its interest in the right of the people of West Irian to self-determination.

This remark captures the point where Papua transitioned from being an issue of decolonization to a postcolonial question. The UNGA decision to close the Papua chapter had a lasting impact not only on Papua but also on global politics. During the decolonization process, West Irian no longer stood out as an international concern. On the contrary, it was made invisible and ascribed to the entity of Indonesia. In Kristeva's (1982: 1) words, Papua was made abject. Papuan agency was disavowed by the Indonesian state and the international community so that Papua came to serve only the Indonesian state's representation of itself as stretching from Sabang to Merauke. This is the nature of Papua's construct within Indonesia, represented not only in words but by military force. A witness from the 1960s expressed his bitter memory as follows:

> When I moved from Tiom [in the highlands] to Jayapura, I saw the Indonesian [army] looting Papuan houses. They treated Papuans as losers so we were like prisoners of war. It was not liberation. So we were treated as enemies since the beginning. This attitude has changed very little to date.[5]

Since the 1949 roundtable conference between the Dutch and Indonesia in The Hague, Papuans have never been given a chance to speak for themselves. Arguing against Indonesia in order to retain Papua as its territory, the Dutch argued that Papuans had not yet arrived at the stage of representing themselves. Ironically, the same argument was used by the Indonesian delegation during the UNGA debate that eventually adopted the result of the Act of Free Choice. In a different form, the same logic was reiterated by then president B. J. Habibie when a team of 100 Papuan representatives presented their aspirations for Papua's independence; his response was "[g]o home and rethink the request" (Hernawan and van den Broek 1999). The argument of incapability and back-wardness is common to colonialism as Robert Young puts it by referring to Spivak: "The colonized speaks only through speaking positions which imperial and other powers permit to its Others" (Pasha 2013: 28). In the current political discourse on Papua, a similar argument remains in response to the aspiration for dialogue with Jakarta. Jakarta's politicians, analysts and public opinion continue to question the capability of Papuans to represent themselves given that there are so many factions, ethnic groups and languages. In other words, Papua's agency is not permitted. The denial of Papua's agency is not only limited to language but, more broadly, also covers political identity, authority over land and demographic composition, as will be further discussed below.

BETWEEN BANDUNG AND THE MSG

If we look back at the 1955 Bandung Conference, we will learn how Papua was mentioned by name as one of the major issues that the new emerging leaders dealt with. In the *Final Communiqué* of the Bandung Conference the former rebel leaders of twenty-nine nations, which had been called "coloured peoples by the West" (Wright 1956: 11), inscribed the case of then West Irian under the subtitle "Other Problems":

> The Asian-African Conference, in the context of its expressed attitude on the abolition of colonialism, supported the position of Indonesia in the case of West Irian based on the relevant agreements between Indonesia and the Netherlands.

The statement captures Indonesia's victory of mobilizing support from African-Asian nations over the unfinished transfer of the sovereignty of Papua by the Dutch. The leaders affirmed that the Papua situation was nothing but the continuation of colonialism, a phenomenon that was condemned and thus had to be abolished (Drooglever 2009: 234). The Bandung Conference therefore bolstered Indonesia's campaign to integrate "West Irian" into Indonesia.

On the sixtieth anniversary of the Bandung Conference, the ULMWP used the powerful wordings of the 1955 Bandung Conference communiqué to claim back its right to self-determination for Papuans:

> On the 60th anniversary of the Bandung conference, it is time for human rights violations in West Papua to end. More than that, it is time for the inalienable right to self-determination of the People of West Papuan to be recognized, respected and implemented, at last. That right has been recognized by the leaders of five Melanesian independent countries.

This is an irony. Sixty years ago, Papuans, who had been framed through the issue of decolonization for Indonesia against the Dutch, had no voice to represent themselves vis-à-vis those disputing parties. Sixty years later, instead of being integrated into the imagined community of Indonesia, Papuans have raised their voices loud and clear to those who were themselves ex-colonial prisoners convening at Bandung in 1955. Not only have the presumably voiceless Papuans articulated their claims but more importantly they have also claimed back their rights to decide for themselves. Drawing on the spirit of decolonization marked by the Bandung Conference, the ULMWP demanded the members of the conference to act on the case of Papua.

The act of reclaiming Papuan history resonates with what Pasha (2013) identifies as the Bandung impulse. The new element of the impulse, however, is that the ULMWP has brought the MSG to the scene, which had not existed sixty years ago. Those who celebrated the spirit of decolonization at the Bandung Conference are no longer in the underdog position; rather, they are in a position to decide. But instead of engaging the Afro-Asian nations, the ULMWP has made the MSG nations its top diplomatic priority as it is only the MSG that recognizes the Papuan impulse, namely the struggle for the rights to self-determination, a repressed colonial history as well as an unfinished history of decolonization.

The words "Melanesia" and "MSG," which were never mentioned by anyone in Papua five years ago or even three years ago, have now become magic words not only for many Papuan activists but also for the government of Indonesia since the Papuan leaders submitted their application for membership of the MSG in 2013. The words capture the desire of indigenous Papuans to express their cultural affiliation with the spirit of Melanesian brotherhood as formally instituted in the MSG. The MSG forum has become the only open space for Papuans to articulate their authentic voice without any fear of being punished, particularly regarding discussions of Papuan decolonization (see Maclellan 2016).

Given this manoeuvre, Indonesia's response has been firm, undertaking systematic attempts to undermine international recognition for Papua. Internally, the Indonesian police repress any public rally convened to raise issues of the MSG. For instance, as recently as 1 May 2015, at least 246 activists of Komite Nasional Papua Barat (KNPB/West Papua National Committee) in five cities in Papua were arrested and detained overnight by the police when they publicly expressed their support for the opening of the 20th MSG summit. This picture poses a stark contrast with thousands of manufacturer labours who organized major rallies in Jakarta and some other big cities in Indonesia to mark "labour day" – on the same day. They found no difficulties or repression from the authorities although the Indonesian police chief was initially rather cautious. While this was a major step for the labour movement in comparison to Suharto's New Order era, which oppressed any attempt to express their views, the democratic space has not infused into Papua's social space. During 30 April–1 June 2015, at least 482 young Papuans were arbitrarily arrested by the police. Although they were released within twenty-four hours, the police action strongly suggested planning and coordination between different jurisdictions.

It is striking that both local and national media were mostly silent about the largest police arrest in Papuan history to date. Such a large-scale mobilization would not have occurred had the police not deployed large state resources. Interestingly, the police did not follow the usual pattern of publicizing their activities in dealing with security-related issues. And we have received no explanation from them to date. Therefore, it might be justifiable to conclude that the incident was carefully crafted to render Papua identity invisible and voiceless. The police action merely prolonged the ongoing practice of state violence against the Papuans.

The denial of Papuan identity by the Indonesian state is further confirmed by the creation of Melanesia-Indonesia (Melindo) as a rival to the ULMWP and a new umbrella for all Papuan political factions that fight for independence. The Indonesian state claims that Melanesian identity is not exclusive to Papua but rather includes four other provinces beyond Papua, namely Maluku, North Maluku, East Nusa Tenggara and West Nusa Tenggara. While the argument attempts to confuse the fundamentals of ULMWP's campaign in the Pacific, it overlooks the fact that none of those provinces expresses its intention to apply for the MSG membership. The most blatant statement has come from the coordinating minister for security and political affairs Luhut

Pandjaitan[6] who made a remark that Papuans who do not want to stay under Indonesia's jurisdiction should go to Melanesia.

SIGNATURES OF COLONIZED PAPUA

In its statement on the anniversary of the Bandung Conference, the ULMWP summarized its sense of living under colonization in terms of the "possession of West Papua," human rights violations, transmigration and identity. While the first problem with regard to the Act of Free Choice in 1969 has been discussed above, the rest will now be detailed.

First, the history of state-sponsored violence against Papuans has been widely documented by both domestic and international bodies but the Indonesian state has done very little to address the issue. The gravity of the violation has reached the level of crimes against humanity (Komnas HAM 2001, 2004, 2014), which is punishable under domestic and international laws. Komnas HAM, non-government organizations, as well as the UN Human Rights Council[7] and the MSG have frequently expressed their concerns over the impunity of ongoing human rights violations. The latest statement of the Solomon Islands prime minister to the 31st Session of the UN Human Rights Council exemplifies these concerns. However, we have yet to see any perpetrator sent to jail for crimes against humanity.

Second, although President Jokowi eventually decided to stop the transmigration programme to Papua,[8] the impact of government-sponsored transmigration has proved enormous.[9] Keerom, Manokwari and Merauke are some of the designated areas where the first generations of transmigrants were resettled in early 1970s. Having lived in the area for four decades, the transmigrants have constituted an integral part of the local population, who are entitled to human rights and rights of citizenship as any Papua resident. This reality poses an ongoing problem of ethnic identity among groups in Papua.

Despite the negative impacts of transmigration on Papua and President Jokowi's decision to terminate the programme, his minister for transmigration, Marwan Jafar, was determined to resume the government-sponsored transmigration to Papua as part of the national transmigration programme from Java to other islands.[10] This determination is reminiscent of the New Order programme that has already caused conflict between the locals and transmigrants because the government grabbed land from traditional landowners and distributed it to transmigration peasants who were relocated to new sites. Another worrying signal comes from the minister of agriculture. He has planned to resume operation of a large agribusiness in Merauke area called Merauke Integrated Food and Energy Estate (MIFEE). These signals have caused disillusions among the Papuan voters as they did not expect that

Jokowi's cabinet would turn to the old school way of dealing with Papua, which even the previous government had avoided.

The third issue that the ULMWP highlights is the danger that Papuans will be a minority in their own land because of the influx of migrants from other parts of Indonesia. While the 2010 government census does not indicate an imbalanced population between Papuans and non-Papuans, the danger is not a fantasy. Both the transmigration programme and economic migration to Papua have largely contributed to the growing tension and often violent clashes between the indigenous and non-indigenous Papuans in recent years, particularly in Sorong and Jayapura areas (Hernawan et al. 2015).

RECLAIMING PAPUAN AGENCY

Postcolonial Papua is an abjected Papua. It is discarded and its agency has been denied and repressed. It is claimed and retained not only to sustain the construct of the Indonesian state but, more importantly, to maintain the geo-political peace of Southeast Asia. Papua is the sacrificial lamb: it is allowed to exist so long as this existence serves the current geopolitical settlement.

The postcolonial nature of Papua can be apprehended through three major patterns that encapsulate this continuing process of abjection. First, its identity is still considered subversive to the Indonesian state as it questions the latter's sovereignty over Papua. The public protests of the young Papuan generation reflect the most prominent example of the ways in which the *memoria passionis* has driven abjected Papuans to reclaim their agency. Second, a population shift is happening. The growth rate of non-Papuan ethnic groups is higher than ethnic Papuans and it has become a growing concern that in twenty years the ethnic Papuans will become a minority in their own land. While statistically ethnic Papuans are the majority in both provinces of Western Papua and Papua, the power relations between non-ethnic Papuan groups and Papuans are imbalanced as the former are in a stronger position in the job market and in the economy outside of the top government positions (law reserves these for ethnic Papuans). Third, the track record of government-sponsored transmigration has contributed not only to the demographic shift but also to land rights issues. It is not uncommon that the government does not consult the Papuans over the rights to land and natural resources.

Papua has struggled for recognition for more than four decades before receiving recognition by the MSG. It has returned to existence. Papuans have voices that the world would do well to listen to and respect. Although the Papuan struggle at the MSG is not inspired by the Bandung Conference, it resonates with the core principle of the Bandung impulse which demands an answer to the unfinished history of decolonization.

NOTES

1. In this chapter, the term "Papua" refers to the western part of New Guinea Island that falls under Indonesia's sovereignty. The name has changed a number of times according to the political regime that rules the area. During the Dutch colonial time, it was named West New Guinea before President Sukarno renamed it West Irian. After President Suharto came to power, it was then renamed Irian Jaya. President Gus Dur gave it its indigenous name: Papua. Currently the area is divided into two administrative provinces: West Papua and Papua provinces. To the West, it is known as West Papua.

2. http://www.un.org/en/ga/search/view_doc.asp?symbol=A/RES/2504% 28XXIV%29.

3. See the communique of the 20th MSG Summit here http://www.msgsec. info/images/LegalDocumentsofCooperation/26%20Jun%202015%20-%2020th%20 MSG%20Leaders%20Summit%20-%20Communique.pdf, accessed on 30 April 2016.

4. Interview with an eyewitness in Merauke on 20 July 2010. Similar unpublished accounts have been collected by local NGOs in Manokwari following the 2nd Papuan Congress in 2000 titled *"Benarkah Bangsa Papua Telah Diberi Kesempatan Untuk Menentukan Nasib Sendiri?: Penuturan tentang Kecurangan PEPERA di Manokwari"* [Is it true that the Nation of Papua has been given a chance to exercise the right to self-determination? Narrative about the deception of the Act of Free Choice in Manokwari] confirms the coercive measure in conducting the Act of Free Choice.

5. Interview with an eyewitness in Manokwari, 4 September 2015.

6. The statement was met with strong reaction (http://nasional.kompas.com/ read/2016/02/19/15131401/Luhut.Pergi.Saja.Sana.ke.Melanesia.Jangan.Tinggal. di.Indonesia, accessed on 30 April 2016).

7. During the 2012 Universal Periodic Review at the UN Human Rights Council, at least twelve UN member states expressed their concerns over the unresolved human rights problems in Papua.

8. http://nasional.kompas.com/read/2015/06/04/18471741/Jokowi.Hentikan. Transmigrasi.ke.Papua (accessed on 30 April 2016).

9. https://tabloidjubi.wordpress.com/2008/03/29/dari-kolonisasi-sampai-transmi-grasi-di-tanah-papua/ (accessed on 30 April 2016).

10. http://jakartaglobe.beritasatu.com/opinion/transmigration-last-thing-papua-people-need/ (accessed on 30 April 2016).

Chapter 16

Bandung as a Plurality of Meanings

Rosalba Icaza and Tamara Soukotta

INTRODUCTION

Our conversations about the 1955 Bandung Conference started in the summer of 2014. Rosalba Icaza (RI) witnessed an informal but intense exchange between Tamara Soukotta (TS) and Walter Mignolo on the contemporary legacies of Bandung. Tamara expressed doubts about Walter's argument on Bandung as setting the historical foundations of decoloniality in global politics, developed in his article "Geopolitics of Sensing and Knowing" (2011).[1]

The present text is the outcome of various conversations that followed this first debate that we held between July 2014 and January 2016. All of our conversations, except the last one, were informal, brief and constantly interrupted by urgent personal-professional concerns. All of them were conducted in English as our lingua franca. Our last conversation was the only one that we agreed to record and transcripts were produced and circulated between us from which a first draft was agreed upon.

As we have known each other for over a period of seven years, starting a conversation was not difficult. However, we realized that it had been extremely rare to find moments and spaces to hold deep conversations about the meanings that each of us attach to Bandung and as part of our own personal-professional-epistemic trajectories. Therefore these conversations have been an opportunity for us to learn about each other as much as we have learnt about the plurality of meanings that Bandung inspires in us as the first international conference of "people of color" and a place of local histories in West Java, Indonesia.

This version of the text also aims to reflect that the meanings that each of us assigns to Bandung are *in relation to* our present interactions as two female colleagues of "Southern" origin doing research in a European University and who share a commitment to struggles for liberation and autonomy of West Papuan people in Indonesia (TS) and of Zapatista communities in Chiapas, Mexico (RI).

Rosalba had already explored auto-ethnography (Icaza 2015; Barbosa da Costa, Icaza and Talero 2015) in a dialogical way as developed by Mexican anthropologist Leyva Solano (2013), who speaks of about it as "a kind of praxis of research of *co-labor* (collaborative research) in which the written text is a dialogue with the spoken and written word, with visuality, with past and present experiences and with the imagined horizon of autonomy." This way of working was agreed upon as our joint reflexive path.

Overall, this text aims to be an account of the multidimensional process of this reflexive path: a dialogue between each other on our different understandings about Bandung but that are nonetheless deeply interconnected to our own political-personal-epistemic trajectories, and to our flourishing friendship as part of a learning community of students and colleagues-friends in the city of The Hague. As such, this chapter aims to demonstrate that our personal accounts of what Bandung means to us are intertwined but are also arising from and in relation to that community of colleagues-friends (see Icaza 2015).

In so doing, this written version of our spoken words uncovers the road travelled in a dialogical process of writing an "academic" reflection. The chosen path is critical self-reflection on the already walked route – our conversations and joint intellectual ruminations – which are rarely visible in "academic" texts, but that nonetheless direct our in-company walking/thinking/sensing. To shed light on this is our way of countering the dominant narratives surrounding the generation of "academic" knowledge as if these were individual(ized) endeavours and coming from no place, no temporality, no memories.

What follows is a dialogue broken in several sections of different extensions that address different themes about Bandung. We chose them keeping in mind a key question: What does Bandung mean to us – the female-teachers-researchers-activists of southern origin based in northern academia?

BANDUNG: LAYING THE HISTORICAL FOUNDATIONS OF DECOLONIALITY?

RI: Let me start this conversation by saying that when I received the invitation to contribute to this book I immediately thought about your conversation with Walter Mignolo on Bandung as a decolonial act.

TS: As you know Mignolo (2013) argues that decoloniality – a different logic to that of modernity/coloniality – has its historical grounding in Bandung conference while modernity, postmodernity and alter-modernity have their historical grounding in the Enlightenment. For him, the Conference didn't represent a "third way" a la Giddens but a delinking from the two main Western macro-narratives of capitalism and communism. I cannot disagree if Bandung is part of decolonization, a part of the political processes taking place after the Second World War when Western colonizers have to leave "their" colonies and these became independent states. Whether Bandung plays foundations for decoloniality, whether this Conference in itself a decolonial act, I am not sure.

RI: Can you elaborate on your hesitations about Bandung as a "decolonial act"?

TS: First of all, it is important to stress diversity of territorial transformations in the processes of political decolonization. The Indonesian nation-state building process was on the basis of unification whereas in the case of Latin America, the postcolonial state was built upon partition.

RI: Yes, but if we understand that underlying both processes – unity or partition – was a modern/colonial "logic" of nation-state building, then both processes were violent impositions over a heterogeneity of languages, people, cosmovisions and so on.

TS: In the case of Indonesia, you need to think on this Archipelago of Islands that were forced to unite. You have peoples who are "ethnically" closer to the indigenous people of Australia, the Pacific or India. There are also smaller Islands. My own province, Maluku – before it was divided into two provinces of Maluku and Northern Maluku – was about 1,000 islands in total, some of them are inhabited and some other not. Within this Archipelago there were many differences and this diversity was "unified" into one nation during the 1945 declaration of Independence of Indonesia.

Our mainstream national history claimed that the Indonesian nation-state building process started earlier, in the 1920s and highlighted as an example the declaration of a Youth Congress (Sumpah Pemuda) in 1928, in which there was an acknowledgement of one nation that is Indonesia and one language of unity that is Bahasa Indonesia. However, there are different views about this Congress. On one hand, some claim that this is definitely part of the nation-state building process led by elites from different parts of the Dutch East Indies coming together and deciding that in order to fight the Dutch a common language was needed and that this shouldn't be Dutch because this was the language of the colonizers. So, these elites decided to adopt one of the local languages *"Melayu Riau"* (Riau Malay) and develop it into a common language. There were different languages at that time and Dutch was one common language spoken by the elites who had Dutch education.

A counter argument emphasizes that the search for a common language didn't mean the creation of one single nation, but that there was a real need of communication between each other. However, the idea of a common language was politically twisted in order to justify the building up of one single nation-state. As a result, unification was imposed by elites but dominant narratives of "our national" history argues that it was the wish of everybody to unify. Unification was envisaged by some as a strategy to get rid of the Dutch without plans for the creation of one nation-state afterwards.

RI: Precisely a decolonial perspective allows me to grasp what you are sharing: the historical movement[2] of modernity of the nation-state brings with it the colonial movement of suppression and annihilation of plural forms of life, being, sense. Mignolo (2010) himself talks about modern/colonial logics as genocidal violence and their concealment as the basis of abstract universality.

TS: My point is that Mignolo argues that the origin of decoloniality was the Third World in its diversity of local histories. But in the case of Indonesia, the host country of Bandung conference, don't you think that the building up of one single nation out of a plurality of "nations" is a colonial act in itself?

RI: For me, a positive answer to your question would mean to understand that despite all its differences and specific characteristics, the Dutch colonial ruling and the Indonesian postcolonial nation-state building share a common ground: a kind of "power over." So, political decolonization by taking the form of a postcolonial nation-state was not exempt of this violent form of control.

TS: Exactly, but in addition to this Mignolo argues that the most enduring legacy of Bandung Conference was delinking, but what about self-reflexivity?

RI: What do you mean by self-reflexivity?

TS: The Indonesian elites, which were educated by the Dutch, decided that a single nation should be built up out of many "nations," for me this was a colonial act. It was an act of forced unity. Our national motto has been translated as "*Unity in Diversity*" but its literal meaning into English is "*Different but One.*" In the process of building that *One*, uniformity was forced instead of embracing the diversity that existed. For example, forms of government shifted into one style, the Javanese style, which for the rest of non-Javanese Indonesians meant that we moved from Dutch colonizers to another form of political control, but control nonetheless. In Indonesia we used the term "*dijajah oleh Jawa*," which literally translated to "colonized by the Javanese"!

RI: I agree with your argument regarding the colonial act of nation-state's logic of forced uniformity. In the last decade, I have been an "IR scholar" engaged with transnational activism supporting Zapatistas autonomy in Chiapas, Mexico and when I hear that a Conference of "Nation-States" bears potentials of delinking and/or grounds decolonial futures, I also have some doubts.

However, we cannot deny that the literature on Bandung, although mainly written in English for an Anglo-Saxon academic audience, including Mignolo himself, is aware of Bandung's antinomies (e.g. Pasha 2013). I read these perspectives as attempts to question the modern/colonial idea of a consistent linear rationality in political events and of the way we in academia try to interpret them under an either/or lens: as decolonial or not, as hegemonic or counter-hegemonic, as revolutionary or not and so on. But what is also important for me is the context in which Bandung happened. What I mean is that Bandung as a political event was unthinkable.

So, Mignolo's ideas help me to understand Bandung as one of the political events grounding decoloniality as a delinking act in its epistemic dimension. This means a break in the narrative of modernity/coloniality, and in particular of the coloniality of being in global politics (see Icaza and Vazquez 2013). This was the first international conference of peoples of color! This is an historical moment in which people of color became politically visible in global politics. Foreign policy analysts started to report about former subjects of Empires as political actors in the international arena. I can also think of this moment in the same way Arturo Escobar talks about the making of the Third World and President Truman's discourse on Asian, African and Latin American people as "underdeveloped." Bandung made epistemically visible the category colored people, which following Mignolo's ideas, means a challenge to the modern/colonial narrative in which non-white people simply didn't exist. I am enthusiastic about this because what I consider crucial from Mignolo's argument is the need to seriously start thinking IR and Global Politics as two disciplines that are founded on the concealment of alterity, including the historical foundations of decoloniality and Bandung.

But of course, we need to think Bandung with extremely critical eyes which for me means to learn from less known versions of Indonesian state building process too. Through this learning, I think, Bandung can be seen as a moment of epistemic rupture through the irruption of the category of "people of color" in global politics, but as all categories this is not exempt of problems as these bring classification as a logic of control and exclusion.

I also think that this perspective connects to the process we have. Being part and product of that is the creation of our own national states (Mexico and Indonesia) from the perspective of our engagement with the struggles of indigenous people there. I personally cannot disassociate genocidal violence and its concealment from the building up of the Mexican national state.

TS: To comment on this I need to go back to Mignolo's emphasis on Bandung as historical grounding of decoloniality and its legacy: delinking. Bandung in itself is problematic but of course we have to understand it in its own context. The act of visibility of people of color in the eyes of dominant powers, although mediated through the nation-state, was extremely important after hundreds of years of colonization and violent dehumanization. I think of Bandung as a source of inspiration to think about decoloniality, to shake the grounds of hegemonic thinking.

RI: You mean a source of inspiration to the present moment?

TS: Yes, but also in 1955 too, because power was shaken. It inspired other decolonization movements as Mignolo says. But having said this, I cannot say Bandung was that or is this now. This is not the focus of the discussion at all for me.

Let me try to explain what the discussion could be about: Bandung as part of the process of ongoing decolonization is not a moment of decoloniality, as one that exceeds the logic of "power over," its genocidal violence and its concealment. This logic is not exceeded but reproduced and extended through the case of West Papua. In 1955, Indonesia was still struggling to take West Papua from Dutch control. By 1965, Sukarno, the first president of Indonesia fell after a coup supported by the US. Some years later, the Netherlands and the US supported by the UN agreed to give West Papua to the Indonesian state instead of granting Papuan Independence. West Papua became part of the Indonesian state as a result of an agreement between the Dutch, the US and the UN. There was a referendum on this, but some of those in West Papua who participated in the referendum that are still alive have said that they were forced to join Indonesia at gun point. And please, do not forget that after the agreement was signed the first contracts with Freeport McMoRan for mining were signed, too. The whole colonial matrix of power in operation! Therefore, when I said that Bandung shook the grounds of Cold War politics, I also think that it provoked violent reactions from Western powers.

RI: So the aftermath of Bandung was also a violent reality for Indonesians.

TS: Yes, we need to think on the aftermath of Bandung in terms of what happened with West Papua. From this perspective, Bandung will not be delinking either because later on the Indonesian Communist Party became extremely strong after Bandung and the US supported the 1965 massacre and coup to suppress that movement. We never actually delinked – we were crushed by the US for moving towards communism, and we have never been actually delinked from global capitalism, either. So, the Bandung Spirit was just born like a fresh budding flower that was killed immediately.

RI: I like the metaphor you used to describe what is the meaning of the Spirit of Bandung for you now: a plant that was planted and killed immediately. Why was it killed immediately? Was it the "pot" of the modern/colonial nation-state that killed it? I would say that it might have been born dead because of the erasure of local histories, of genocidal violence contained in the representation of the Indonesian state as one single nation.

TS: Plus that we were caught between decolonization and neo-colonization and US neo-imperialism building up their relations with former colonies through growing capitalism and mining exploitation just like in the case of West Papua.

WHO ARE WE AS AN "US"?

RI: Tamara you are bringing a local history perspective on Bandung's aftermath. You as an Indonesian linked to West Papuan independence activism bring to the discussion what has been produced as inexistent by the dominant narratives of Indonesian nation-state building.

TS: I think I am bringing a perspective about Bandung from the memories and histories of localities of the Eastern part of Indonesia.

RI: What does it mean for you to speak about Bandung from the Eastern part of Indonesia?

TS: It means marginalization after independence. I come from Maluku, a neighbouring province to West Papua, and this was a place of privilege during the colonial period; for example, many got educated within the Dutch system of education. After independence, we Malukans – like many others – paid a high price. As the capital was moved to Java, developmental projects too and there was a kind of Javanization of the whole Archipelago. This is how we see independence from the Dutch in the Eastern part of Indonesia. I see the nation-state differently. I was not born and raised in Jakarta, the capital, and I don't come from the main ethnic group but from one that was marginalized after independence and also forced into being one nation.

Then, there is the question of racism. Because of our different heritage, some of us Malukans are darker than the Javanese, but in general we are always seen as darker even if we are not. I studied in Jakarta, I am not a fair Indonesian but not very dark either, and I don't have curly hair, which is the stereotype of Eastern Indonesian: we should have curly hair and black skin. When I am there and people ask me where I come from, they are surprised that I am not black or curly, but still I am perceived as dark. In this hierarchy of skin colours that exists in Indonesia, the Eastern part occupies the darker side.

Moreover, the Southern Republic of Maluku was proclaimed in 1950 and tried to separate between the 1950s–1960s and it was crushed, like other parts of Indonesia who tried to separate before Bandung. Like many other women of my generation-social class-ethnic origin – I was educated to be a proud nationalistic person. I started to change as the history and the process of Indonesian nation-state building was revealed as a colonial act, too.

Therefore, my understanding of Bandung is about the moment when Indonesia presented itself to the world as one single nation. During that moment, within Indonesia and probably in the other participating countries, diversity was crushed. So, the question for me is not if Bandung is a decolonial act or not, but the underside, what was not "represented" there. If I could take this violence out, then I could agree and say that Bandung is a historical grounding of decoloniality, because power in Cold War politics was questioned – but I can't. We shouldn't, indeed. I might be able to do it if I was an "outsider" observer – but this is not the case, and I cannot get rid of this feeling. I am thinking from the gut here.

RI: We say *senti-pensar* in Spanish, which translates as "sensing-thinking."

TS: Maybe if I have not born into the memories and the experiences of being marginalized and pushed from the centre to the periphery I wouldn't have any doubt about Bandung being a decolonial possibility. As an Indonesian national, I cannot separate Bandung from Indonesia as a nation-state. We hosted the conference as a nation-state, whether I like it or not – in this sense even as a moment of globalism, Bandung for me is tethered to Indonesia as a nation-state.

WHO WAS THE AUDIENCE?

RI: I would like to share something else with you in the form of a question, not to be answered, but as a device to think further about Bandung's plural meanings that include perspectives from local histories of marginalization in Indonesia.

I think that Bandung can also show us the limits of focusing on changing the terms and content of the conversation *with* power. I mean, whose ground shifted? One could say that global political dynamics among national elites controlling state power shifted. But, whose ground was shattered by the "Spirit of Bandung," by the flower that was planted and instantly killed?

Bandung as an International Conference changed and affected people's lives in concrete terms. I am not denying that. Do you remember University of Leiden's Conference on Bandung that we attended together?[3] We actually heard the eyewitnesses' experiences of Francisca Pattipeilohy who was involved in the Afro-Asian Journalist Association and of Ibrahim Isa who was involved in the Afro-Asian People's Solidarity Organization. They shared their testimonies about the emerging solidarity between people of color, but also about their lives being shattered in the aftermath of Bandung because they were caught in Cold War politics and forced into exile.

What I am trying to ask is whose grounds were challenged when the conversation is mainly with power? For me Bandung as an international conference has as target audience – elites within the participant countries and other elites in the West. The audience was power. Bandung participants were speaking to power, even if for some this was unintentional like in the case of Francisca and Ibrahim. Hence, we need to remember that when you speak to power sometimes you use the same language and might end up reproducing the same logics.

Sixty years after Bandung, Mignolo (2013) speaks of an emergent "communal logic" as something different from capitalism, communism or neo-liberalism that is simply not speaking to power, that is not a kind of power over and doesn't have power as a target audience. When common people learn that power is not listening, autonomy becomes the horizon. I would like to say that this is the experience I have witnessed and learnt from in Zapatista autonomous communities. This might help us to understand the limitations of Bandung and to learn from the limitations of speaking to power, of creating categories (people of color) that have power as a target audience.

Nonetheless, Bandung set the grounds for people of color, the majority of the world indeed, to speak to power. Unfortunately, power was/is not listening; hence we cannot be naïve when speaking to power.

TS: Because power speaks back.

RI: I don't want to be unfair to Bandung, but after sixty years, its spirit seems to me a good example to learn from on how not to be naïve when building up autonomy and delinking projects. Bandung then becomes pedagogy for speaking to power and for learning about the limitations this option has. Something

I have learnt from listening to Zapatistas on how they have been building their autonomy is that they soon realized power was not listening or was twisting their message. Over the years, their main audience became the communities themselves. They started to learn how to talk to each other, and today young generations of Zapatistas are able to speak two or three Maya languages plus Spanish.

TS: I really like the question you posed before: whose ground was shattered by Bandung? Yes, it might have shattered global elites ground, but at the same time, the plurality of local histories was destroyed.

BANDUNG SPIRIT AS PRESENCE AND ABSENCE

RI: I heard about Bandung for the second time in my life thanks to the 2006 World Social Forum (WSF) Bamako Appeal controversy. The Bamako Appeal launched by Samir Amin and other "organic intellectuals" stimulated a debate among WSF participants about the need for a WSF manifesto or consensus in which neoliberalism became identified as the main "enemy" of progressive leftist global forces. At that time, I was doing research *about* Mexican transnational activism against free trade and on the WSF politics. For me the most important aspect of the Bamako Appeal was its call for a "People's" Bandung. The inclusion of "people's" meant to me an invitation to think how limiting was to understand "the international" and "global politics" from the exclusive dimension of nation-states dynamics.

It was also equally important for me that Bandung was present again. Please, bear in mind that I was coming from Mexican IR academia in which Bandung as a key geopolitical event was erased from IR BA 1990s curricula. This had important implications for a whole generation of "Mexican" – and I would say Latin American – internationalists.

TS: Did you receive any teaching about South East Asia at all?

RI: Yes, but with a specific perspective that Arlene Tickner (2003) explains as IR in Latin America as Anglo-Relations (and to lesser extent European) but not "international." In the 1990s, I was an IR student in a neoliberal university. Bandung was simply erased from the curricula. How can I explain this? Well, this is the decade of consolidation of the TINA ideology (There is No Alternative to neoliberalism) in the country and in IR academia meant the prevalence of neoliberal institutionalism theory in IR while dependentistas were left behind, "revolutions" and "emancipations" had failed and liberation movements or autonomy projects were simply unthinkable. Adapt, integrate to the global economy or perish! That was the motto.

Nonetheless, I was lucky enough to have as a teacher the only Mexican expert on the Philippines who is an historian. In her class "History of International Relations" I read about the two "World Wars" as Inter-European Wars in the eyes of an Indian scholar, we read Nehru's discourses, and read about Bandung.

So, it was a matter of luck that I read about Bandung, Sukarno, Nasser, Nehru, and so on. This was an exception not the rule.

In this context, the Non-Alignment Movement as an off-spring of Bandung was understood in IR curricula as an example of "Mexican populism of President Luis Echeverria" who belonged to the Partido Revolucionario Institucional, the political party that stayed in power for over seventy years and that has recently came back. So, the Spirit of Bandung became a nightmare!

President Echeverria, the national champion of the Non Alignment Movement who received a nomination to the Nobel Prize in 1974 due to his efforts in promoting the Letter on the Duties of the Rights and Duties of the States, was the man who organized the 1968's killing of students in Tlatelolco!

This framed my learning about Bandung and the Non-Alignment Movement discourses with a lot of initial distrust. Nonetheless, to have the opportunity to read about South-East Asian and Indian perspectives on "the international" instigate in me an appetite for challenging the limits of the Anglo-Saxon canon in IR, and later on of my own disciplinary boundaries. The very possibility of opening local histories became very powerful for me and has been with me since then.

So, for me what is at stake in the meanings of Bandung is also the colonization of the mind, which entails the incapacity to think, and theorized beyond the Western/Anglo-Saxon canon in IR. Colonization of the imagination is very present in a generation of IR scholars in Mexico and other Latin American Countries. But then in this context, Bandung becomes part of the hidden histories in International (Anglo) Relations in Mexico.

TS: I think that the same caution you have for the Non-Alignment Movement due to your own formative-personal experiences is the same caution I have about Bandung.

RI: Is it because the way you were educated about it? Because we were educated about other historical facts in foreign policy such as the Cuban-US missile crisis, it is part of the curricula. Did you ever hear about it?

TS: This is exactly where I want to move now. So, you knew about Bandung just because you were lucky enough to have a teacher who had an interest in Asia. It was not part of the curricula, like Latin American issues are not part of our curricula in Indonesia. We, of course learnt about European history as they were our colonizers; we learnt about the US. We don't really study India; I educated myself about Indian history, but because some parts of Indonesia have shared legends with India. But, are we educated about African countries and nations history? No, nothing. Are we educated about Latin American countries, nations or struggles? No, of course, nothing.

RI: So, Bandung Spirit has not really landed in BA or high-school curricula after sixty years?

TS: Well, I actually have to go back to my high-school history books but as far as I remember it was taught as an International Conference organized by the

Indonesian nation-state. Indeed, what I have learnt about the history of my country and its plurality of peoples, I learnt it here, when I came to the Netherlands, to ISS. Please bear in mind that I was not a student of IR, so maybe IR students received more materials regarding Bandung conference.

If I knew something about Latin America it was not in the University as a BA but because of my activism with Franciscans' commission of Justice and Peace in Jakarta who introduced me to ideas of Monsignor Romero and Liberation Theology. Then I knew, there are other alternatives, there are other versions. But, it was an encounter from which I was lucky too, in a context in which Liberation Theology etc. was seen as "leftish," and often associated with "communist," which is banned in Indonesia.

BANDUNG EVENT/PLACE

RI: Which is the dominant narrative in official Indonesian education about Bandung?

TS: We learnt about the conference as an event in which "our country" played a very important role. It is introduced early in primary or secondary school. It is taught in way that at the end it is taken for granted. Interestingly, nothing was said or at least it was not emphasized that it was the first international conference of people of color. I learnt and understood its relevance about it here doing my research on Dutch colonialism in Indonesia.

Therefore, Bandung is taught as part of the process of nation-state building. For me History is telling stories of your own people. But, when we learnt History of Bandung Conference is about events, dates and how important it was for Indonesian nation-state building. We actually never spoke about "Bandung Conference." We learnt and spoke about it as KAA (*Konferensi Asia-Afrika*, Asian-African Conference). Bandung was just the venue for us, and Bandung has so many meanings for me/us in Indonesia.

RI: Exactly, Bandung means so many things! In IR academic community it is immediately related to the conference.

TS: But Bandung means so many things in the history of Indonesia. Bandung for Indonesians means the place, the city, while for the IR community that you mention, Bandung is the conference. Furthermore, Bandung as a place is so related to colonial history. It was the *Paris of Java* (or *Parijs van Java* in Dutch) during colonial times. It was a beautiful place to which people used to go to enjoy their Villas and the cooler weather. Plantations also surrounded the place, of course. Now, Bandung is part of West Java and the popular-racist claim is that "the most beautiful women" come from this region because of the mix with the Dutch. In the plantation area, the Dutch had formal concubines that were kept within the house or "informal" concubines in the sense that they were women they raped.

After the independence, Bandung was almost captured by the British and their allies, so the Revolutionaries decided to burn out the city. The Northern part of Bandung was eventually captured, and the Southern part was evacuated and set on fire. Bandung is also about evacuation and destruction by the "Revolutionary" fire known as *Bandung Lautan Api* (Bandung The Sea of Fire).

RI: Bandung as a place of colonial violence in the form of labor and sexual exploitation, as the place of destruction by Revolutionary fire.

TS: Today Bandung is a place near Jakarta where people go to enjoy cooler weather. So, when I am asked what is the meaning of Bandung, it is also about the local history of the place and its peoples.

RI: Bandung is not only an event but also a place.

TS: This is very important, because your understanding of Bandung is of an event, a political one with epistemic delinking possibilities, whereas I understand it as a place shaped by local histories.

RI: Yes, from this perspective, one of the multiple meanings of Bandung is of a top-down inter-state event, that as a global design erases the plurality of incarnated local experiences such as the colonial sexual and labor exploitation and of nationalities and ways of being.

This becomes important because then our understandings of Bandung, as a place in which a political event of people of color took place become richer. I think so. Bandung the event that might contribute to challenge the dominant narrative of modernity/coloniality can be read as an act of resistance that didn't happen in the abstract vacuum of the modern/colonial objectivity of the no place, no body. It sits in a plurality of incarnated experiences of coloniality.

TS: The place in itself is not empty or free from histories. The origin of the city of Bandung sits in a local legend of *Sangkuriang* and his mother *Dayang Sumbi* which local people share with outsiders.

RI: What I learnt from all of this is to think Bandung as the place, with all the politics of incarnated local histories and violences, a place with local legends. I think that this dimension will add to the readings of Bandung that are focused in the geopolitics of knowledge, by thinking it from what decolonial feminist Maria Lugones will refer to as a "place of vulnerability" as concrete incarnated experiences which decentre the dominant thinking from the nowhere of abstraction and that turns the world into "systems."

TS: Yes, talking about Bandung in the context of the Cold War is one epistemic location. Looking at it from the continuous colonization process would be another epistemic location. When the context is just one of these dimensions, for me it is depoliticization that results in taking for granted local histories.

I don't want to give the impression that there should be "one" way of understanding the Bandung and its legacies. What I try to say is that the meanings we attach to this conference might change if we know the whole plurality of histories, for example: by understanding that Bandung does not always mean the 1955 conference to people based in Bandung, the place. So, for me this is an option not a claim.

RI: I would like to finish by emphasizing that for me Bandung is both: event in the history of speaking to power and in this way of challenging it; but it is also a place. From this perspective, to revive "the Spirit of Bandung" in a critical way means that these two dimensions become visible. The question is not about de-romanticizing Bandung, or defining if it is delinking or not, but to understand how as an event it shattered the lives of many people and as a place in its plurality of histories.

Tamara, this conference has been read as the first International Conference of peoples of color. Does this resonate with your own activism on West Papua?

TS: I would like to finish by saying that learning about Bandung even with all the problems I already spoke about, make me think of how much we have been forced to move back! Bandung resonates in the following way. I would like to understand how we moved from this claim of a "peoples of color" conference to now. In betraying this idea, we betrayed ourselves. Papua was given to Indonesia because there was disbelief that Papuans could survive as an independent nation. I am currently trying to understand the historical origins of the racialization of some people in Indonesia and of the idea of Javanese people as the right way to be Indonesian because of their lighter skin and straight hair.

In one of the demonstrations in Jakarta in the early 2000s, we gathered with West Papuan students outside the Parliament and I overheard the national intelligence referring to West Papuan students as "monkeys." The East Timorese, the West Papuans – they are labelled "the monkeys." This is the kind of racism that we have in Indonesia.

So, if Bandung is about delinking what about self-reflexivity? This is one of the strongest points of speaking/thinking decolonial. Look back critically into yourself. I think that Bandung the event of "peoples of color," was looking critically to just one side. West Papua is just one of the experiences of this lack of self-reflexivity.

NOTES

1. See also "Decolonizing the 'Cold War' / Be.Bop 2013. Black Europe Body Politics." https://decolonizingthecoldwar.wordpress.com/.

2. For Vazquez (2014) understanding modernity/coloniality as two different movements or forms of relationship with reality, and not "two structural logics" makes possible to highlight their different locus of enunciation: the historical movement of modernity as from which hegemony and privilege has named reality, whereas the historical movement of coloniality is understood as the locus from which the negation of realities and worlds otherwise that exceed the dominant modern geo-genealogy of modernity takes place.

3. "Bandung at 60: Toward a Genealogy of the Global Present," 18 June 2015.

CONCLUSIONS

Chapter 17

The Bandung Within

Mustapha Kamal Pasha

This leprous daybreak, dawn night's fangs have mangled –
This is not that long-looked-for break of day,
Not that clear dawn in quest of which those comrades
Set out, believing that in heaven's wide void
Somewhere must be the stars' last halting-place,
Somewhere the verge of night's slow-washing tide,
Somewhere an anchorage for the ship of heartache.

—Faiz (1947: 123–125)

THE BANDUNG MOMENT

The decolonial impulse for a non-Eurocentric habitation within IR has rarely produced its own archive. Neglected, erased or silenced, the "Bandung moment" (Pasha 2013) has seen rebirths and reversals in equal measure. New decolonized spaces have attracted swift campaigns of pacification, seeking to restore the natural order. Yet, the Bandung moment *within* has stubbornly resisted its own passing. How is it possible to probe the contexts of this impulse within IR, linking it to the memory of Bandung in world politics? Is it thinkable to produce a narrative that parallels yet avoids a strict analogue between Bandung and the imprint of varied struggles in the discipline for alter self-affirmation? Can the Bandung *within* furnish resources for contesting and denaturalizing Western IR?

Bandung enters the political senses principally as memory – a world of promise, but also of loss; of great expectations diminished by co-optation and compromise, yet hopes never completely fading in the face of imperial subterfuge. Lighting up the horizons of new ex-colonials and those still aspiring to be free, Bandung sits apart from time's linear pathway. Once a footnote in the Cold War's high drama, Bandung presents a liberation from the (colonial) past. But, it also evokes mixed responses, as aspiration and failure. Unable to overcome the historical burden of subordination, ex-colonials sought refuge in the ideology of non-alignment. This was not the terrain of capitulation. The failure ultimately resided in their confinement in the Westphalian prison-house with its internal logics of nationalism and embrace of the teleology of development. Neither the fiction of homogenized political space conceived in European theories linking blood with identity nor the myth of material salvation within fixed spaces produced an alternative world or a different humanism (Fanon 2004). Forgotten in the euphoria of political independence was the logic of coloniality, as thought, structure and practice. The postcolonial world never arrived, as the great South Asian poet Faiz muses.

Political independence was no trivial achievement after decades and centuries of dehumanizing European domination. Not merely foreign dominion over territory or resources, nor the enlightened passage of the savage to civilization, colonialism was subjection without selfhood, separating the colonized body from its soul. Imperial nostalgia paints a picture of gift-giving in which the colonizer displays astonishing generosity towards unfamiliar natives. The gift is a most spectacular one since it is not simply about its material worth, but its symbolic, cosmological and ideational properties which have transformative effects on materiality: notions of property and selfhood, manners and etiquette, science and reason, and a religion of Salvation. In short, a new (superior) mode of being. In return, the natives are merely asked to part away their means of material sustenance, including land and labour, an (inferior) culture and their primitive selves attached to magic, superstition or apostasy.

The myth of "colonialism as gift-giving" persists. Critics are placed in the impossible position of acknowledging the "mixed" blessings of colonialism. Often the argument goes as follows: After all, many postcolonial regimes have failed or are failing; they lag behind their former colonial masters in the area of "human" rights, diminished by crippling postcolonial institutions and corruption. Through this interpretative trickery, the contrast is supposed to legitimize the past. Overlooked in this dominant narrative is the impregnation of colonial violence in the structure of world politics and its cognate expressions in thought and being. The specificity of this violence resides in perpetuating a colonial order of humanity, a racialized gradation of cultures and populations expressed in uneven access to citizenship, rights and wealth.

Imperial historiography glorifies the pedagogical role played by Europe in uplifting the natives from their childlike state into maturity. The education of the colonial world, however, also produced the Bandung generation, one that could hold back the mirror to the educator and demand equality on the international stage. This apparently surprising development was a worrisome sign for both the erstwhile colonizing powers and the emerging hyper-power. Bandung spoke a universal language in a vernacular postcolonial dialect. No measure of revisionism could jettison the intrinsic value of anti-colonial struggle and its legacies. Ideas of self-determination and self-governance, despite elite reversals, had given the Bandung generation the capacity to aspire for a better future. Political independence, as the conference unfolded, negated the colonial denial of being. Above all, the notion of solidarity was an anathema to the Westphalian scheme that only acknowledged rival national identities and interests. How could former colonials forge a common language seeking an alternative world order? Bandung sought deliverance from the colonial form of the Westphalian order.

Bandung, however, cannot be placed as a datum on modern time's linear canvass. Linear time allows few thinking spaces to fully comprehend Bandung's significance or its living legacy. In contrast to the empty time of received consciousness, Bandung's real meaning lies on the trajectory of *political* time, a register of breaks interrupting the smooth flow of routine. A revolt against "imperial time" (Pasha 2013), Bandung reconstructs the standard historical European narrative of progress by connecting modernity with coloniality (Quijano 2000), giving subaltern faces and voices a global stage to be seen and heard. An alternative to chronological time, political time captures the experience of both immediacy and transcendence, allowing the past to surrender to an anticipated, if unrealized, future. In coming together collectively to seek alternatives to the established order, the ex-colonials at Bandung were defying colonial expectations of conformity to the world order they had produced (Prashad 2007). Admittedly, the aims were modest, yet equally revolutionary in the symbolism alone. The claim by "new" nations for sovereign equality promised by the European-based Westphalian system was radical enough (Lee 2010). More drastic was the call for non-alignment, a willingness to stay away from the Manichean ideological divisions of the Cold War. Nominally, little defiance can be adduced from a meeting of ex-colonials in a provincial city of a former Dutch colony. Yet the ability to converse with self-confidence about the contours of an alternative world, in the face of Western political and cultural hegemony which authorized the right to speak, ruptured imperial time.

The Cold War was "cold" only for its progenitors, not for the Third World still confronting active colonialism in most parts of the African continent, South East Asia and the South Pacific. Political independence had only arrived in a handful of nations; decolonization was forcefully resisted by European colonialism as future events in Algeria and South Africa would clearly demonstrate. On the other side, as the theatre of violent "proxy" conflicts engineered by the two superpowers threatened humanity with nuclear weapons, the "developing world" was swiftly becoming the actual battleground of "hidden" wars. Non-alignment was not a mere token gesture, but an expression of an alternative stance for constituting a different international society shared by the former colonies. The Cold War, far in excess of what the Bandung leaders had warned, proved to be a deadly affair, accounting for the deaths of over 20 million people (Halliday 1990). Ironically, the end of the Cold War also evidenced the demise of the Third World and solidarities forged in its name. However, the Bandung impulse did not entirely face the same fate. The decolonial expectation congealed in the singularity and boldness of its assertion continues to unsettle the colonial order of things.

From the vantage point of realist statecraft, the Bandung Conference was simply a postcolonial Melian cry for equality and justice, a short-lived and largely unsuccessful effort in generating an alternative world order. There would be other moments such as the calls for an New International Economic Order (NIEO), but these proved to be transient. Non-alignment was problematic even at the time of the historic meeting in 1955 and despite growth in numbers of those nations hitching their public stance to that label, superpower alignment remained the paramount force in driving international relations. However, even in its presumed failure, the basic principles and code of conduct (Tan and Acharya 2008) promoted by the Bandung delegates continue to produce a different vision to Western intervention and interference usually in the name of rights, democracy and humanitarianism. The emphasis on dialogue, not conflict, envisioned at Bandung presents an enduring counter-legacy to the simplistic verities of the "clash of civilizations."

THE BANDUNG WITHIN

Is there an analogue to the Bandung moment in IR? To the degree that "theories of international relations are more interesting as aspects of contemporary world politics that need to be explained than as explanations of contemporary world politics" (Walker 1993: 6), their presumed neutrality is questionable. As a part of the discursive formation fabricating and reproducing the "West" and its "Others," Western IR remains central to the ideational and real divide in world politics. Hegemony now travels from the West to non-West, concluding the Hegelian story of progress in which the journey was once in the opposite direction. In the service of power, IR has played a significant role on this great voyage, alongside anthropology and sociology.

The question of complicity can be controversial. However, it is difficult to refute the continued colonial frame deployed in Western IR – in discourses of development and state-building, political stability and violence, nationalism and cosmopolitanism, human rights, responsibility to protect, or the clash of civilizations. The (former) colonial world is not simply imagined in colonial terms but is expected to relate to the West, knowing its subordinate place. Exceeding the horizon "gifted" by the West to the former colonies, as in Bandung, can invite scorn, sanction or even intervention and conquest. Against this image, the postcolonial moment is "not that long-looked-for break of day." Despite the "reflexive" turn in IR, the foundational categories and practices it has helped spawn, reflect a colonial order of being or the "colonial present" (Gregory 2004). The conceptual apparatus of IR continues to supply both the frame and rationale to maintain an uneven world order in which the majority of the world's inhabitants endure more refined forms of coloniality.

The glass is not entirely half-empty, though. Disciplinary IR's legendary refusal to address both coloniality as the historical past of the contemporary world order and coloniality's instantiation as racially differentiated spatio-temporal "international" relations, is increasingly catechized in postcolonial and decolonial thought. Greater representation of non-Western thought (Shilliam 2010) previously marginal to the discipline, as well as sensitivity to different "national" IRs (Tickner and Wæver 2009) have taken noteworthy steps to overcome IR's provincialism. Interventions in historical sociology (Hobson 2012) or critical security studies (Barkawi and Laffey 2006) build upon earlier work (Darby and Paolini 1994) designed to open up the conversation. Within the Anglo-American centres of knowledge production more generally, reflexivity is a rite of passage for demonstrating scholarly literacy. Both anthropology and sociology, as well as history, have their own stories to tell about resistance and struggle, insurrection and appeasement.

Reception to critiques of Eurocentrism within IR's liberal academy is no longer exceptional, but progressively normalized. It affirms the existence of diversity and forbearance in sync with the changing cultural order of *political* hegemony. Unlike the world in which Bandung germinated, the disciplinary spaces within today's Western academic public sphere are more hospitable, compared to an earlier "postcolonial" period. However, postcolonial critique is embraced principally as *spectacle, not politics*. Postcolonial thinking appears in its ideal-typical form as personified alterity. As with domesticated critique more broadly, postcolonial critique is estranged from politics, inseparable from the "native" informants within a largely orientalist cultural economy. Dissent is strictly professionalized, unconnected to the wider terrain of politics. Unavoidably, membership has its privileges and responsibilities, especially the expectation of sustained self-orientalized performativity by knowledgeable native experts. Many "postcolonial" voices, like their erstwhile critical partners in the academy, accept the seduction of this address, fully recognizing the rules of the craft. Self-orientalism and coloniality can, hence, go hand in hand. The former allows the circulation of alter-identities; the latter ensures that established rules are never broken. Hence, the easy flow of self-orientalized alter-identities preserves the colonial order, which is, in fact, the former's condition of possibility.

The Bandung moment in IR as analogue is a turn towards multilingualism, both in terms of greater reflexivity as well as an acknowledgement of difference. Unlike Bandung's singular temporality, however, the IR complement takes the profile of multiple ruptures, often overlapping but following manifold, albeit non-linear, temporal pathways. Reflexivity takes the appearance of dissidence towards normal science, congealed principally in critiques of the realist canon, and its primal affinities with liberal imaginings of state and society, or their presumed absence in international space (Ashley and Walker 1990). In essence, the battles have raged over Western meta-theory, over the potency or infirmity of categories designed to provide reliable accounts of the social and political worlds. Drawn from a series of crises, both existential and philosophical, IR has been busily catching up translating Western angst reflected in Anglo-American sentience of the scale of horrors of the two world wars, the Holocaust and Việt Nam. The "colonial deficit" in these delayed exercises of awareness, is significant, but unsurprising. Critical theory's reflexivity swiftly reveals its cultural limits as soon as it reaches the edges of the non-West, the zone of unassimilable difference. Culturally myopic, claims of reflexivity parallel theological disputations within recognized monotheistic boundaries. Unaware of its own cultural limits, critical theory's alleged insurgency against IR's holy empire appears against the burden of history as mostly self-serving, merely advancing the liberal project of orchestrated dissent. Perhaps, this characterization is too harsh. What is undeniable, though, is how unreflective critical IR is in approaching non-Western alterity.

On balance, the discipline appears more relaxed about acceding greater representation to "dissident" voices and recognition of difference. With institutional openness and celebration of plurality and in accord with the spirit of liberal philanthropy, critical perspectives do not need to be banished (Ashley and Walker 1990). These perspectives now serve, like vegetarian options, as alternative dishes on the liberal *carte du jour*. Only a generation ago, however, it was not the spirit of benevolence that described this dramatic shift, but concrete intellectual scuffles forcing real consequences. In its hegemonic methodological form, especially, the history of Western IR is dotted with strategies of exile, silencing, marginalization or erasure towards critical interventions. Each of these strategies, either in union or independently, produced real material and symbolic effects for several of those who harboured unorthodox views about the shape of the international and challenged the hegemonic paradigms helping constitute it. Combining sustained interrogation of the canon with the stratagem of intellectual embarrassment, critical IR scholars made significant contributions to unshackle IR from monolingualism. The inheritors of the fruits of past labours need not worry about being written off from IR's stage for espousing Foucauldian or Derridian prose. Rather, the more critical the voice, greater is the recognition for assumed theoretical erudition. Neither silence nor exile awaits academic subjects in the neo-liberal university.

Ironically, the key challenge facing decolonial thought is that difference can now be entertained in IR's institutional corridors, coexisting with established perspectives, but only in *domesticated* spaces. Self-assured in its Enlightenment potential, IR has successfully rediscovered and reinvented itself. A part of this rediscovery and reinvention has been to allow different voices to be heard; representation and recognition of alternative perspectives can only help fortify the institutional fortresses. Unfettered by critique, hegemonic IR can display magnanimity without compromising on essentials: the West as a universal reference for claims of justice and human rights, cosmopolitanism and democracy, or development and societal form. It is the universalism of Western IR that requires permanent deconstruction, not in the self-referential deconstructive, but decolonial mode.

The postcolonial predicament faced by the Bandung nations also confronts IR: to forge alternative visions of the world while operating with colonial space. However, this is only a part, albeit salient part, of the problem. A more serious issue lies with the character of critical thinking itself, chiefly its refusal to escape the disciplinary prison-house of what constitutes theory. Decolonial thought is not only interdisciplinary, but also transdisciplinary; it does not subscribe to received attachments to Western cosmological, ontological, or methodological regulative principles; those principles themselves continue to produce the seeds of hegemony. They ensure that alternative cultural horizons remain subordinate in order to be noticed. But critical theory itself has been reluctant to discard Eurocentrism. Even in critiquing Eurocentrism, it has relied on Eurocentric modes of thought.

A principal task of revitalizing the Bandung spirit within IR is to discover new pathways connecting critiques of Eurocentrism to producing a self-subsistent decolonial archive. This project would necessarily entail a repudiation of the colonial matrix of power (Quijano 2000): the recognition that despite hegemonic claims of plenitude, anti-colonial struggles, both hidden and revealed, have created affective, symbolic, and material registers of alterity that need not depend on either Western sovereign authorization or complicity with power to be sustainable. In repudiating the deep structure of knowledge production, which is premised on the tacit agreement that the wellsprings of knowledge, including critique, flow from Europe, a decolonial archive would also produce alternative genealogies of critical thought, taking postcolonial and decolonial thinking not as derivations of post-structural, or more broadly, postmodern critique, but as reflections on the colonial problem as thought and practice, inseparable from the historical conditions of its germination and legacy.

The project of producing an alternative decolonial archive, however, remains incipient, an unfulfilled promise. Paradoxically, the consolidation of domesticated postcolonial dissent often serves as the principal obstacle to creating decolonial thinking spaces. Located strictly within sites of managed diversity, postcolonialism can effortlessly pass the test, not as an adversary, but as liberalism's ally. This tacit alliance ensures that no professional sacrifice or pain for its subsidiary (postcolonial) partners is extracted. The first task for creating decolonial zones, therefore, is *reflexive disentanglement* from self-orientalized performativity, including exposure of the limits and pitfalls of self-orientalism. Trapped within the thinking zones of received language and syntax, mimicry or mere gesturing readily materialize as available options. These are typically embraced in attempts to forge alternative avenues of thought.

By contrast, other idioms need to be deployed to make the language of IR correspond to subaltern histories, subjectivities and political desires. Ultimately, though, a decolonial archive is unimaginable without the invention of a new language, one that rests on a refusal to see the world only through Western eyes or to cater to Western taste. It would not only seek to uncover the distortions inherent in hegemonic frames, but actively take other spatio-temporal horizons not merely as alternatives, but as coeval and equal perspectives of the world. These perspectives are not simply remnants of past images available for decoding, but living world designs inhabiting life-worlds of the many who refuse assimilation into a singular cultural vortex. Drawn from other or mixed genealogies, these world perspectives sustain different political and personal desires for sociability and community, not fulfilling a preordained project of history. A decolonial archive cannot simply be found in the recesses of critical theory, but in the rediscovery of anticolonial contestations and struggles, in projects of excavating different ontological moments of emancipatory thought and action (e.g. the Haitian Revolution, not simply the French Revolution); in recognizing other actors and movements writing historical scripts and in other languages and vernaculars; and in identifying alternate understandings of what constitutes humanity or the meaning of what it means to be human. A decolonial archive would depend upon reviving the Bandung impulse, not merely as remembrance or commemoration, but through sustained interrogation of the colonial problem that has refused to fade away with the arrival of the "global" modern or globalization and liberal dreams of cosmopolitanism and a "flat" world.

How can the Bandung impulse be sustained within IR? The growing professionalization of postcolonial/decolonial thinking is unlikely to produce a decolonial archive. Without forging links with actual decolonial struggles, both within the neo-liberal academy and the wider world of alterities, decolonial thought can merely become yet another pathway towards individuated professional achievement, not decentring the colonial matrix of power, but actually reinforcing it. The greater the move towards professionalization, the greater is the peril of surrender. Neither appeals for a more reflexive IR nor calls to make Bandung speak to the world can resolve the essential dilemma facing decolonial thought: the immanent liberal universe in which claims of transcendence can be made without much discomfort. The real Bandung would show a way out.

To the extent that Bandung is not merely a moment of arrival, but a moment of being and becoming, decolonial thought needs to look closely at what transpired in that singular temporality. Bandung recognized the actuality of colonialism in places that remained unrepresented. The spectral presence of incomplete decolonization was not distant from those that were fortunate to be at Bandung. They understood colonialism, not as an abstraction, but as fact. The actuality of existing colonialism, not the illusive charms of political independence, stirred the Bandung dreamers. Foremost on their minds was decolonization. Can this be said about the interlocutors of current decolonial thought?

A tangible strategy to realize the promise of decolonial thinking lies in recognizing the differentiated states of being within the academy, while pursuing the project of undoing hegemonic thinking. The spaces within the academy are largely averse to difference.

Demographics can be deceptive, but in this instance they gesture towards a larger problem of silence. The accumulated poverty of absence now appears in stark detail. Without addressing the politics of *this* silence, it is inconceivable that decolonial thought can accomplish what it seeks. Hence, the need to link decolonial thought with a political engagement with *colonial* spaces. To avoid the pitfalls of self-referential critique, the Bandung spirit can once again attach itself to the project of decolonization. In this instance, it is the academic world itself.

Chapter 18

Afterword

Bandung as a Research Agenda

Craig N. Murphy

I first wrote about the 1955 Bandung Conference in my doctoral dissertation, a political history of the ideas underlying the New International Economic Order (NIEO) proposals of the 1970s. The connections I made between Bandung and the NIEO were not as rich as those made by Heloise Weber in this volume, but I was writing more than thirty years ago. I described Bandung as a reaction to the eroding commitment of the military victors in the Second World War to principles they had affirmed throughout the war as a way of encouraging support among the largely subject peoples of Asia and Africa (and among the "non-combatant United Nations," independent countries primarily in Latin America). The Bandung conferees emphasized decolonization, the commitment to provide development assistance to others no matter what their economic system, the imperative that the postwar UN system quickly becomes and remains universal, and the UN Charter and fundamental human rights as the unity within which the desirable diversity of national systems should thrive (Murphy 1984, 37–46). As Sam Okoth Opondo reminds us in this volume, the Bandung principles were taken back to the UN for universal reaffirmation by the General Assembly in 1957.

At Bandung, the Third World alliance that was beginning to emerge did not question Enlightenment modernism and had not yet agreed on the desirability of non-alignment between the Cold War adversaries, or even the ubiquity and significance of the global colour line, even though some of the principal speeches at the conference pointed in these directions, as Anna Agathangelou notes in her chapter. Moreover, all of the conferees were well schooled in years of scepticism of the liberal and internationalist intentions of the great powers. In a typical 1943 article on "Post-War Economic Planning," the director of the Bengali Institute of Economics, Benoy Kumar Sarkar gave a great deal of attention to the anti-colonial, anti-racist, and pro-development views of liberal American pundits, but concluded that within five years of the end of the war, more traditional American views would come to dominate policy: "neither de-imperialization nor de-albinization is envisaged." A militarized world of competitive imperialism (called "neo-colonialism") with the Soviets likely ruling their own adjacent empire was all but inevitable, and, "neo-colonialism is not in for world peace" (Sarkar 1943, 186).

Sarkar's forecast may have been more accurate than those of any of the principals at Bandung. Nasser imagined his fellow North Africans and Southwest Asians would continue to be regarded as privileged "whites." Nehru believed that non-alignment would become a real third force in world politics, one that would tame militarization. Sukarno expected that substantive "unity" really could arise out of the diversity of people united within the colonial borders of his, and many other postcolonial countries.

On the other hand, while I am not certain, I doubt that any – except perhaps Sukarno – anticipated the range and depth of the meanings that would become attached to the conference after two generations. It is no longer just one of dozens of surprisingly similar conferences, dozens of points in the lines of development of non-alignment, the NIEO or the revolt of the Global South. It is a symbol and a political myth, a meaningful story told scores of different ways, to different audiences, to different effects. This book tells us a great deal about this larger Bandung, but there is much more to study, much more to learn.

Here are five suggestions, taken from this book, for future scholars of Bandung, what came before, and what came after.

1. Dig where you are standing.[1]

Rachmi Diyah Larasati, Rahul Rao, Rosabla Icaza and Tamara Soukotta all in this volume point out different ways that this can be done. All provide personal, connected narratives that demonstrate particular aspects within the changing solidarity within the Global South and the ubiquity of global fault lines of Bandung. I suspect that every reader could do the same.

In my own case, I know that I wrote a dissertation at the University of North Carolina that touched upon Bandung because as an undergraduate at a small Iowa college I had gone to Ghana to study the impact of an international commodity agreement on local farmers. I was interested in Ghana in part because Sherin Kamal, a junior high-school friend in Norway, had told me all about Nasser. Sherin's father, the Egyptian ambassador, had been part of the Free Officers' Movement. I also was curious about Ghana because, when I was a child, my father, a US Air Force officer, always pointed out to me the stories in the newspaper about the new countries in Africa that had just become independent. We located them on the map and my father always reminded me that his close friend, my godfather Richard P. McCormick had gone to graduate school at the University of Pennsylvania with Francis Nkrumah, now Kwame – "Africa's George Washington" – while my father navigated bombers between England and Germany.

For most of us, perhaps, the more interesting stories are not personal, but institutional. It is here where all readers are likely to find Bandung stories right where they are standing. I realized this by accident while reading Robert Vitalis's (2015) outstanding *White World Order, Black Power Politics: The Birth of American International Relations*. I wondered about whether W. E. B. Du Bois, Ralph Bunche and others Vitalis discusses had ever published on international relations in journals that included authors more sympathetic to the black scholars' views than the racist liberal internationalists in charge of *The Journal of Race Development* (later known as *Foreign Affairs*). I quickly found three such people in my own backyard. Anti-imperialist socialists of Du Bois's generation on the Wellesley faculty, women who were friends of Rosa Luxemburg and Karl Leibknecht, campaigners against the US occupation of Haiti and parts of Central America, whose students included a leading Filipina revolutionary, and who were fired or excluded from the faculty of international relations after they were caught up in the Red Scare of the First World War (Murphy 2015). I had taught IR at Wellesley for thirty years and had only heard the story of one of these three women. This seemed particular surprising because Wellesley has a strong, frequently recalled, Anglican social gospel-oriented tradition and one of these scholars, Vida Scudder, who was both a Marxist and an Episcopalian, is recognized on the liturgical calendar: October 10th; her saint's day conveniently replacing the national "Columbus Day" celebration.

Scudder and her colleagues turned out to be only the first of many generations of Wellesley international relations scholars who were socialists and many of whom collaborated with African, African American and Afro-Caribbean scholars in Vitalis's book. The Wellesley women have been forgotten, even in the place where I stand, because, through the 1960s, all were subjects of one or more of the United States' successive Red Scares. Randolph Persaud in this volume and others makes it clear that the histories of anti-racist/anti-colonial solidarity and radical socialist activism cannot be separated. Wellesley's little story is another instance.

2. Look for longer cultural (and other) connections.

The stories of the forgotten black and socialist scholars are not only about the suppression of ideas within the field of international relations, but they are also stories of forgotten or misremembered solidarities. Siba Grovogui and Mustapha Pasha in this volume both emphasize what has been forgotten

Craig N. Murphy

or left out as part of what is really a cultural analysis of IR. It is worthwhile to read their contributions alongside both Rachmi Diyah Larasati's personal deconstruction of one of the thousands of popular cultural sharings that have political import and that take place across the world every day, and Amy Niang's discussion of the shift in African independence discourse after Bandung. Taken together, they suggest to me that future scholars of Bandung should be willing to look almost anywhere for connections between colonized communities that may have had political import.

I am reminded of another, later "Bandung story" I discovered among the IR community at Wellesley. In 1960 a later generation of Wellesley scholars on the left from various departments invited various other scholars and political activists (Julius Nyerere was perhaps the most prominent) to come to the college to talk about the future of Africa. The initiative seems to have emanated from Gwendolen Carter, who started her career at Wellesley and was one of the founders of African studies in the United States. The first session was led by Carter's friend Ralph Bunche, the former Howard University professor who is often credited with inventing UN peacekeeping and who had received the Nobel Peace Prize ten years earlier.

During the session Melville Herskovits, the man who was already happy to be identified as *the* founder of African studies in the United States pontificated a bit about how pan-Africanism was really something that only involved British Africa; the French had a cultural sort of thing that was very different, and there was nothing like this kind of solidarity movement in Lusophone Africa, and that none of these things really mattered because Africans weren't yet very good at such international cooperation.

Bunche along with Carter quietly objected, reminding Herskovits of Du Bois and other African and Caribbean Americans, suggesting that perhaps the difference between the cultural and the political was being overdrawn, and saying that he wasn't sure that anyone in the room knew enough about the Portuguese-speaking black world to draw Herskovits's conclusion. Bunche ended with, "I don't share Mr. Herskovits's concern about this, because I think it is true that there is more real internationalism in thought and approach in the African continent than anywhere in the world." Of course, Herskovits had to have the last word: "Yet we must be very careful not to generalize on this case" (*Symposium on Africa* 1960, 38).

There are many ironies here. Perhaps the largest is that in the months immediately preceding and especially the months following this conference, pan-African nationalists launched coordinated armed struggles across Portugal's African colonies. Amilcar Cabral, perhaps the greatest intellectual leader of that movement, who always spoke about the unity among the different movements across Africa (and even farther away, near Bandung, in Timor-Leste) was linked to a cultural movement that began around the same time as the Francophone Négritude movement. Due perhaps to the greater repressiveness of the Portuguese government, the cultural movement was not centred in the metropole, in Lisbon, but in the Brazilian northeast, where the revolutionary Cape Verdean Luís Romano de Madeira Melo published *Famintos: romance do Povo*, perhaps the first novel in an "African" Portuguese. While the novel may have energized Cabral's troops, it was a late development in a revolutionary pan-African cultural tradition that had existed for more than a generation, but a tradition that observers wouldn't find if they looked only in Africa (Hamilton 1975).

This leads to the third suggestion:

3. Look for those who have been overlooked.

Icaza and Soukotta's and Budi Hernawan's chapters emphasize stories of Bandung from the points of view of those that are most often left out of the narrative. Those stories are usually the most revealing. From the point of view of anyone on the non-Javanese periphery of Indonesia, the story of the Bandung Conference has to seem bizarre and tragic. The unified but diverse country that Sukarno hoped to create looks like an exchange of one imperial master for another. Moreover, some of the specifics of the thwarting of national independence are clearly a matter of inter-imperial collusion. This is as much the case with Washington, Lisbon and Jakarta in Timor-Leste as it is with the Dutch, the Western powers and the UN in Papua. Moreover, like many other complex multinational societies, Indonesia still suffers from a hypocritically uneven system of regional autonomy. Timor-Leste has won independence; Aceh has a significant degree of economic and cultural autonomy; while Papua and West Papua are under a more paternal kind of "autonomy" regime, with significantly increasing resources from the centre, but less local control.

There are many places in the world that are isolated, rugged, sparsely populated and even a bit of a nuisance to their central government and to the UN system. In the 1940s, Jorge Barbosa, another one of those Lusophone African authors who helped build solidarity in that part of the Afro-Asian world, described them as the places ignored by "the World Health Organization, Red Cross, Caritas, Salvation Army" and "the elegant ladies later praised by the magazines with photos in Ektachrome displaying collars and crosses shining in their naked breasts" (Barbosa 1986, 82); today it would be enough to say those ignored by Bono and Angelina Jolie.

It is especially useful to try to hear the views of our unequal world of people from such places, but it is also important to remember that those who are isolated and overlooked are not always disconnected. In one of Robbie Shilliam's most evocative and significant short pieces, "Spiritual Bandung," he reminds us that Jamaica's Leonard Percival Howell, known as Tuff Gong, physically isolated with his community in the hills, "enjoyed regular visitations from Rabindranath Tagore. And Reasoned together on anti-colonialism, the nature of reality, the heights." (Shilliam 2014). Tagore also shows up all throughout the pages of Pankaj Mishra's (2012) intellectual history of the early decolonization movements in Asia (and North Africa). Khadija El Alaoui in this volume found him across the Arab world. When I was trying to dig for Bandung in the organizations where I've stood, I found Tagore in the middle of Iowa, as far away from a major city as one can be in the American Midwest. He was visiting Subhinda Bose, a man from Keotkhali, near Dacca, who began teaching "world politics" at the University of Iowa in 1913, studied militarism and the arms trade, corresponded with W. E. B. Du Bois for many years, wrote "Musings on Race Prejudice" comparing the Indian and American versions, and global ramifications, of what Du Bois had called "The Problem of Problems" (Biswas 2008).

So this is the fourth piece of research advice:

4. Look for the people who make the connections among people.

Why do people like Tagore matter? It is not just that they teach isolated people who are potential intellectual and political leaders about the similar concerns and shared struggles of distant others. It is more that the people who make the connections are likely to learn from these many others. Tagore, for example, was a very strange sort to be a globally prominent intellectual in the first decades of the twentieth century. He certainly didn't believe in a few of the core principles of the historical Bandung Conference. For him, both nationalism and modernism were anathema – sources of absurd conflict, of real and spiritual death. Nonetheless, this book is full of voices that are a lot like Tagore's. Himadeep Muppidi writes about a deep and rich sense of the politics of the world that goes beyond Jean-Paul Sartre's and Richard Wright's somewhat self-absorbed reactions to Bandung and the larger processes of which it was a part. Narendran Kumarakulasingam wants us to look beyond the ways governments and rebel armies conceive of national conflicts suppressed by Bandung's state-level "Different but One" motto to the solidarity *and* difference that regularly has arisen in local communities, places where people still "have the ear to listen." Giorgio Shani wants us to remember the "missed opportunity" of Bandung to define a new form of political community, something other than the storm "we call progress." Tagore, and others like him, may know these things because they have talked with the isolated, they have listened to those who still know how to listen, they have met with those who are creating and preserving sacred spaces in high places far enough above the storm that they can look forward rather than back.

So, the fifth and final suggestion for those who will study both future and past Bandungs, both as history and as myth, is:

5. Look for what has been overlooked.

That is to say, look for what has been overlooked by the leaders at the conferences, however courageous and honourable they may be. With them, it may be good to begin where Aida Hozić ended in her chapter. Consider what they did in the same way you would consider what they *remember* about it. Both are evidence of their aspirations; aspirations that might reflect their best selves. In that way, there may still be beautiful parts of the grand disaster of modern history.

NOTE

1. The phrase Sven Lindqvist (1979) uses to name and describe the method of the popular history movement he founded.

Bibliography

Abraham, Itty. 2008. "From Bandung to NAM: Non-alignment and Indian Foreign Policy, 1947-65." *Commonwealth & Comparative Politics* 46 (2): 195–219.
———. 2014. "Prolegomena to Non-Alignment: Race and the International System." In *The Non-Aligned Movement and the Cold War: Delhi –Bandung – Belgrade*, edited by Mišković, Nataša, Fischer-Tiné, Harald, and Boškovska, Nada. New York: Routledge.
Acharya, Amitav. 2014. "Who Are the Norm Makers? The Asian-African Conference in Bandung and the Evolution of Norms." *Global Governance* 20: 405–417.
Acharya, Amitav, and Barry Buzan (eds.). 2007. "Why Is There no Non-Western International Relations Theory: Reflections on and from Asia." *Special Issue of International Relations of the Asia-Pacific* 7 (3): 287–312.
Achebe, Chinua. 1994. *Things Fall Apart*. Anchor Books: New York.
Afro-Asian Peoples' Solidarity Organization. 2005. *Vision of Bandung after 50 years: Confronting the New Challenges*. Cairo: AAPSO publication.
"Afro-Asian Conference." 1955. *Afro-American*, April 9.
Agathangelou, Anna. 2011. "Making Anew an Arab Regional Order? On Poetry, Sex, and Revolution." *Globalizations* 8 (5): 581–594.
———. 2012. "The Living and Being of the Streets: Fanon and the Arab Uprisings." *Globalizations* 9 (3): 451–466.
Agathangelou, Anna, and Kyle D. Killian. 2006. "Epistemologies of Peace: Poetics, Globalization and the Social Justice Movement." *Globalizations* 3 (4): 459–483.
Ahmad, A. 1994. *In Theory: Classes, Nations, Literatures*. London: Verso.
Al-Abnudi, A. 2002. "Our Revolution." *Al-Ahram Weekly*, 18–24 July. http://www.mafhoum.com/press3/nas105-15.htm [Accessed on 26 March 2016].
Al-Kabli, A. n.d. "Asia and Africa's Song." *Arabic Song*. http://www.sm3na.com/audio/87a5394a9c3d [Accessed on 26 March 2016].
Al-Refa'i, H. 1985. *The Complete Collected Poems of Hashem Al-Refa'i*. Al-Zarqa, Jordan: Al-Manar.
Al-Sharqawi, A. R. 1953. "A Message to President Truman from an Egyptian Father." In *Abdel Rahman Al-Sharqawi 1920-1987*, edited by Murwat, Karim, *Al-Ahram*,

31 May 2014. Arabic. http://www.ahram.org.eg/NewsPrint/291017.aspx [Accessed on 14 May 2015].

Al-Udhari, A. ed. 1986. *Modern Poetry of the Arab World*. London: Penguin Books.

"An African British Subject Tells of Ethiopia." 1936. *New Times and Ethiopia News*. 14th November 5–6.

Amin, Samir. 1990. *Delinking: Towards a Polycentric World*. London: Zed Books.

———. 2015. "From Bandung (1955) to 2015: Old and New Challenges for the States, the Nations and the Peoples of Asia, Africa, and Latin America (draft)." *Bandung Spirit*. http://www.bandungspirit.org/IMG/pdf/samir_amin-bandung_oct_2015.pdf.

Ampiah, Kweku. 2007. *The Political and Moral Imperatives of the Bandung Conference of 1955: The Reactions of the US, UK and Japan*. Folkestone, UK: Global Oriental.

Anand, Mulk Raj. 1940. *Untouchable*. London: Penguin.

Anderson, Benedict. 1983. *Imagined Communities*. London: Verso.

Anghie, Antony. 1993. "'The Heart of My Home': Colonialism, Environmental Damage, and the Nauru Case." *Harvard International Law Journal* 34 (2): 445–506.

———. 2004. *Imperialism, Sovereignty and the Making of International Law*. Cambridge: Cambridge University Press.

Appadorai, Angadipuram. 1955. *The Bandung Conference*. New Delhi: Indian Council of World Affairs.

Appiah, Kwame Anthony. 1992. *My Father's House: Africa in the Philosophy of Culture*. New York: Oxford University Press.

Armstrong, Elisabeth. 2016. "Before Bandung: The Anti-Imperialist Women's Movement in Asia and the Women's International Democratic Federation." *Signs* 41 (2): 305–331.

Arroyo, Jossianna. 2013. *Writing Secrecy in Caribbean Freemasonry*. New York: Palgrave McMillan.

Asia-Africa Speaks from Bandung. 1955. Djakarta: The Ministry of Foreign Affairs, Republic of Indonesia.

Ashley, Richard K., and R. B. J. Walker. 1990. "Conclusion: Reading Dissidence/ Writing the Discipline: Crisis and the Question of Sovereignty in International Studies." *International Studies Quarterly* 34 (3): 367–416.

Assie-Lumumba, N'Dri. 2015. "Behind and Beyond Bandung: Historical and Forward-looking Reflections on South-South Cooperation." *Bandung: Journal of the Global South* 2 (11): 1–10.

Baldwin, James. 1998. *Baldwin: Collected Essays*. Edited by Toni Morrison. Library of America.

Bandaranaike, Sirimavo R. D. 1976. "The Non-Alignment Movement and the United Nations." *The Black Scholar* 8 (3): 27–38.

Barbosa da Costa, Larisa, Rosalba Icaza, and Angelica Ocampo Talero. 2015. "Knowledge about, Knowledge with: Dilemmas of Researching Lives, Nature and Genders Otherwise." In *Practising Feminist Political Ecologies*, edited by Harcourt, Wendy and Nelson, Ingrid, 260–285. London: Zed Books.

Barbosa, Jorge. 1986. "Crianças/Children." Jorge Barbosa in English/em Inglés, Rendall Leite (ed. and trans.). Mindelo: Instituto Caboverdeano do Livro, 81–91.

Barkawi, Tarak, and Mark Laffey. 2006. "The Postcolonial Moment in Security Studies." *Review of International Studies* 32 (2): 329–352.

Beckert, Sven. 2014. *Empire of Cotton: A Global History*. New York: Vintage Books.

Berger, Mark T. 2004. *The Battle for Asia: From Decolonization to Globalization*. London: Routledge.

Beisner, Robert L. 1968. *Twelve Against Empire: The Anti-Imperialists 1898-1900*. New York: McGraw-Hill.

Benjamin, Bret. 2015. "Bookend to Bandung: The New International Economic Order and the Antinomies of the Bandung Era." *Humanity: An International Journal of Human Rights, Humanitarianism, and Development* 6 (1): 33–46.

Bennabi, M. [1956] 1981. *L'Afro-Asiatisme*. Trans. Abdel Assabur Shahin. Damascus: Dar Al-Fikr.

———. [1954] 2006. *Vocation de l'Islam*. NP: Editions ANEP. https://www.fichier-pdf. fr/2014/04/11/vocation-de-l-islam-malek-bennabi/ [Accessed on 1 January 2016].

———. [1961] 2012. *Reflections*. Damascus: Dar Al-Fikr.

———. [1966] 2015. *Memoirs of a Witness of the Century*. Vol. 1 & 2. Damascus: Dar Al-fikr.

Bidwai, Praful. 2005. "Bandung is More Than a Nostalgia Trip." *Khaleej Times*, May 1.

Benjamin, Walter. 2007. *Illuminations: Essays and Reflections*. Translated by Harry Zohn. Edited with and introduction by Hannah Arendt. New York: Schocken Books.

Bier, Laura. 2011. *Revolutionary Womanhood: Feminisms, Modernity, and the State in Nasser's Egypt*. New York: Stanford University Press.

Bissio, Roberto. 2016. "Bandung in Latin America: The Hope for Another World." *Inter-Asia Cultural Studies* 17 (1): 19–26.

Biswas, P. 2008. "Colonial Displacements: Nationalist Longing and Identity among Early Indian Intellectuals in the United States." PhD dissertation in History. Los Angeles: University of California.

Blain, Keisha N. 2015. "'[F]or the Rights of Dark People in Every Part of the World': Pearl Sherrod, Black Internationalist Feminism, and Afro-Asian Politics during the 1930s." *Souls* 17 (1–2): 90–112.

Borstelmann, Thomas. 2006. *The Cold War and the Color Line: American Race Relations in the Global Arena*. Cambridge: Harvard University Press.

Brecher, Michael. 1963. "International Relations and Asian Studies: The Subordinate State System of Southern Asia." *World Politics* 15 (2): 213–235.

Bull, Hedley, and Adam Watson (eds.). 1984. *The Expansion of International Society*. Oxford: Clarendon Press.

Burke, Roland. 2010. *Decolonization and the Evolution of International Human Rights*. Philadelphia: University of Pennsylvania Press.

Burton, A. 2010. "Epilogue, The Solidarities of Bandung: Towards a Critical 21st Century History." In *Making A World After Empire: The Bandung Moment and its Afterlives*, edited by Lee, C. J. Athens: Ohio University Press.

Bush, Andrew, Andrew Davison, and Himadeep Muppidi. 2009. "Openings." In *Europe and Its Boundaries: Words and Worlds, Within and Beyond*, edited by Davison, Andrew and Muppidi, Himadeep. London: Lexington Books, xi–xvii.

Calhoun, Craig, Frederick Cooper and Kevin W. Moore. 2006. *Lessons of Empire: Imperial Histories and American Power.* New York: New Press.

Carter, Martin. 1951. "Shines the Beauty of My Darling." http://www.poemhunter.com/poem/shines-the-beauty-of-my-darling/.

Certeau, Michel de. 1984. *The Practice of Everyday Life.* Berkeley: University of California Press.

Césaire, Aimé. 2001. *Notebook of a Return to the Native Land.* Middletown, CT: Wesleyan University Press.

———. 2010. "Culture and Colonization." *Social Text* 28 (2): 127–144.

Chaar-Pérez, Kahlil. 2013. "'A Revolution of Love': Ramón Emeterio Betances, Anténor Firmin, and Affective Communities in the Caribbean." *The Global South* 7 (2).

Chakrabarty, Dipesh. 2000. *Provincializing Europe: Postcolonial Thought and Historical Difference.* Princeton, NJ: Princeton University Press.

———. 12 November 2005. "Legacies of Bandung – Decolonisation and the Politics of Culture." *Economic and Political Weekly* 40 (46): 4812–4818.

———. 2010. "The Legacies of Bandung: Decolonization and the Politics of Culture." In *Making a World after Empire: The Bandung Moment and its Political Afterlives*, edited by Lee, Christopher. Athens: Ohio University Press.

Chatterjee, Partha. 1991. *The Nation and Its Fragments: Colonial and Postcolonial Histories.* Princeton, NJ: Princeton University Press.

———. 1999. *Nationalist Thought and the Colonial World: A Derivative Discourse?* New Delhi: Oxford University Press.

———. 2005. "Empire and Nation Revisited: 50 Years after Bandung." *Inter-Asia Cultural Studies* 6 (4): 487–496.

———. 2012. *The Black Hole of Empire: History of a Global Practice of Power.* Princeton: Princeton University Press.

Chomsky, Noam. 1992. *Deterring Democracy.* London: Vintage.

Cohen, Benjamin J. 2007. "The Transatlantic Divide: Why Are American and British IPE So Different?" *Review of International Political Economy* 14 (2): 197–219.

Cooper, Brenda. 2008. "Returning the Jinns to the Jar: Material Culture, Stories and Migration in Abdulrazak Gurnah's *By the Sea.*" *Kunapipi* 30 (1): 79–95.

Daniel, Valentine. 1997. *Chapters in an Anthropography of Violence; Sri Lankans, Sinhalas, and Tamils.* Delhi: Oxford University Press.

Darby, Phillip, and Albert J. Paolini. 1994. "Bridging International Relations and Postcolonialism." *Alternatives* 19 (3): 371–397.

Datta-Ray, Sunanda K. 2015. "Coloured People's Gala – A New Strategic Partnership Between Asia and Africa." *The Telegraph*, April 23.

Devare, Aparna. 2011. *History and the Making of a Modern Hindu Self.* New Delhi: Routledge.

Devetak, Richard, Tim Dunne, and Ririn Tri Nurhayati. 2016. "Bandung 60 Years on: Revolt and Resilience in International Society." *Australian Journal of International Affairs* 70 (4): 358–373.

Dhanapala, Jayantha. 2010. "The Foreign Policy of Sirimavo Bandaranaike." In *Sirimavo: Honouring the World's First Woman Prime Minister*, edited by Jayatilaka, Tissa. Colombo: The Bandaranaike Museum Committee.

Didanović, Vera. 2007. "Tajna sa Dedinja." *Vreme.* May 4. Available at http://www. vreme.com/cms/view.php?id=451714 [Accessed on 26 April 2016].

Dieng, Amady Aly. 2009. *Les grands combats de la Fédération des étudiants d'Afrique noire: de Bandung aux indépendances, 1955-1960.* Paris: L'Harmattan.

Dinkel, Jürgen. 2014. "'To Grab the Headlines in World Press': Non-Aligned Summits as Media Events." In *The Non-Aligned Movement and the Cold War. Delhi – Bandung – Belgrade,* edited by Mišković, Natasa, Fischer-Tiné, Harald and Boskovska, Nada. Routledge: London.

Diouf, Khar N'Dofene et al. 1958. *Le Sang de Bandoëng.* Paris: Présence Africaine.

Dinas, Sedjarah Militer Kodam XVII/Tjendrawasih. 1971. *Irian Barat dari Masa ke Masa.* Djajapura: Dinas, Sedjarah Militer Kodam XVII/Tjendrawasih.

Dirlik, Arif. 2015. "The Bandung Legacy and the People's Republic of China in the Perspective of Global Modernity." *Inter-Asia Cultural Studies* 16 (4): 615–30.

Djilas, Milovan. 1980. *Tito: The Story from Inside.* Translated by Vasilije Kojić and Richard Hayes. New York and London: Harcourt Brace Jovanovich.

Drooglever, P. 2009. *An Act of Free Choice, Decolonization and the Right to Self-Determination in West Papua.* Oxford: One Word.

Dubois, W. E. B. 1917. "To the Nations of the World." In *My Life and Work,* edited by Walters, Alexander. New York: Fleming H. Revell Co.

Dubois, W. E. B. 1994. *The Souls of Black Folks.* New York: Dover Publications.

Dubois, W. E. B. 1996. "Introduction by Herb Boyd." *The Souls of Black Folk.* New York: Modern Library.

El-Hamri, J. 2016. "Malek Bennabi: When Islam Makes History." *French Academy of Islamic Thought.* 30 January 2016. https://www.youtube.com/watch?v= 5ZN4B2r49DE [Accessed 9 March 2016].

Eslava, Luis, Michael Fakhri, and Vasuki Nesiah (eds.). Forthcoming. *Bandung, Global History and International Law: Critical Pasts and Pending Futures.* Cambridge: Cambridge University Press.

Espiritu, Augusto. 2006. "'To Carry Water on Both Shoulders': Carlos P. Romulo, American Empire, and the Meanings of Bandung." *Radical History Review* 95: 173–190.

Faiz, Ahmed. 1947. *Poems by Faiz.* Translated by Kiernan, Victor G. London: George and Unwin.

Fanon, Frantz. 1956. "Racism and Culture." *Presence Africaine,* 8–10.

———. 1963. *Black Skins, White Masks.* New York: Grove Press.

———. 1967. *The Wretched of the Earth.* New York: Grove Press.

———. 2004. *The Wretched of the Earth.* Translated by Richard Philcox. Foreword by Homi Bhabha and Preface by Jean-Paul Sartre. New York: Grove Press.

Farid, Hilmar. 2016. "Rethinking the Legacies of Bandung." *Inter-Asia Cultural Studies* 17 (1): 12–18.

Fernando, Radin. 1999. "In the Eyes of the Beholder: Discourses of a Peasant Riot in Java." *Journal of Southeast Asian Studies* 30 (2): 263–285.

Finnemore, Martha. 1996. "Constructing Norms of Humanitarian Intervention." In *The Culture of National Security,* edited by Katzenstein, Peter. New York: Columbia University Press, 309–321.

Foner, Philip S. (ed.). 1978. *Paul Robeson Speaks: Writings, Speeches, Interviews, 1918–1974*. New York: Brunner/Mazel Publishers.

"Former 'first lady of the Non-Aligned Movement' dead." 2013. *The Hindu*. October 21. Available at http://www.thehindu.com/todays-paper/tp-international/former-first-lady-of-the-nonaligned-movement-dead/article5255667.ece [Accessed on 21 October 2016].

Fraser, Cary. 2003. "An American Dilemma: Race and Realpolitik in the American Response to the Bandung Conference 1955." In *Window on Freedom: Race, Civil Rights, and Foreign Affairs, 1945–1988*, edited by Plummer, Brenda Gayle. Chapel Hill: University of North Carolina Press.

Frazier, E. Franklin. 1956. "The New Negro." *The Nation*, 183.

Friedkin, Noah E. 2001. "Norm Formation in Social Influence Networks." *Social Networks* 23: 167–189.

Fromkin, D. 1990. *A Peace to End All Peace: The Fall of the Ottoman Empire and the Creation of the Modern Middle East*. New York: Avon.

Gallicchio, Marc. 2000. *The African American Encounter with Japan & China*. Chapel Hill: The University of North Carolina Press.

Gardiner, Robert K. A. 1967. "Race and Color in International Relations." *Daedalus* 96 (2): 296–311.

Ghazal, Amal N. 2010. *Islamic Reform and Arab Nationalism: Expanding the Crescent from the Mediterranean to the Indian Ocean (1880s-1930s)*. London: Routledge.

Glissant, Édouard. 1997. *Poetics of Relation*. Detroit: University of Michigan Press.

Goldstein, Slavko, and Ivo Goldstein. 2015. "Dr. Kušić: Druže Tito, Jovanka boluje od paranoidnog poremećaja." *Jutarnji List*. May 30. Available at http://www.jutarnji.hr/dr--kusic---quot-druze-tito--jovanka-boluje-od-paranoidnog-poreme-caja-quot-/1355853/ [Accessed on 26 April 2016].

Goswami, Manu. 2012. "Imaginary Futures and Colonial Internationalisms." *American Historical Review* 117 (5): 1461–1485.

Gregory, Derek. 2004. *The Colonial Present: Afghanistan, Palestine, Iraq*. Oxford: Blackwell.

Grovogui, Siba. 2006. "Mind, Body, and Gut! Elements of a Postcolonial Human Rights Discourse." In *Decolonizing International Relations*, edited by Gruffydd Jones, Branwen. Lanham, MD: Rowman & Littlefield, 179–196.

Grovogui, Siba. 2011. "To the Orphaned, Dispossessed, and Illegitimate Children: Human Rights Beyond Republican and Liberal Traditions." *Indiana Journal of Global Legal Studies* 18 (1): 41–63.

Guevara, Che. 1967. "Vietnam Must Not Stand Alone." *New Left Review* I/43: 79–91.

Guha, Ranajit. 2009. "The Small Voice of History." In *The Small Voice of History: Collected Essays*, edited by Chatterjee, Partha. Delhi: Permanent Black.

Gurnah, Abdulrazak. 2002. *By the Sea*. London: Bloomsbury.

Halliday, Fred. 1990. "The Ends of the Cold War." *New Left Review* 180 (April–June): 5–23.

Hamilton, Russell G. 1975. *Voices from an Empire: A History of Afro-Portuguese Literature*. Minneapolis: University of Minnesota Press.

Hardt, Michael. 2004. "Today's Bandung." In *A Movement of Movements: Is Another World Really Possible?* edited by Mertes, Tom. London: Verso, 230–236.

Harvey, David. 2007. *Neoliberalism: A Brief History.* New York: Oxford University Press.

Heikal, M. H. 1976. *The Suez Files: The Thirty Years War.* Arabic. Cairo: Al-Ahram Center for Publishing and Translation.

Hernawan, Budi. 2013. "From the Theatre of Torture to the Theatre of Peace: The Politics of Torture and Re-imagining Peacebuilding in Papua, Indonesia." PhD thesis, The Australian National University.

———. 2015. "Torture as a Mode of Governance: Reflections on the Phenomenon of Torture in Papua, Indonesia." In *From "Stone-Age" to "Real-Time": Exploring Papuan Temporalities, Mobilities and Religiosities*, edited by Slama, Martin and Munro, Jenny. Canberra: ANU Press.

Hernawan, Budi, and T. van den Broek. 1999. "Dialog Nasional Papua, Sebuah Kisah 'Memoria Passionis' (Kisah Ingatan Penderitaan Sebangsa)." *TIFA Irian*, No. 12.

Hernawan, Budi, M. Verawati, Ari Yurino, and K. Mezariani. 2015. *Dari Dekolonialisasi ke Marjinalisasi: Potret Kebijakan Pemerintah di Tanah Papua selama 46 Tahun Terakhir.* Jakarta: ELSAM.

Herrera, Rémy. 2005. "Fifty Years After the Bandung Conference: Towards a Revival of the Solidarity between the Peoples of the South? Interview with Samir Amin." *Inter-Asia Cultural Studies* 6 (4): 546–556.

Hicks, James. 1955. "Dark Nations Assert Power: Vote of 27-27 on Algeria Puts U.S. on the Spot." *Afro-American*, October 8.

Hikmet, Nazim. 1962. "To Asian and African Writers." Translated by Nilüfer Mizanoglu Reddy. https://www.scribd.com/doc/16184991/Nazim-Hikmet-Some-Poems [Accessed 23 June 2015].

Hobson, John M. 2012. *The Eurocentric Conception of World Politics: Western International Theory, 1760-2010.* Cambridge: Cambridge University Press.

Horne, Gerald. 2000. *Race, Woman: The Lives of Shirley Graham Du Bois.* New York: New York University Press.

Icaza, Rosalba. 2015. "Testimony of a Pilgrimage. (Un)learning and Re-learning with the South." In *Women in Academia Crossing North-South Borders: Gender, Race and Displacement (Latin American Studies)*, edited by Barahona, Melba and Arashiro, Zuleika, 1–26. Lanham, MD: Lexington Books.

Icaza, Rosalba, and Rolando Vázquez. 2013. "Social Struggles as Epistemic Struggles." *Development and Change* 44 (3): 683–704.

Inayatullah, Naeem, and David L. Blaney. 2004. *International Relations and the Problem of Difference.* New York and London: Routledge.

"Interview with Chou En-Lai." 1955. *Times of India*, April 20.

Jackson, Robert. 2005. *Classical and Modern Thought on International Relations.* London: Palgrave Macmillan.

James, C. L. R. 1989. *Black Jacobins. Toussaint L'Ouverture and the San Domingo Revolution.* New York: Vintage.

Jasanoff, Sheila. 2003. "In a Constitutional Moment: Science and Social Order at the Millennium." In *Social Studies of Science and Technology: Looking Back, Ahead*, edited by Joerges, Bernward and Nowotny, Helga. Dordrecht: Kluwer, 155–180.

Jokanović, Žarko. 2013. *Jovanka Broz: moj život, moja istina*. Blic: Beograd.

Jones, Matthew. 2005. "A 'Segregated' Asia? Race, the Bandung Conference and Pan-Asianist Fears in American Thought and Policy, 1954-1955." *Diplomatic History* 29 (5): 841–868.

Kahin, George McTurnan. 1956. *The Asian-African Conference, Bandung, Indonesia, April 1955*. Ithaca: Cornell University Press.

Kamugisha, Aaron (ed.). 2013. *Caribbean Political Thought: The Colonial State to Caribbean Internationalisms*. Kingston, Jamaica: Ian Randle Publishers.

Kaviraj, Sudipta. 2010. "Outline of a Revisionist Theory of Modernity." In *Indian Political Thought*, edited by Singh, Aakash and Mohapatra, Silika. London and New York: Routledge.

Keleny, Anne. 2013. "Captain Jovanka Broz: Partisan and rifle woman who became First Lady of Yugoslavia." October 21. Available at http://www.indepen-dent.co.uk/news/obituaries/captain-jovanka-broz-partisan-and-riflewoman-who-became-first-lady-of-yugoslavia-8895181.html [Accessed on 28 April 2016].

Kinzer, Stephen. 2003. *All the Shah's Men: An American Coup and the Roots of Middle Eastern Terror*. New Jersey: John Wiley.

Kofele-Kale, Ndiva. 1978. "The Policy of Non-Alignment in an Age of Alignment Politics: Africa Twenty Years after Bandung." *Civilizations* 23 (3–4): 251–268.

Komnas, H. A. M. 2001. *Laporan Akhir KPP HAM Papua/Irian Jaya*. Komisi Nasional Hak Asasi Manusia, Jakarta.

———. 2004. *Laporan Penyelidikan Tim Ad Hoc Penyelidikan Pelanggaran HAM yang Berat di Papua*. Jakarta: Komisi Nasional Hak Asasi Manusia.

———. 2014. *Ringkasan Eksekutif Laporan Penyelidikan Pelanggaran Hak Asasi Manusia Berat*. Jakarta: Komisi Nasional Hak Asasi Manusia (Komnas HAM).

Kothari, S. 1996. "Whose Nation? The Displaced as Victims of Development." *Economic and Political Weekly* 31 (24): 1476–1488.

Kristeva, J. 1982. *Powers of Horror, An Essay on Abjection*. New York: Columbia University Press.

Kumar, Corinne (ed.). 2011. *Asking, We Walk: The South as New Political Imaginary*. Bangalore, India: Streelekha Publications.

———. 2004. "From a Corner on the Arab Street." http://snellings.telenet.be/wom-eninblackleuven/cornerArabstreet.htm [Accessed on 6 November 2015].

Lee, Christopher J. 2009. "At the Rendez-Vous of Decolonisation." *Interventions* 11 (1): 81–93.

———. 2010. *Making a World after Empire: The Bandung Movements and Its Political Afterlives*. Athens: Ohio University Press.

Lindqvist, Sven. 1979. "Dig Where You Stand." *Oral History* 7 (2): 24–30.

Leyva Solano, Xochitl. 2013. "Y/osotras ¿Mi/nuestras Luchas Epistémicas Creativas?" In Obra Colegiada del Seminario Virtual Internacional. http://www.encuentrored-toschiapas.jkopkutik.org/index.php/es/xochitl-leyva-solano [Accessed 29 August 2016].

Mackie, J. 2005. *Bandung 1955: Non-Alignment and Afro-Asian Solidarity*. Singapore: Editions Didier Millet.

Maclellan, N. 2016. "Pacific Diplomacy and Decolonisation in the 21st Century." In *The New Pacific Diplomacy*, edited by Fry, Greg and Tarte, Sandra. Canberra: ANU Press, 263–281.

Malcolm, X. 1963. "Message to Grassroots," November 10.

Malkki, Liisa. 1995. *Purity and Exile: Violence, Memory and National Cosmology among Hutu Refugees in Tanzania*. Chicago: University of Chicago Press.

Mamdani, Mahmood. 2001. "Beyond Settler and Native as Political Identities: Overcoming the Political Legacy of Colonialism." *Comparative Studies in Society and History* 43 (4): 651–664.

———. 2012. *Define and Rule: Native as Political Identity*. Cambridge: Harvard University Press.

Manuel, Peter. 2002. "From Scarlatti to Guantanamera: Dual Tonicity in Spanish and Latin American Musics." *Journal of the American Musicology Society* 55 (2): 311–336.

"Marshal Tito's Wife Vanishes from Public View, and Belgrade Whispers of Her Arrest for Meddling." 1977. *People*. November 14. Available at http://www.people.com/people/archive/article/0,,20069527,00.html [Accessed on 28 April 2016].

Martinsson, Johanna. 2011. *Global Norms: Creation, Diffusion, and Limits*. Washington, DC: The World Bank. Available at http://siteresources.worldbank.org/EXTGOVACC/Resources/FinalGlobalNormsv1.pdf.

McDougall, Derek, and Antonia Finnane (eds.). 2010. *Bandung 1955: Little Histories*. Caulfield: Monash University Press.

McMichael, Philip. 2016. *Development and Social Change: A Global Perspective*. London: Sage.

Menon, Dilip M. 2014. "Bandung is Back: Afro-Asian Affinities." *Radical History Review* 19: 241–254.

Mignolo, Walter D. 2000. "The Many Faces of Cosmo-Polis: Border Thinking and Critical Cosmopolitanism." *Public Culture* 12 (3): 721–748.

———. 2010. "Delinking: The Rethoric of Modernity, The Logic of Coloniality and the Grammar of Decoloniality." In *Globalization and the De-Colonial Option*, edited by Mignolo, Walter and Escobar, Arturo, 303–368. London: Routledge.

———. 2011. "Geopolitics of Sensing and Knowing: On (De) Coloniality, Border Thinking and Epistemic Disobedience." *Postcolonial Studies* 14 (3): 273–283.

———. 2013. "Geopolitics of Sensing and Knowing On (De) Coloniality, Border Thinking, and Epistemic Disobedience." *Confero: Essays on Education Philosophy and Politics* 1: 129–150.

Mignolo, Walter, and Rolando Vasquez. 2013. "Decolonial Aesthesis: Colonial Wounds/Decolonial Healing." *Social Text*. Available at http://socialtextjournal.org/periscope_article/decolonial-aesthesis-colonial-woundsdecolonial-healings/.

Mishra, Pankaj. 2012. *From the Ruins of Empire: The Revolt against the West and the Remaking of Asia*. New York: Picador.

Mudimbe, V. Y. 2013. *On African Fault Lines: Mediations on Aalterity in Politics*. Scottsville: University of Kwa-Zulu Natal Press.

Mudiraj, K. K. 1934. *Pictorial Hyderabad*, vol. 2. Hyderabad: Chandrakanth Press.

Muhr, Thomas. 2012a. "(Re)constructing Popular Power in Our America: Venezuela and the Regionalization of 'Revolutionary Democrary' in ALBA-TCP Space." *Third World Quarterly* 33 (2): 225–241.

Muhr, Thomas. 2012b. "The Politics of Space in the Bolivarian Alliance for the Peoples of Our America – Peoples' Trade Agreement (ALBA-TCP): Transnationalism, the Organized Society, and Counter-Hegemonic Governance." *Globalizations* 9 (6): 767–782.

Mullen, Bill V. 2003. "Du Bois, Dark Princess, and the Afro-Asian International." *Positions* 11 (1): 217–239.

Muppidi, Himadeep. 2012. *The Colonial Signs of International Relations.* London: Hurst.

———. 2014. *Politics in Emotion: The Song of Telangana.* London: Routledge.

Muralidharan, S. 2014. "Alternate Histories: Hyderabad 1948 Compels a Fresh Evaluation of the Theology of India's Independence and Partition." *History and Sociology of South Asia* 8 (2): 119–38.

Murphy, Craig N. 1984. *The Emergence of the NIEO Ideology.* Boulder, CO: Westview Press.

———. 2015. "The Point of IR: Understanding Industrial-Age Global Problems." Paper presented at the University of Sussex Conference: "What's the Point of IR?" December 10.

Nandy, Ashis. 2004. "Towards a Third World Utopia." In *Bonfire of Creeds: The Essential Ashis Nandy.* New Delhi: Oxford University Press.

———. 2005. "The Idea of South Asia: A Personal Note on post-Bandung Blues." *Inter-Asia Cultural Studies* 6 (4): 541–45.

———. 2009. *The Intimate Enemy: Loss and Recovery of Self under Colonialism.* New Delhi: Oxford University Press.

Naylor, P. C. 2006. "The Formative Influence of French Colonialism on the Life and Thought of Malek Bennabi." *French Colonial History* 7: 129–142.

Negm, A. F. 1974. "We'll Sing." http://elfagoomy.blogspot.com/2011/01/blog-post_7382.html. Text in Egyptian Colloquial [Accessed 13 April 2016].

Nehru, Jawaharlal. 1955. "World Peace and Cooperation." *Speech in the Closed Session of the Asian-African Conference.* Bandung, 22 April. File SI/162/9/64-MEA.

———. 1955. "Recollections of the Conference." *Speech at a Closed-Door Meeting of Members of the Congress Parliamentary Party,* May 3. From AICC tapes.

———. 2001. *Selected Works of Jawaharlal Nehru, Volume 28.* Second Series. Edited by Kumar, Ravinder and Sharada Prasad, H. Y. New Delhi: Jawaharlal Nehru Memorial Fund; Oxford: Oxford University Press. Available at http://www.claudearpi.net/maintenance/uploaded_pics/SW28.pdf.

———. 2003. *The Discovery of India.* New Delhi: Oxford University Press.

Nelson, C. 1996. *Doria Shafik, Egyptian Feminist: A Woman Apart.* Gainesville, FL: University Press of Florida.

Nesadurai, Helen E. S. 2008. "Bandung and the Political Economy of North-South Relations: Sowing the Seeds for Re-visioning International Society." In *Bandung Revisited, The Legacy of the 1955 Asian-African Conference for International Order,* edited by Tan, Seng and Acharya, Amitav. Singapore: NUS Press, 68–101.

Niaah, A. H. Jahlani. 2016. "On the Edge of Bandung: Folk Fellowship and Repair." *Inter-Asia Cultural Studies* 17 (1): 158–161.

Niang, Amy. 2015. "A Community Out of Empire: The French Union (1946–58) as a Postcolonial Experiment in Multinational Polity." *WISH Seminar*, WISER, 9 March.

———. 2016. "Blaise Compaoré in the Resolution of the Ivorian Conflict: From Belligerent to Mediator-In-Chief." *African Peacebuilding Network Working Paper Series* N.6, March.

Nigam, Aditya. 2016. "Afro-Asian Solidarity and the 'Capital' Question: Looking Beyond the Last Fronntier." *Inter-Asia Cultural Studies* 17 (1): 33–51.

Nora, Pierre. 1989. "Between Memory and History: Les Lieux de Mémoire." *Representations* 26 (Spring): 7–24.

———. 2002. "Reasons for the Current Upsurge in Memory." Available at http://www.eurozine.com/articles/2002–04-19-nora-en.html [Accessed on 13 February 2015].

Onuf, Nicholas. 2012. *A World of Our Making: Rules and Rule in Social Theory and International Relations*. London: Routledge.

Paisley, Fiona. 2009. *Glamour in the Pacific: Cultural Internationalism and Race Politics in the Women's Pan-Pacific*. Honolulu: University of Hawaii Press.

"Pan-African Conference." *The Daily News* (UK), 24 July 1900.

Parker, Jason. 2006. "Cold War II: The Eisenhower Administration, the Bandung Conference, and the Reperiodization of the Postwar Era." *Diplomatic History* 30 (5): 867–92.

Pasha, Mustapha Kamal. 2013. "The 'Bandung Impulse' and International Relations." In *Postcolonial Theory and International Relations: A Critical Introduction*, edited by Sanjay Seth. Oxford: Routledge, 144–165.

———. 2009. "After Imperial Reason: Gandhi and the New Cosmopolitanism." Lecture at Centre for Postcolonial Studies, University of London, March 3.

Persaud, Randolph B. 2001. "Re-Envisioning Sovereignty: Marcus Garvey and the Making of a Transnational Identity." In *Africa's Challenge to International Relations Theory*, edited by Dunn, Kevin C. and Shaw, Timothy M. New York: Palgrave, 103–128.

———. 2001. *Counter-Hegemony and Foreign Policy: The Dialectics of Marginalized and Global Forces in Jamaica*. Albany: State University of New York Press.

———. 2003. "Reconceptualizing the Global South's Perspective: The End of the Bandung Spirit." In *The Foreign Policies of the Global South: Rethinking Conceptual Frameworks*, edited by Braveboy-Wagner, J. A. Boulder: Lynne Rienner, 49–64.

Phạm, Quỳnh N. and María José Méndez. 2015. "Decolonial Designs: José Martí, Hồ Chí Minh, and Global Entanglements." *Alternatives: Global, Local, Political* 40 (2): 156–173.

Pitts, Jennifer. 2010. "Political Theory of Empire and Imperialism." *Annual Review of Political Science* 13: 211–235.

Plummer, Brenda Gayle. 1996. *Rising Wind: Black Americans and U. S. Foreign Affairs, 1935-1960*. Chapel Hill: University of North Carolina Press.

———. 1998. "Firmin and Martí at the Intersection of Pan-Americanism and Pan-Africanism." In *José Martí's "Our America": From National to Hemispheric*

Cultural Studies, edited by Belnap, Jeffrey and Fernández, Raúl. Durham: Duke University Press, 210–227.

Prashad, Vijay. 2007. *The Darker Nations: A People's History of the World*. New York: The New Press.

———. 2012. *The Poorer Nations: A Possible History of the Global South*. London: Verso.

Proctor, Robert and Londa Shiebinger (eds.). 2008. *Agnotology: The Making and Unmaking of Ignorance*. Stanford: Stanford University Press.

Quijano, Anibal. 2000. "Coloniality of Power, Eurocentrism, and Latin America." *Nepantia: Views from the South* 1 (3): 533–580.

Radwan, Noha M. 2012. *Egyptian Colloquial Poetry in the Modern Arabic Canon: New Readings of Shi'r Al'Ammiyya*. New York, NY: Palgrave Macmillan.

Ramazani, Jahan. 2009. *Transnational Poetics*. Chicago: University of Chicago Press.

Rancière, Jacques. 2008. "Aesthetic Separation, Aesthetic Community: Scenes from the Aesthetic Regime of Art." *Art & Research: A Journal of Ideas, Contexts and Methods* 2 (1): 1–15.

Raja Keesara Venkatappayya, and others v. Rajah Nayani Venkata Ranga Row (Madras) [1928] UKPC 92 (23 November 1928).

Rajagopal, B. 2003. *International Law from Below – Development, Social Movements and Third World Resistance*. Cambridge: Cambridge University Press.

Raza, Ali, Franziska Roy and Benjamin Zacharia (eds.). 2015. *The Internationalist Moment: South Asia, Worlds, and World Views, 1917–39*. New Delhi: SAGE Publications India Pvt Ltd.

Rao, E. K. 2013. *The Kisan Struggles in Andhra Pradesh: A Study of Kisan Struggles of Munagala and Challapalli Zamindaries*. Thesis submitted to Acharya Nagarjuna University. Available at http://hdl.handle.net/10603/8104.

Rey, Matthieu. 2014. "'Fighting Colonialism' versus 'Non-Alignment': Two Arab Points of View on the Bandung Conference." In *The Non-Aligned Movement and the Cold War: Delhi – Bandung – Belgrade*, edited by Mišković, Nataša, Fischer-Tiné, Harald and Boškovska, Nada. New York: Routledge.

Reyes-Santos, Irmary. 2013. "On Pan-Antillean Politics: Ramón Emeterio Betances and Gregorio Luperón Speak to the Present." *Callaloo* 36 (1): 142–157.

Rist, Gilbert. 1997. *The History of Development: From Western Origins to Global Faith*. London: Zed Books.

Roberts, Brian Russell and Keith Foulcher. 2016. *Indonesian Notebook: A Sourcebook on Richard Wright and the Bandung Conference*. Durham, NC: Duke University Press.

Rogers, J. A. 1966. "Bandung is Product of 500 Years." *Pittsburgh Courier*, April 23.

Rollins, Judith. 1985. "Part of a Whole: The Interdependence of the Civil Rights Movement and Other Social Movements." *Phylon* 47 (1): 61–70.

Romulo, Carlos P. 1956. *The Meaning of Bandung*. Chapel Hill: The University of North Carolina Press.

Roosevelt, Kermit. 1979. *Counter Coup: The Struggle for the Control of Iran*. New York, NY: McGraw-Hill.

Rubinstein, Alvin Z. 1970. *Yugoslavia and the Non-Aligned World*. Princeton, NJ: Princeton University Press.

Rudwick, Elliott M. 1959. "W.E.B. DuBois and the Universal Races Congress of 1911." *The Phylon Quarterly* 20 (4): 372–378.

Sakar, B. K. 1943. "World-Politics and Post-War Economic Planning." *The Indian Journal of Political Science* 5 (2): 161–90.

Saltford, J. 2003. *The United Nations and the Indonesian Takeover of West Papua, 1962-1969, The Anatomy of Betrayal.* 1st edn. London and New York: RoutledgeCurzon.

Said, Edward. 1977. *Orientalism.* London: Penguin.

Said, S. 2011. "The Arab Freedom Anthem" 28 January 2011. https://www.youtube.com/watch?v=Y05tWiATaXU [Accessed on 13 April 2016].

Saleh, H. 2007. "The Banned" Documentary. *Al-Jazeera Arabic.* http://www.aljazeera.net/programs/thebanned/2007/5/14/ [Accessed on 3 January 2016].

Sarkar, S. 1973. *The Swadeshi Movement in Bengal: 1903–1908.* New Delhi: People's Publishing House.

Saull, Richard. 2005. "Locating the Global South in the Theorisation of the Cold War: Capitalist Development, Social Revolution and Geopolitical Conflict." *Third World Quarterly* 26 (2): 253–280.

Savigliano, Marta E. 1995. *Tanggo and Political Economy of Passion.* Colorado: West View Press.

Scarry, Elaine. 1985. *The Body in Pain: The Making and Unmaking of the World.* Oxford: Oxford University Press.

Scott, David. 2004. *Conscripts of Modernity: The Tragedy of Colonial Enlightenment.* Durham: Duke University Press.

Sen, A. 1983. "The Food Problem: Theory and Policy." In *South-South Strategy,* edited by Gauhar, A. London: Third World Foundation, 91–103.

Shani, Giorgio. 2008. "Toward a Post-Western IR: the Umma, Khalsa Panth, and Critical International Relations Theory." *International Studies Review* 10: 722–734.

———. 2014. *Religion, Identity and Human Security.* Abingdon, Oxon. and New York: Routledge.

Shapiro, Michael J. 2000. "National Times and Other Times: Re-Thinking Citizenship." *Cultural Studies* 14 (1): 79–98.

Shepperson, George and St. Clare Drake. 2008. "The Fifth Pan-African Conference, 1945 and the All African Peoples Congress, 1958." *Contribution in Black Studies: A Journal of African and Afro-American Studies* 8 (5): 1–32.

Sherman, T. C. 2007. "The Integration of the Princely State of Hyderabad and the Making of the Postcolonial State in India, 1948-56." *Indian Economic & Social History Review* 44 (4): 489–516.

Shilliam, Robbie. 2008. "What the Haitian Revolution Might Tell Us About Development, Security, and the Politics of Race." *Comparative Studies in Society and History* 50 (3): 778–808.

———. 2010. *International Relations and Non-Western Thought: Imperialism, Colonialism and Investigations of Global Modernity.* London and New York: Routledge.

———. 2013. "Intervention and Colonial-Modernity: Decolonising the Italy/Ethiopia Conflict Through Psalms 68:31." *Review of International Studies* 39 (5): 1131–1147.

————. 2014. "Spiritual Bandung." https://robbieshilliam.wordpress.com/2014/03/
30/spiritual-bandung/.

————. 2015a. *The Black Pacific: Anti-Colonial Struggles and Oceanic Connections.*
London: Bloomsbury.

————. 2015b. "Colonial Architecture or Relatable Hinterlands? Locke, Nandy,
Fanon, and the Bandung Spirit." *Constellations* 1–11.

Shimazu, Naoko. 2011. *"Diplomacy as Theatre": Recasting the Bandung Conference
of 1955 as Cultural History.* Singapore: Asia Research Institute, National University of Singapore.

Sikkink, Kathryn and Martha Finnemore. 1998. "International Norm Dynamics and
Political Change." *International Organization* 52 (4): 887–917. Available at http://
home.gwu.edu/~finnemor/articles/1998_norms_io.pdf.

Sivasundaram, Sujit. 2013. *Islanded: Britain, Sri Lanka & the Bounds of an Indian
Ocean Colony.* Chicago: University of Chicago Press.

Skocpol, Theda. 1979. *States and Social Revolutions: A Comparative Analysis of
France, Russia, and China.* Cambridge: Cambridge University Press.

Spira, Tamara. "Intimate Internationalisms," Lecture at UC Berkeley, 21 November
2011.

Stoddart, Theodore L. [1920] 2012. *The Rising Tide of Color Against White World-
Supremacy.* London: Forgotten Books.

Strong, Tracy B. and Helene Keyssar. 1985. "Anna Louise Strong: Three Interviews
with Chairman Mao Zedong." *The China Quarterly* 103: 489–509.

Sullivan, Shannon and Nancy Tuana (eds.). 2007. *Race and the Epistemologies of
Ignorance.* Albany: SUNY Press.

Symposium on Africa. 1960. Barnett Miller Foundation. Wellesley, MA: Wellesley
College.

Tageldin, Shaden. 2011. *Disarming Words: Empire and the Seductions of Translation
in Egypt.* Berkeley: University of California Press.

Tagore, R. 1917. *Nationalism.* London: Macmillan.

Taj Al-Sir, A. 1956. "Asia and Africa's Song." Arabic. Arab Institute for research and
Arabic studies. http://www.airssforum.com/forum [Accessed on 26 March 2016].

Tan, Seng and Amitav Acharya. 2008. *Bandung Revisited: The Legacy of the 1955
Asian-African Conference for International Order.* Singapore: NUS Press.

Tarling, Nicolas. 1992. "'Ah-Ah': Britain and the Bandung Conference of 1955."
Journal of Southeast Asian Studies 23 (1): 74–112.

Tebay, N. 2009. *Dialog Jakarta-Papua: Sebuah Perspektif Papua*, 1st edn. Jayapura:
Sekretariat Keadilan dan Perdamaian, Keuskupan Jayapura.

Thomas, C. 1985. *New States, Sovereignty and Intervention.* Aldershot: Gower Publishing Company.

Tickner, Arlene. 2003. "Hearing Latin American Voices in International Relations
Studies." *International Studies Perspectives* 4: 325–350.

Tickner, Arlene B. and Ole Wæver (eds.). 2009. *International Relations Scholarship
around the World.* London and New York: Routledge.

Trouillot, Michel-Rolph. 1997. *Silencing the Past: Power and the Production of
History.* Boston: Beacon Press.

Uyangoda, Jayadeva. 1998. "Biographies of a Decaying Nation-State." In *Culture and Politics of Identity in Sri Lanka*, edited by Thurchelvam, Mithran and Dattathreya, C. S. Colombo: International Centre for Ethnic Studies.

"Uz vojne počasti pokopana Jovanka Broz." 2013. *Aljazeera*. October 26. Available at http://balkans.aljazeera.net/vijesti/uz-vojne-pocasti-pokopana-jovanka-broz [Accessed on 26 April 2016].

Vadivelu, A. 1908. *The Aristocracy of Southern India*, vol. 2. Madras: Vest & Co.

Vincent, R. J. 1982. "Race in International Relations." *International Affairs* 58: 4.

Vitalis, Robert. 2013. "The Midnight Ride of Kwame Nkrumah and Other Fables of Bandung (Ban-doong)." *Humanity: An International Journal of Human Rights, Humanitarianism, and Development* 4 (2): 261–288.

———. 2015. *White World Order, Black Power Politics: The Birth of American International Relations*. Ithaca: Cornell University Press.

"Vremeplov: Beograd je svet, 1961." 2011. B92. September 5. Available at http://www.b92.net/info/vesti/index.php?yyyy=2011&mm=09&dd=05&nav_id=539676 [Accessed on 26 April 2016].

Waberi, Abdourahman A. 2005. "Intimate and Colossal Fragments." In *The Land Without Shadows*, translated by Garane, Jeanne. Charlottesville: University of Virginia Press.

Wagner, Rudolf G. 2012. "Don't Mind the Gap!: The Foreign-language Press in Late-Qing and Republican China." *China Heritage Quarterly* 30–31. Available at http://www.chinaheritagequarterly.org/features.php?searchterm=030_wagner.inc&issue=030.

Walker, R. B. J. 1993. *Inside/Outside: International Relations as Political Theory*. Cambridge: Cambridge University Press.

Wardaya, Baskara T. 2005. "Global Solidarity against Unilateralism." *Inter-Asia Cultural Studies* 6 (4): 476–486.

Wa Thiongo, Ngugi. 1991. *Moving the Centre: The Struggle for Cultural Freedoms*. Nairobi and London: EAEP and James Currey.

Weber, Heloise. 2007. "A Political Analysis of the Formal Comparative Method: Historicizing the Globalization and Development Debate." *Globalizations* 4 (4): 559–572.

———. 2015. "Is IPE just 'Boring', or Committed to Problematic Meta-Theoretical Assumptions? A Critical Engagement with the Politics of Method." *Contexto Internacional: Journal of Global Connections* 37 (3): 913–943.

Weber, Heloise and P. Winnati. 2016. "The 'Bandung Spirit' and Solidarist Internationalism." *Australian Journal of International Affairs*. Forthcoming.

West, Michael O., William G. Martin and Fanon Che Wilkins (eds.). 2009. *From Toussaint to Tupac: The Black International since the Age of Revolution*. Chapel Hill: The University of North Carolina Press.

Wight, Martin. 1987. "An Anatomy of International Thought." *Review of International Studies* 13 (3): 221–227.

Wood, Gillen D'Arcy. 2008. "The Volcano Lover: Climate, Colonialism, and the Slave Trade in Raffles's *History of Java* (1817)." *Journal for Early Modern Cultural Studies* 8 (2): 33–55.

Wright, Richard. 1956. *The Colour Curtain: A Report on the Bandung Conference*. London: Dobson Books.

Wright, Richard. 1956. *The Color Curtain: A Report on the Bandung Conference*. Jackson: Banner Books, University Press of Mississippi.

Young, Robert J. C. 2005. "Postcolonialism: From Bandung to the Tricontinental." *Historein* 5: 11–21.

Zangari, Sotene M. 2009. "Straightjacketed into the Future: Richard Wright and the Ambiguities of Decolonization." *The Black Scholar* 39 (1–2): 78–83.

Zee, Tyler. 2014. "Burn Down the Prison: Race, Property, and the Ferguson Rebellion." *Unity and Struggle*, December 11.

Zhou, Enlai. 1955. "Speech to the Political Committee of the Afro-Asian Conference, April 23, 1955." *New York Times*, April 25.

Zubrzycki, J. 2006. *The Last Nizam: The Rise and Fall of India's Greatest Princely State*. London: Picador.

Index

Cover Image **"El Tercer Mundo," by Wifredo Lam (1902–1982).** Colección del Museo Nacional de Bellas Artes de la Habana – Cuba

CPSIA information can be obtained
at www.ICGtesting.com
Printed in the USA
BVOW04s1939291016

466371BV00002BA/3/P